About This Book

Why is this topic important?

It's been two decades since my first job as a director of human resources. Many aspects of the field haven't changed much. However, there have been some very significant changes in other aspects. For people engaged in HR management, consulting, and education, there is a need to remember where the field has been. More important, though, is the need to work within the new parameters that have developed. Even for managers and executives whose functional responsibility is not HR, there is a need to stay up-to-date.

What can you achieve with this book?

You can stay up-to-date. The second *Annual* in this field provides a wide variety of information and knowledge needed by anyone in the field or anyone who comes in contact with the field. This book places at your fingertips options for increasing hands-on knowledge about a wide variety of issues and approaches. In short, this book has something for everyone.

How is this book organized?

This book has two sections. The first section describes successful efforts of HR practitioners inside organizations. These writings offer first-hand experiences that experts have shared. The second section is much more opinion-oriented. This section includes writings from experts who have given special thought to what they have written. They provide much food for thought.

About Pfeiffer

Pfeiffer serves the professional development and hands-on resource needs of training and human resource practitioners and gives them products to do their jobs better. We deliver proven ideas and solutions from experts in HR development and HR management, and we offer effective and customizable tools to improve workplace performance. From novice to seasoned professional, Pfeiffer is the source you can trust to make yourself and your organization more successful.

Essential Knowledge Pfeiffer produces insightful, practical, and comprehensive materials on topics that matter the most to training and HR professionals. Our Essential Knowledge resources translate the expertise of seasoned professionals into practical, how-to guidance on critical workplace issues and problems. These resources are supported by case studies, worksheets, and job aids and are frequently supplemented with CD-ROMs, websites, and other means of making the content easier to read, understand, and use.

Essential Tools Pfeiffer's Essential Tools resources save time and expense by offering proven, ready-to-use materials—including exercises, activities, games, instruments, and assessments—for use during a training or team-learning event. These resources are frequently offered in looseleaf or CD-ROM format to facilitate copying and customization of the material.

Pfeiffer also recognizes the remarkable power of new technologies in expanding the reach and effectiveness of training. While e-hype has often created whizbang solutions in search of a problem, we are dedicated to bringing convenience and enhancements to proven training solutions. All our e-tools comply with rigorous functionality standards. The most appropriate technology wrapped around essential content yields the perfect solution for today's on-the-go trainers and human resource professionals.

Pfeiffer
www.pfeiffer.com   *Essential resources for training and HR professionals*

The Pfeiffer Annual Series

The Pfeiffer Annuals present each year never-before-published materials contributed by learning professionals and academics and written for trainers, consultants, and human resource and performance-improvement practitioners. As a forum for the sharing of ideas, theories, models, instruments, experiential learning activities, and best and innovative practices, the *Annuals* are unique. Not least because only in the *Pfeiffer Annuals* will you find solutions from professionals like you who work in the field as trainers, consultants, facilitators, educators, and human resource and performance-improvement practitioners and whose contributions have been tried and perfected in real-life settings with actual participants and clients to meet real-world needs.

> *The Pfeiffer Annual: Consulting*
> Edited by Elaine Biech
>
> *The Pfeiffer Annual: Human Resource Management*
> Edited by Robert C. Preziosi
>
> *The Pfeiffer Annual: Training*
> Edited by Elaine Biech

Call for Papers

How would you like to be published in the *Pfeiffer HRM Annual?* Contributions may fit into one of two broad categories:

- Current Practices: presentations of specific HRM approaches used in a particular organization
- Insights and Perspectives: general position papers that offer critical thinking and/or analysis

Possible topics encompass those included in this volume as well as others related to the HRM field.

To discuss possible topics or submission requirements, contact editor Bob Preziosi at preziosi@huizenga.nova.edu.

Robert C. Preziosi, EDITOR

The *2006* Pfeiffer ANNUAL

HUMAN RESOURCE MANAGEMENT

Pfeiffer
A Wiley Imprint
www.pfeiffer.com

ISBN-10: 0-7879-7824-8
ISBN-13: 978-0-7879-7824-2
ISSN: 1046-333-X

Acquiring Editor: Martin Delahoussaye
Director of Development: Kathleen Dolan Davies
Developmental Editor: Susan Rachmeler
Production Editor: Dawn Kilgore
Editor: Rebecca Taff
Manufacturing Supervisor: Becky Carreño
Editorial Assistant: Leota Higgins
Composition and Technical Art: Leigh McLellan Design

Printed in the United States of America

Printing   10   9   8   7   6   5   4   3   2   1

Contents

Insights and Perspectives   **141**

Preface

There was an article recently in my hometown newspaper about the "richness" in books that isn't found at websites, on CDs, or even on television. Perhaps it is because reading a book offers both visual and tactile stimulation (unless you're on an exercise bike and it is mechanically propped up). You can't even get that from a computer unless your tactile stimulation comes from touching the words on your screen (that would make it hard to read).

So this HRM *Annual* provides a richness that you may not get from any other medium. This is true because of the nature of other mediums, as well as the special content of books.

The content in this *Annual* is quite special. There are articles on a wide variety of individual topics. You can prioritize your reading based on more immediate to less immediate needs to know. As you do that, you will notice the unique nature of each writing. You probably won't find anything quite like any of these articles.

Thus, your path to increased knowledge about current thinking and practices is one of your own choosing. In many ways this *Annual* is like a buffet dinner. Everything has been prepared for you and presented in an organized fashion. However, you get to choose how and where everything lands on the plate. You have everything from everyone.

One of the things that occurs during all buffets is a great deal of relaxed conversation. This *Annual* provides a wonderful opportunity to have such conversations. Get a group together. It could be your HR department, a networked group of consultants, or a gathering of academics. All in the group could read the same article and get together to discuss its implications for the workplace. A second option would be to assign people different articles and have them lead discussions on their individual articles.

Make the Annual work for you! It will work for you, thanks to the work of the authors. Thanks to all of them for doing such a wonderful job. The folks at Pfeiffer were great, also. A huge thanks to Martin Delahoussaye, Susan Rachmeler, Dawn Kilgore, and Rebecca Taff.

Most important of all is a big thank you to my family—Kitty, Lauren, and Carly. They are a great source of strength. Kitty keeps me excited about achieving greater professional success. Lauren reminds me that optimists are the most successful. Carly reinforces my belief that my role is to serve.

Robert C. Preziosi, Editor
September 2005

Introduction
to The 2006 Pfeiffer Annual: Human Resource Management

There continues to be a great deal of writing and conversation about the leadership deficit. The issue has been referred to in many other ways, but the bottom line is that many current and future leaders aren't prepared to fulfill the role. The noise comes from all quarters. It is not unique to any kind of organization, gender, generation, job level, ethnic group, etc. HR has an opportunity to be the driving force in developing leaders.

Leadership education, training, and development are all subject to influence from HR. In some cases, organizations have decided to place such outcome-oriented activities directly on the shoulders of the HR department. Whatever the organizational structure, HR needs to be in the forefront, because leadership is mostly a "human" set of competencies.

At the same time, HR must be setting the pace in helping organizations attain visible results that will satisfy the various stakeholder groups that HR is linked to. This requires adding economic value to the organization via the unique role of HR. The folks who've written articles for this *Annual* will help you add value if you act on what you think is most important about what they've had to say.

What's in This Annual?

The Annual is divided into two sections: Current Practices, which focuses on actual cases or experiences of the contributors, and Insights and Perspectives, which allows contributors to present ideas, theories, and models that can be used to help expand or improve the practice of HR. It starts with Laurie Bassi and Dan McMurrer, who shed more light on the what and how of HR measurement in providing a framework as well as an application. Tom Cairns' article on self-help HR was chosen because greater use of technology for administrative purposes can mean more time to handle the HR issues that must be dealt with person to person. Lindsey Craig-Willis' article provides solid examples of successful client-consultant partnerships for success in dealing with certain HR issues.

Jack Howard's article provides keen insight on how HR can learn from the actions it takes so that past mistakes are not replicated in the future. My colleague and friend Dick Kropp has skillfully outlined the importance of human resource planning, while at the same time discussing his organization's approach to such. I was fortunate to get Bob Losyk to write for the *Annual.* His suggestions on how HR can help the stress issue in America's workforce goes to the heart of how billions of dollars could be saved if organizations would accept the need to take action to alleviate this problem.

Linda Raudenbush provides very useful tools that any one of us can use to identify appropriate external resources. The practice of hiring retirees, which is one answer to talent shortages, is presented with lessons for us all by Jim Rhodes and Bahaudin Mujtaba. This is followed by Roslyn Vargas' report on how she implemented performance management in an environment where it was much needed.

Margaret Vickers and Melissa Parris wrote the final article on Current Practices. It reports a much-needed framework for understanding the feelings aspect of behavior that has become increasingly an important issue in HR.

The Insights and Perspectives section kicks off with Doug Buck's update on free agency employment. It's here to stay, and Doug points out how to address it. The article on storytelling by Elizabeth Doty and Kat Koppett was chosen because HR must be a powerful force in organizational learning. Storytelling is a great learning tool.

Ron Fetzer's contribution of building a case for HR's role in creating open communications environments is very well stated in a way that all of us can benefit from. Jack Kondrasuk's treatment of HR's need to be well-positioned in a terrorism mentality is full of useful perspective. Steve Paskoff's article on things HR managers should avoid is another perspective as important as dealing with terrorism.

Rick Rocchetti's article on getting off to a good start suggests how we can strengthen the approach to bringing in good talent so that they can be real individual contributors from the word "go." John Sample's update on BARS is most valuable. As John suggests, greater use of BARS can only help HR's impact on the need to measure performance more objectively.

A full copy of the text of this *Annual* is available on the accompanying CD.

Introduction
to the Current Practices Section

There seems to be renewed interest in creativity and innovation. It's been at least ten or fifteen years since I've observed such heightened interest in these two factors of effectiveness in business, government, and education. It certainly makes sense to me. The first real engagement with these two factors took place for me over thirty years ago. I thought then, as I do now, that both were essential for organizational success. Unfortunately, there have been peaks and valleys of interest.

They're on the front burner now, though. They should be. I was once told that a Committee on Industrial Competitiveness at a renowned university considered creativity the most important human characteristic for increased American competitiveness. Innovation has been called the fuel of American business. Every year now, many major business magazines devote a large section to innovation in one of their issues.

In this Current Practices section, there are excellent writings that reflect how HRM has responded to the need for greater creativity and innovation. What makes the writings so important is that they represent how individual organizations have chosen to respond. As you read what has been written, you will be telling yourself one of two things: either you'll be glad to hear that someone else has tried something that you wanted to try and you can learn from it or you'll be exposed to something that you might want to import to your organization.

There is no better time than now for HR to be creative and innovative. HR might find unique responses for numerous situations and issues. Reading through the section on current perspectives and taking new actions will increase HR's contribution to business results.

This section contains the following articles:

Beyond Employee Satisfaction, ROI, and the Balanced Scorecard:
Improving Business Results Through Improved Human Capital
Measurement, by Laurie Bassi and Daniel McMurrer

Beyond Employee Satisfaction, ROI, and the Balanced Scorecard:
Improving Business Results Through Improved Human Capital Measurement

Laurie Bassi and Daniel McMurrer

Summary

The authors discuss the need for changes in human capital measurement systems. Problems with current systems are presented. This paper goes on to address attributes that such systems need and how to systematically weave them into current systems. The authors also discuss how certain measurement methods can be used. A case study from a Fortune 500 company is presented.

We stand at a great juncture in economic history—the point at which human capital has overtaken both physical capital and natural resources as the primary source of prosperity and wealth creation. Given the infrequency with which such junctures occur (the last such juncture was the transition from an agricultural to an industrial economy), it is difficult to quickly sort out the opportunities and perils that they create. But this much is clear: the rules that heretofore governed wealth creation are in the midst of being turned upside down and inside out.

Previously it was ownership and superior management of either physical capital or natural resources that generated wealth. This, in turn, determined how human capital was managed and rewarded. Now that human capital has become the primary source of prosperity and wealth creation, the reverse is true. It is the superior management of human capital that determines rewards in the marketplace.

In addition to this reversal of roles, there is one enormously important distinction between the current knowledge era and preceding eras. Unlike physical capital and natural resources, human capital cannot be "owned" by employers. Consequently, an enormous premium now accrues to those organizations that have developed superior capacity for managing human capital. In fact, a growing body of research points to human capital management as the single most important predictor of an organization's ability to outperform its competition (McBassi & Company, 2004).

The sea of change that is taking place as developed economies continue to become more knowledge-intensive is requiring senior executives to focus on human capital management as never before. This, in turn, requires measurement systems that can help them optimize their return on people. The current state of human capital measurement within most organizations, however, typically consists of some (mostly unhelpful) combination of the following:

- Traditional "HR metrics" (which are, at best, lagging indicators of business results and, at worst, have nothing to do with business results) that have simply been relabeled as "human capital metrics"

- Employee satisfaction surveys with no known connection to business results

- Simplistic "balanced scorecard" measures, such as percentage of managers who have been through a development program (while these measures are intended to be forward-looking and predictive, few actually meet these criteria)

- Historic "ROI" measures (too often designed primarily for budget justification and typically unable to provide any guidance for how to improve an organization's return on people)

Thoughtful executives are desperate to change this state of affairs and to begin using a new generation of human capital measurement systems, which can actually serve as a guide to organizations seeking better business results through the improved management of their people.

This article provides guidance for senior executives on how to create such a system. The first section delineates the essential attributes that such next-generation human capital measurement systems must possess. The next section then maps these attributes onto currently available measurement systems, thereby providing a systematic basis for assessing their strengths and weaknesses. The third section outlines the content that should be captured by next-generation human capital measurement systems, and the fourth section outlines basic measurement methodologies that can be used to create powerful, actionable insights. The fifth section provides an example of how such a system has been deployed in a Fortune 500 firm. The final section provides some concluding thoughts on the subject.

Essential Attributes of Human Capital Measurement Systems

Six key attributes must be possessed by a human capital measurement system if it is to be of maximum use to executives in managing and deploying people effectively within an organization. The system must be:

1. *Descriptive*—at a minimum, a measurement system should produce summary statistics that provide a clear and succinct summary for each issue of interest. Descriptive data tend to focus on the occurrence of a phenomenon, its frequency, or its intensity. For example, descriptive statistics can help an organization monitor the degree to which an important best practice is (or is not) actually being implemented throughout the organization. While necessary, in and of itself descriptive data is insufficient since it typically measures only "inputs" or "process," but provides no information on outcomes or results.

2. *Credible*—a measurement system must be designed to provide the credible and unbiased insights needed to improve business results. Typically, any system designed primarily for the purpose of self-justification is quickly seen as suspect and is given little credence by senior executives. Many ROI initiatives, for example, fall into this category. Similarly, measurement systems designed by consulting firms can suffer from credibility issues if there is the perception (or the reality) that the system is designed to justify the sale of the consulting firm's products or services.

3. *Predictive*—a measurement system must produce statistics that help an organization predict where it is headed. Predictive measures are those that have been linked to the organization's desired business results. If the descriptive data generated by a measurement system have not been (or cannot be) linked to business results, then the usefulness of the underlying data is of questionable value. In short, "input" or "process" data that have no known impact on organizational success will be of little value to senior executives who need insights that will help them to improve organizational performance.

4. *Detailed*—the information produced by a measurement system must be sufficiently detailed and disaggregated to provide the insight needed on where action should be taken. For example, many types of information must be available across departments or business units in order to allow for a possible intervention to be targeted on those areas where it might be most successful. Consequently, data on an organization that is gathered from a single

individual or function will not be sufficiently detailed to provide a basis for action. HR Scorecards typically suffer from this shortcoming.

5. *Actionable*—a measurement system should focus on those issues over which an organization can exert influence; other items (however interesting they may be) are unhelpful in enabling action to drive business results. The best example here is a counter-example; one well-known measurement system (the Gallup Q12) measures whether or not employees "have a best friend at work." While this is indeed an interesting descriptive statistic (and might even be predictive and detailed), it is not an actionable piece of information and hence should not be an area of focus within a measurement system.

6. *Cost-effective*—as important as a powerful measurement system is to a well-managed business, it must be cost-effective if it is to be sustainable.

Attributes of Currently Available Measurement Systems

In the discussion that follows, we rank a variety of commonly used measurement systems from 1 to 5 on each of those six attributes. (A "1" indicates that the attribute is absent and a "5" indicates that the attribute is fully present.)

Balanced Scorecard

The Balanced Scorecard movement started with the best of intentions—to help organizations focus on the leading indicators of future business results (rather than focusing primarily on financial results, which are lagging indicators). Despite these good intentions, most Balanced Scorecard initiatives have fallen well short of their promise when it comes to the "people" component. Since few organizations have done the analysis to know definitely which people-related measures are the important drivers (predictors) of future business results, these initiatives end up providing relatively inane descriptive statistics (e.g., percentage of managers who have been through a leadership development course).

Descriptive	3
Credible	3
Predictive	1
Detailed	1
Actionable	1
Cost-effective	1

Employee Satisfaction Surveys

Employee satisfaction surveys typically have the capacity to provide highly detailed, descriptive data. Rarely, however, is the necessary analysis undertaken to determine whether the descriptive information is actually predictive. Hence, the information often receives less attention than it might because it is not viewed as significant.

Descriptive	5
Credible	5
Predictive	1
Detailed	5
Actionable	1
Cost-effective	3

Gallup Q12

Unlike most employee satisfaction surveys, Gallup has a research-based measurement tool that has identified a core set of measures that predict business results. This work, however, has three primary shortcomings: (1) it is based on the implausible assumption that twelve key attributes are equally important in all organizations; (2) some of the information (e.g., do employees have a best friend at work?) is simply not actionable; and (3) it is designed to be sold as a part of Gallup's consulting services (which undermines the appearance of being an unbiased and impartial measurement system).

Descriptive	5
Credible	2
Predictive	3
Detailed	5
Actionable	3
Cost-effective	1

HR Scorecard

HR Scorecards are typically used to analyze and benchmark the efficiency of an organization's HR function. As such, they are descriptive—but not at all predictive (since the efficiency with which HR transactions are accomplished has little discernible impact on either overall organizational costs or value creation).

Descriptive	3
Credible	3
Predictive	1
Detailed	1
Actionable	1
Cost-effective	2

Kirkpatrick Levels 1 Through 4

Kirkpatrick's four levels of evaluation have been used to evaluate the impact of training interventions. Although it is certainly necessary to know whether investments in training are generating their intended impacts, these evaluations typically fail to answer an equally important set of questions about the cause of the results. So while they can produce actionable information as to whether or not a training course should be continued, they typically fail to produce actionable insight into how to improve outcomes. These evaluations also have credibility problems (especially at levels 3 and 4) when they have not been well-designed. Careful design and execution, however, can be quite expensive.

Descriptive	4
Credible	3
Predictive	2
Detailed	4
Actionable	2
Cost-effective	2

ROI

Return on investment evaluations are sometimes used to evaluate training interventions (often referred to as "Level 5" evaluations), as well as other HR initiatives. Such evaluations are quite difficult to do well, however, because they require an accurate and credible estimate of what would have happened in the absence of the intervention. Moreover, too often ROI estimates are undertaken as a means of justifying budgets or staff positions. When they are motivated by any purpose other than providing the information and insight necessary for improving organizational outcomes, the results are seen as highly suspect. Even when properly done, however, their historical focus means that they typically fail to produce actionable information about future outcomes.

Descriptive	3
Credible	2

Predictive	2
Detailed	1
Actionable	1
Cost-effective	1

Watson Wyatt Human Capital Index

Like Gallup, Watson Wyatt has a well-researched measurement methodology. As is the case with Gallup, it suffers from the following shortcomings: (1) it is based on the implausible assumption that a single set of human resource practices and policies are equally important in all organizations; (2) all of the information on which it is based is provided by a single individual, and hence no disaggregated detail is available; and (3) it is designed to serve as a business development tool for Watson Wyatt (undermining the appearance of unbiased impartiality).

Descriptive	3
Credible	2
Predictive	3
Detailed	1
Actionable	2
Cost-effective	5

Summing Up

Although none of the commonly used measurement systems possess all of the essential attributes described in the previous section, the mapping outlined above begins to point to a path forward for creating next-generation human capital measurement systems that possess all of these attributes. By embedding research-based, predictive measures into employee surveys (and avoiding the potential credibility problems associated with consulting firms), it is possible to create vastly improved, forward-looking measurement systems.

Key Human Capital Measures That Every Organization Should Track

Research (ours and others') has shown that there are four general types of human capital management factors that consistently predict business results (Bassi & McMurrer, 2005; Becker, Huselid, & Ulrich, 2001; Buckingham & Coffman, 1999). These represent a "core set" of measures that organizations should track through their human capital measurement systems. The predictive measures can be broken into five categories, as follows[1]:

1. *Leadership practices* include managers' and leaders' communication, performance feedback, supervisory skills, demonstration of key organizational values efforts, and ability to instill confidence;

2. *Workforce optimization* includes an organization's success in optimizing the performance of its workforce through the establishment of essential processes for getting work done, provision of good working conditions, strong hiring decisions, and emphasis on accountability;

3. *Learning capacity* includes an organization's overall ability to learn, innovate, and continually improve;

4. *Knowledge accessibility* includes an organization's "collaborativeness" and its capacity for making knowledge and ideas widely available to employees; and

5. *Employee engagement* includes an organization's capacity to engage, retain, and optimize the value of its employees.

The best way to measure these factors within an organization is through a thoughtfully constructed survey of employees. Note that such a survey would vary considerably from the typical "employee satisfaction survey," which has little (if any) proven linkage to business results. The most important distinction between a more thoughtful survey and the typical survey is the maintaining of an intense focus on the links between the factors being measured and key business outcomes.

Using statistical techniques (such as those that are briefly described in the following section), each of the five human capital categories—as well as their specific components—can be linked to a variety of alternative measures of business outcomes. Such linkages provide senior executives with a clear prioritization—a road map of sorts—of the human capital management initiatives that will generate the greatest improvement in business results.

---

[1]Because of space limitations, we are unable to include a detailed description of each of the factors that constitute these five indices. Such a description is, however, available from the authors on request.

Measurement Methodologies That Identify the Drivers of Business Results

Have a system in place that's providing you with detailed, trustworthy information on your organization's human capital management—but not sure how to make the best use of the data? The most fundamental point to recognize is that, nine times out of ten, the information you have will be most useful to you after you've linked it with your organization's business results—either financial ones (growth rate, revenues generated) or non-financial ones (safety, customer satisfaction)—to determine which of your people-related factors are driving your business results.

A few basic statistical techniques can be employed quite effectively to link these human capital measures to business results in a way that is both credible and actionable.

Inputs and Outcomes

The central challenge in doing so is to isolate how one factor (e.g., training investments or the effectiveness of managers' communications) causes another factor (e.g., revenues or safety) to change.

After gathering information on a given set of factors (through a measurement system and employee survey of the type described above), the effects of each factor can typically be isolated by applying the principles of a "quasi-experimental design." This identifies and quantifies causal relationships between "inputs" and "outcomes."

Consider for a moment a drug dosage experiment wherein patients (all of whom have the same ailment) are given varying dosages of a medicine. The severity of the patients' illness varies, and each is different along a variety of dimensions (e.g., gender, weight, age). A statistical technique called regression analysis can be used to isolate the effect of the medicine on the "outcome" of interest (improved health), while controlling for both the variations in the dosages of the medicine (the "input" of interest) and the effects of "confounding variables" (gender, weight, age).

Similarly, the effect of human capital management "inputs" on business "outcomes" can be isolated by controlling for the effects of "confounding variables" that affect different parts of your organization in different ways (e.g., age of plant and equipment, local economic conditions, exchange rates).

Take Advantage of Multiple Offices/Locations

This can be done by identifying and making use of the "natural experiment" that exists within every organization. Suppose your organization has twenty-five sales offices (or factories, or branches, or locations) and that you have comparable outcomes measures (e.g., sales per employee, safety) available for each office.

By "regressing" the input measures—such as those that might be measured through an employee satisfaction survey or by documenting varying "dosages" of training—on the outcome measures, it is possible to determine the magnitude of the effect (and its statistical significance) of each input of interest on the outcome of interest after eliminating the confounding effects of other factors that also affect outcomes.

Maximizing the Power of Your Data

Your ability to estimate such impacts with statistical precision will increase with the number of different units being analyzed. In addition, the capacity to eliminate the effects of confounding variables is enhanced if outcomes (and inputs, if possible) are observed on more than one occasion for each unit. This allows for the "differencing out" of the effects of unit-specific confounding factors. (For additional information on the statistical techniques described in this section, see Kmenta, 1997, or Chiang, 1984.)

When the number of units (e.g., sales offices) is not large enough to support regression analysis, alternative statistical techniques are available, such as differences of means (t-tests) and correlation analysis (Pearson coefficients). Or you might consider using a different "unit of analysis." Instead of using outcomes for each sales office overall, you could use individual managers' or employees' outcomes (e.g., absentee rates, turnover, or sales productivity). This would significantly increase the number of units available for analysis, thereby vastly increasing your ability to identify and isolate effects.

Examining Other Links

The statistical techniques described here can also be used to analyze the circumstances under which the impacts of interest are particularly large or small (e.g., certain types of learning interventions might be effective only in units with high scores on learning capacity). This analysis generates insights into why the results are as they are and hence is useful in determining what actions should be taken to optimize organizational performance.

Summing Up

In sum, it is possible to rigorously quantify how an organization's management of human capital affects business results when multiple (disaggregated) observations of both outcomes and inputs exist. The type of analysis outlined above essentially combines the strengths (and eliminates the weaknesses) of the balanced scorecard, employee surveys, and ROI analysis.

If you have training investment data and/or can undertake a thoughtfully constructed employee satisfaction survey (as described in the previous section), techniques are readily available that allow executives to be provided with the information they need to improve business results through enhanced human capital management.

An Example from a Fortune 500 Firm

American Standard, an established global manufacturer in the areas of air conditioning systems, bath and kitchen products, and vehicle control systems, has tracked the five human capital indices within the organization over the past three years and has used them to manage its talent across and within its major business units. The indices have become an integral component of American Standard's strategic management process, feeding into and improving its balanced scorecard measures and its performance management system.

We worked with American Standard to examine the relationship between the human capital indices and a key internal American Standard measure that was designed to summarize the financial results and growth trends of the U.S. sales offices within one of its major business units. The analysis found a clear relationship between the indices and the summary sales measure, pointing to the importance of human capital factors in shaping sales success. Sales, of course, is a fundamental determinant of business success—or failure.

For each of the five indices, the sales offices that were in the top 50 percent of all offices in their score on the given human capital index also had a higher median summary sales score. Depending on the specific index, the median sales scores were between 6 and 35 percent higher for offices in the top half of the human capital distribution (see Figure 1). The largest differences were seen between the top half and the bottom half in their scores on Learning Capacity and Knowledge Optimization.

The combination of summary findings like those included in Figure 1, with more detailed information (not shown here) on individual sales offices' scores on each index (and on the specific items that comprise each index), provides American Standard with information on the links between human capital and sales success, pointing to a clear method to identify specific human capital initiatives that would be expected to bring about the greatest improvements in sales productivity.

The senior vice president for human resources at American Standard, Lawrence Costello, describes the impact of these findings in this way:

> "For the past three years, American Standard has been creating a much more strategic process for investing in the development and management of our people. The missing piece for us was a way to link our investments to bottom-line results.

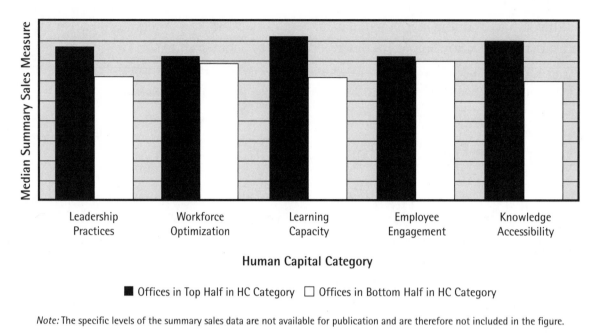

Figure 1.   Median Summary Sales Office Measure for American Standard

Our human capital measurement methodologies created that link, helping us to develop a clear road map for improving business results. Equally important is our improved capacity to persuade managers to make the necessary investments by providing them with compelling evidence on the bottom-line impact that results from improved development and management of their people."

In short, understanding the actual business impact of human capital investments was a crucial advance for American Standard in its efforts to improve the effectiveness and targeting of those investments.

Concluding Thoughts

The quality of human capital management is now the single most important predictor of an organization's business results. Given its importance, the measurement systems that most organizations use to evaluate and improve the effectiveness of human capital management and its impact on their business outcomes are grossly inadequate. Successful organizations are moving toward a "next generation" measurement system that provides executives with credible, actionable insights for driving business results through the improvement of their human capital management. Organizations like American Standard can now identify the human capital investments that are most closely tied to their sales—a key business outcome. A system that reliably provides such insights is well within the reach of most mid- to large-size organizations. All that is required is a thoughtfully constructed employee survey that focuses on human capital metrics that are known to predict business results, some basic statistical tools, and the will to move beyond traditional "HR metrics."

References

Bassi, L., & McMurrer, D. (2005). What to do when people are your most important asset. *Handbook of business strategy*. Bradford, England: Emerald Group Publishing.

Becker, B., Huselid, M., & Ulrich, D. (2001). *The HR scorecard: Linking people, strategy, and performance*. Cambridge, MA: Harvard Business School Press.

Buckingham, M., & Coffman, C. (1999). *First, break all the rules: What the world's greatest managers do differently*. New York: Simon & Schuster.

Chiang, A. (1984). *Fundamental methods of mathematical economics* (3rd ed.). New York: McGraw-Hill/Irwin.

Kmenta, J. (1997). *Elements of econometrics* (2nd ed.). Ann Arbor, MI: University of Michigan Press.

McBassi & Company. (2004). *The impact of U.S. firms' investments in human capital on stock prices*. [Online]. Available: www.mcbassi.com.

Laurie Bassi *is the CEO of McBassi & Company, a workforce strategy and benchmarking company, and the chairwoman of the board of Bassi Investments, an investment company that invests in companies that invest in their employees.*

Daniel McMurrer *is the vice president for research at McBassi & Company and the chief research officer at Bassi Investments. His principal research interests are in identifying empirical linkages between firms' human capital investments and practices and their subsequent business results.*

Changing the Way HR Departments Do Business Through Employee Self-Service

Thomas D. Cairns

Summary

The growth of the Internet in the 1990s dramatically changed the way companies did business. Human resource (HR) professionals seized on this new enabling technology to help change the way HR functions and activities were performed. HR began using internal intranets to transfer certain transactions/ activities to employees, calling it "employee self-service" (ESS). This article reviews the factors to consider when implementing an ESS program, the advantages and disadvantages of ESS, and the continuing impact that technology and ESS has had on employees and management.

"The arrival of the Internet has been compared to the Industrial Revolution, the automobile, and the Gutenberg printing press" (Sullivan, 2001, p. 13). However, it was not until 1991, when British scientist Tim Berners-Lee invented the World Wide Web (WWW), that the Internet revolution really began (Grossman, 2003).

As this promising technology was burgeoning, entrepreneurs and venture capitalists sought to exploit every opportunity this technology seemed to offer. The presumption was that typical brick-and-mortar companies would be a thing of the past, replaced by a virtual company delivering goods and services via the Internet. The uses of the Internet were perceived to be limitless—and indeed they were and are. Yet it has yet to replace traditional brick-and-mortar companies.

While the technology advanced, companies continued to look for ways to apply the Internet to their businesses. The initial focus was on using it to market products and services to customers. In doing this, companies soon realized that the Internet was not only a great marketing tool but that it also enabled customers to complete transactions without leaving their homes. As the technology improved, websites became more elegant and robust with information. Large and small businesses, government agencies, universities, churches, and essentially anyone was able to use the Internet to market their products and/or services. It almost certainly is not an exaggeration to state that nearly every business has some kind of presence on the Internet.

One of the major uses of the Internet by consumers is to search for products and services. Several companies are vying to be the number one provider in this space. One of those companies is Google. According to an executive at Google, its "mission is to organize the world's information." The technology certainly exists or will exist to enable Google to achieve this goal (Wegner, 2004, p. 3B). Its success will depend on obtaining the information.

Information is the key to the success of anyone who uses the Internet to market goods or services. Consequently, massive efforts are underway to digitize every form and kind of data possible. If the three rules in retail are location, location, and location, then the analogous rules in technology must be digitization, digitization, and digitization.

As organizations were focusing on the uses of the Internet for their external customers, they began to explore its uses with their internal customers, that is, managers and employees. As stated previously, Google's goal is to organize the world's information. Many companies have tried to do this on a much smaller scale—to organize data (employee information) and make it available to employees via an intranet. Companies use Internet technology but limit access to the site to employees only.

What Is Employee Self-Service?

The American consumer understands the concept of self-service. Whether at a gas pump, grocery store, cafeteria, or wherever, the idea of self-service offers the consumer a certain level of speed and control. The Internet feeds on that notion. An intranet, a by-product of the Internet, offers the same idea to internal customers.

The concept of employee self-service first emerged as an opportunity for human resource (HR) departments to transfer certain HR transactions/activities to employees through an intranet. This would allow HR to focus less on administrative tasks and more on strategic, value-added processes. The initial focus of most HR-related intranet activities was on the employee benefit process. This process was manual, very transactional, labor-intensive, and high volume. By automating the process and using an intranet, the idea of employee self-service (ESS) began. ESS set off a "change in the fundamental paradigm of how employees would interact with information they need and information they would own" (LaPointe, 1998, p. S13).

Current Practices

19

The Basis for ESS

The rationale for companies to implement ESS was obvious. Because HR processes could be streamlined on an intranet, organizations could improve service to employees and reduce costs. Printing and distributing company policies, corporate directories, employee handbooks, forms, and other work could be replaced by posting these materials on an intranet, thereby reducing the costs of materials, equipment, and labor. The number of specialists and the amount of time that HR would need to assist employees with simple transactions such as changes of address, emergency contact information, and beneficiary information could be dramatically reduced—and in some cases eliminated. Employees could immediately access the necessary information and implement changes instantly.

According to a survey conducted of one hundred companies in 2000, over 60 percent of them allowed employees to complete their annual benefit enrollment processes online (Elswick, 2001). The number of companies doing this is most likely increasing yearly. Corresponding to this is that, due to ESS, human resource departments have experienced a "75 percent reduction in everyday benefit-related questions" (Ascentis Software, 2003, p. 82).

Fundamental Questions When Implementing an ESS Program

When a company is considering implementing an ESS program, a number of factors must be considered.

1. Does the company have the internal resources (information technology) to create and support an intranet, or will it need to use the services of an outside vendor?

2. How comfortable are employees with using technology, and do employees have access to such technology (Lampron, 2002)?

3. How will the company "persuade" employees that ESS is a benefit to them (Crosby, 2004)?

4. Is the company prepared to invest in training employees on how to use ESS (Employee Self-Service, 2002)?

5. What applications will the company first offer to employees (Crosby, 2004)?

The responses to these questions will vary from company to company, but the need to adequately prepare for the implementation of an ESS program will not. The "decisions are easy, but hard to implement. Gaining cooperation within the human resource and information technology departments requires effort. In addition, understanding which processes to impact and then making them consistent across the organization is no small challenge, not to mention getting people to accept a new way of doing things" (Roberts, 2004, p. 158). Therefore, it seems obvious that HR should focus its efforts on those areas that are value-added and easy to implement. Once the easy-to-implement areas are flawlessly executed, a company can move into the more complex value-added areas. See Table 1 for a matrix that can be used to determine what activities have the most impact and ease of implementation.

Table 1. ESS Value–Added and Ease of Implementation Matrix

	Simple	Complex
High Value	• Basic employee info (change of address, etc.)	• Performance appraisals
	• Annual benefits enrollment	• Employee opinion surveys
	• Company policies	• Time and attendance info
	• Employee handbook	• Training programs
	• Vacation tracking	
Low Value	• Company directories	

Advantages and Disadvantages of ESS

Human resource departments need to remind themselves, as increasingly more is pushed to ESS, that an intranet is a tool to facilitate improved employee service. It does not replace the need for solid human resource benefits, policies, and practices. A good intranet site does not make up for a poorly designed benefits enrollment process, training program, employee handbook, or other function. Nor does a well-designed benefits enrollment process, training program, or employee handbook negate the need for a fully integrated intranet system. There are clear advantages and disadvantages to ESS for both the employer and employee. The following are examples of both:

Advantages for the Employer

- Reduced expense of:
    - Printing materials, forms
    - Distributing materials
    - Processing information, paperwork
    - Administrative support staff
    - Expert support staff
    - Storing information
- Provide employees access to pertinent information
- More accurate and timely information
- Improve communication to employees
- Ability to use an intranet for other applications:
    - Employee performance assessments
    - Training (compliance, workplace violence e.g.)
    - Employee opinion surveys
    - Time and attendance records
    - Compensation planning
    - Succession planning

Advantages for Employee

- Instant access to information
- More accurate information
- Personal control of information
- Privacy
- Repository of important information and documents
- Use when convenient

Disadvantages for Employer

- Reduced expenses attributed to an intranet have not been realized. Some companies have been able to reduce the number of support staff; however, the need to invest in human resource technology has offset some of the expected gains.

- Expense of creating and supporting IT infrastructure

- Training employees to use the intranet

- Not all employees have access to the intranet

- Communicating to employees the need to keep information current

- Need to allow employees access to experts as support without replacing the requirement to use the intranet

- Ensuring that employees access their information and make pertinent changes

- Printed materials and forms still need to be available

- Ensuring that employees receive important communication they need to act on

- Tendency to put everything on the intranet

- Overload employees with requests for information and feedback

- Changes are confirmed but not always validated

- Less interaction with employees about matters important to them

Disadvantages for Employee

- Information overload

- Less interaction with experts

- Limited access to experts

- May miss important deadlines

- Not always computer-savvy

- Perception that "Big Brother" is watching

- Relying solely on electronically filed data

Strategic Approach to ESS Is Key to Success

As technology continues to advance, progressively more human resource applications can be delivered on the intranet. Human resources will need to be strategic in selecting what HR applications to move to an intranet. The majority of HR tasks that have been moved to ESS have been predominantly transactional and administrative. What is left are the more complex yet highly value-added tasks that have direct effects on the manager-employee relationship that is, compensation planning, succession planning, training programs, and so forth. Since successful implementations of ESS have been "tactical," a strategic approach will be necessary in the future "if ESS is going to be a key factor in the paradigm-shifting transformation of the HR function" (LaPointe, 1998, p. S13). ESS is well on its way to being institutionalized in organizations today; however, the continued success of ESS will be dependent on HR continuing to communicate to employees that ESS is employee "empowerment" and employees agreeing that it is not an "imposition" and that their needs are being met (Roberts, 2004).

American Honda Motor is strategically using ESS to provide skills training to its employees. After evaluating what skills employees needed to ensure quality customer service, American Honda concluded that effective problem-solving skills and decision-making skills were the key components. These two skills were the basis of "rational thinking skills" that American Honda had trained employees in for years through a standard workshop format. However, American Honda looked for ways to blend e-learning with the more traditional classroom setting. The result was taking the features of the workshop training that did not require instructor interaction and delivering it online (Stottler, 2004).

For example, training on the concepts of effective problem solving and decision making could be delivered online at the employee's own pace and be monitored by an instructor. Once this phase was completed, the employee would then learn how to apply the skills to real work situations. This action learning would take place in a classroom setting. Once the training is completed, the employee returns to his or her job and starts applying the learning in day-to-day situations. American Honda then uses ESS to review progress and provide online "support tools and information" (Stottler, 2004, p. 36).

More than three hundred American Honda employees have gone through the "high-tech and high-touch" training in the past couple of years. American Honda believes the blended training has been successful in helping employees retain and use the skills learned. Although no formal study has been conducted to evaluate the long-term effectiveness of the training methodology, the strategic use of ESS to improve the quality of customer service is value-added (Stottler, 2004).

Another area for the strategic use of ESS is in employee performance management. Since the Intranet can store significant amounts of employee performance information, many companies have placed their employee evaluation forms on the intranet. Employees and managers can be notified automatically about the need to complete performance appraisals. Employees are able to complete their portions of the performance appraisal online and submit it to their managers. The manager can access an employee's self-evaluation and complete his or her portion of the appraisal. Once the initial review is completed, the next step in the process is approval at the next level of management and then formal feedback to the employee. When this process is complete, there is a documented record of employee performance. This not only documents employee performance but also can provide a history of the employee's past performance. The record can further include information on employee development and training. For example, information about training courses the employee has completed can be stored on an intranet.

The value of having the performance appraisal process online is that it facilitates performance feedback. Employees are empowered to complete their performance appraisals. The bottleneck in the performance appraisal process is usually with the manager. Most managers need help in preparing a quality performance review and how to conduct an effective employee feedback session. Using ESS in the performance management process enables HR to focus on these more value-added activities.

The Continuing Impact of Technology on Management and ESS

The Internet and its offspring, the intranet, continue to have a profound effect on the work environment. The Internet and its enabling technology have helped create information-based organizations. Through the implementation of ESS, human resource professionals facilitate employees "learning to use information generated by a computer—data that has been analyzed, synthesized, and organized in useful ways" (Cetron & Davies, 2001, p. 39).

As technology advances, one of the "greatest benefits of an HR self-service platform is that it can help an organization move to a broader employee portal, allowing employees to access a range of other applications and services, from industry news to facilities information and financial metrics" (Rodgers, 2003, p. 4). Additionally, ESS and the evolving manager self-service (MSS) will transform the traditional manager-employee relationship, from one that relies on management structure to convey daily work direction to one with less control and more goal and expectation setting, allowing employees to determine how to achieve their goals (Roberts, 2004). If technology has changed the way business is conducted, it has also changed the way employees are managed.

Conclusion

Human resource departments were some of the early adopters of intranets. The initial interest was to reduce operating expenses while improving employee services. Human resource departments seized the opportunity to convert many of their transactional functions and activities to ESS. However, the cost benefit of implementing ESS has not been achieved, due to the costs of entry and the continuing support of the new web-enabling technology. However, it has achieved improved employee communication and delivery of HR services. Yet these gains are difficult to quantify. Employees have accepted ESS, but further research is necessary to determine the level of employee satisfaction.

Human resource departments continue to shift from administrative functions to being strategic business partners. Human resource executives have a unique opportunity to provide leadership in the new information-based organization. Human resources will need to continue to monitor the impact that ESS has on the manager-employee relationship. Technology may assist good leadership, but it will never replace it.

References

Ascentis Software. (2003, June). Special advertising section: 2003 product showcase. *Workforce, 82*(6), 82.

Cetron, M.J., & Davies, O. (2001). Trends now changing the world: Technology, the workplace, management, and institutions. *Futurist*, pp. 27–42.

Crosby, A. (2004). Persuading workers to serve themselves. *National Underwriter Life & Health, 108*(30), 29.

Elswick, J. (2001, September 15). Employee self-service soars, but ROI lags. *Employee Benefit News*, pp. 1–2.

Employee self-service. (2002). *Strategic Finance, 83*(12), 19.

Grossman, L. (2003, March 31). How the web was spun. *Time, 161*(13), A66.

Lampron, F. (2002). Is ESS right for your company? *HR Magazine, 47*(12), 77.

LaPointe, J.R. (1998). Seven steps to successful ESS. *HR Focus, 75*(4), S13–14.

Roberts, B. (2004). Empowerment or imposition. *HR Magazine, 49*(6), 157–166.

Rodgers, K. (2003, May 7). Do-it-yourself HR functions reap benefits: Employee self-service. *The Financial Times*, p. 4.

Stottler, W. (2004). Improving service quality at Honda. *Quality Progress, 37*(10), 33–38.

Sullivan, B. (2001). Internet founder working on secret optical brew. *ISP Business News, 7*(2), 13.

Wegner, J. (2004, July 14). Study shows internet now beginning to pay off for firms after initial costs. *USA Today*, p. 3B.

Dr. Thomas D. Cairns *is senior vice president of human resources for NBC Universal. He has responsibility for all HR functions for digital, television, and studio operations. He has published a number of HR-related articles and teaches HR leadership at the graduate level. His interests are mainly in labor relations, HR leadership, and HR team building.*

Strategies and Methods for Competency–Based Selection and Leadership Development:
Four Case Studies
Linsey Craig-Willis

Summary

This paper discusses four different organizations—three private sector companies and one governmental organization. It highlights the various consulting strategies and methods used for each to effectively design, develop, and implement its competency-based promotional selection and/or leadership development programs. The specific methodologies, data-collection process, assessment process components, and administration of each process are summarized.

We know that to be successful in consulting we must listen to the voice of the customer. We must also be willing and able to jump through hoops to get the job completed to the customer's specifications. At times we even find ourselves providing extra services that are not strictly written in the contract document. Also, regardless of the type of consulting project we are working on, occasionally extenuating circumstances create problems. Other difficulties also arise that cause ripples in what was expected to be a smooth operational process.

Examples of these circumstances include:

1. Some of your client's staff do not want you there;
2. Some of the subject-matter experts (SMEs) favor the status quo;
3. The resources promised at the start of the engagement change or no longer exist; or
4. Politics always creeps into any consulting engagement.

This can be the case even when the human resources department is working collaboratively with the consultant. Included in the case studies are the various strategies utilized to ensure a smooth and collaborative working relationship with each client while securing successful competency-based selection and leadership development projects.

Thus, the purpose of this paper is to examine the various strategies that were used to effectively deliver competency-based personnel selection and leadership development consulting services to the various clients and to review and discuss each of the specific competency-based assessment process components. Each case discusses the problem(s) each client organization faced, summarizes the process, and reviews the outcomes for each project.

A main theme and similar methodologies link these diverse projects together. First, each consulting project has something to do with competency-based and personnel selection leadership development, which is a very hot topic in the human resources profession. A lot of books and articles have been written on competencies, which are also referred to in the standard job description as part of the KSAOs (knowledge, skills, abilities, and other personal characteristics) or as skill dimensions when conducting an assessment center. Second, a strategy of using assessment center methodology for selection and/or development was used for each project design and implementation.

Originating from the work of German psychologists in the 1900s, an assessment center is a method for identifying management potential that has been used for over thirty years in the public and private sectors. The many different components that comprise an assessment center include the employee's characteristics (interpersonal skills, organization and planning, decision making, and others) and a means of measuring that incorporates various types of simulation exercises. The process also requires the use of a trained staff to administer and interpret the performance behaviors (competencies) observed.

The candidate's competencies (also referred to as abilities or skill dimensions) are evaluated by means of simulation exercises designed to mirror the management position as closely as possible without putting the person in the position and monitoring his or her performance for several months. Exercises are, in a sense, "snapshots" of the position. The job simulation exercises are designed based on job analysis data collected from the subject-matter experts (SMEs), paperwork, organizational charts, and other data.

In some selection systems, personnel are selected based on the degree to which they demonstrate certain competencies, for example, demonstrating interpersonal competence (such as providing emotional support, demonstrating concern and interest for the employee), planning and organizing, problem analysis, and decision making. Ultimately, the competencies employees are expected to demonstrate should be part of a comprehensive and integrated system, starting with the recruitment and selection process, moving to the performance management system, and ending with management/leadership training and development and succession planning.

Overview of Case Study Selection Criteria

The range of recent consulting projects, descriptions of the competency-based selection and leadership development programs and processes, relative similarities, difficulties, and lessons learned with each project are covered in the following case reviews. The private sector companies and government agency chosen for the case studies were carefully selected based on responses to the following questions:

1. Were competencies a main component of the project?

2. Was the use of competency-based development/personnel selection a way to improve the management/leadership of the organization?

3. Would successful completion of the project resolve a current problem in the organization?

4. Was data collected in the process of designing, developing, and implementing the program?

5. Was there collaboration between the organization and the consulting firm in the development of the program?

If the answers were yes to those questions, then the organization was included as one of the case studies.

The Organizations

The four client types range in size from small (1 to 250 employees) to large (more than 1,000 employees) and include the following:

- Mortgage brokerage firm catering to residential home buyers in Florida;

- Bank: medium-size regional bank located in Florida with seventy-three locations that provide services to individuals, small businesses, and large corporations;

- Clerk of the Circuit Court: a large county clerk of the circuit court office located in the southeastern United States; and

- Resort hotel chain: a large resort hotel chain with eleven locations in a warm region of the Western hemisphere.

Utilization of Similar Methodologies for Client Projects

As stated previously, each consulting project was completed using a similar project methodology. Table 1 lists each client in the order each is discussed in the paper. The table includes the project type and client strategy used for working with the client, data-collection methodology, process design, and the process outcomes.

Customization of the materials would not have been possible without gathering and reviewing organizational data. The most important data collected is the job analysis data collected by interviewing the SMEs, reviewing current job descriptions, and gathering and examining work samples (organizational charts, forms, notes, reports, and so on). Also, in terms of management/leadership development, the consultant must always find out something about the background and training/development received by the participants in the past. She or he must also obtain historical information about the client's selection and development processes.

A careful review and examination of the data collected is utilized to develop the management/leadership selection and training materials. Even though much of the management/leadership selection and training material on the market is generic, a universal application, or has been done elsewhere, the consultant should do some customization for delivery of a quality product unless the client indicates that she or he prefers an off-the-shelf product. This is an excellent strategy because the employees relate better to the assessment or development materials because the competencies, situations, and exercises are based on their company data (job descriptions, performance competencies, situations, and so forth), not something off-the-shelf.

Utilization of Different Strategies to Effectively Deal with the Client and Complete a Successful Project

Although the methodology used to design, develop, administer, or implement each project for each client was similar, the strategies employed to interact with the clients and ensure successful completion of each project were different. Four strategies, which will be discussed in more detail when each case is outlined, were the following:

- Lend a Helping Hand

- Listen to the Voice of the Customer

- Validate a Competency Model

- Adapt to an International Culture

Table 1. Comparison of Client Projects

Project Type and Client	Strategy for Dealing with Client	Data Collection	Process Design	Process Outcome
1. Personnel Selection (Mortgage Company)	Lend a helping hand	Conduct interviews with incumbent and president; review organizational data and work samples	Develop CBSSI; write job description; prepare newspaper advertisement; conduct rater training; coach president on reference checking process	New hires; new hiring model; very favorable
2. Management Training (Regional Bank)	Listen to the voice of the customer	Conduct one-on-one interviews; review organizational data, job descriptions, competency model	Review competency statements; develop questions and response standards; conduct mock interviews	New hires; new hiring model; voted best module
3. Executive Selection (County Clerk of the Circuit Court's Office)	Validate a competency model	Complete job analysis; conduct interviews with SMEs; review organizational data and work samples; conduct SME review of material	Develop PC exercise; develop LGD exercise; develop CBSSI; train in-house staff to administer	In-house person selected; very favorable
4. Leadership Development (International Resort Hotel Chain)	Adapt to an international culture	Review mission statement, employee handbook, and other organizational data	Review competencies; develop LGD exercise; develop group/team exercises	Very favorable

Legend: CBSSI: Competency-based structured situation interview questions; LGD: Leaderless group exercise; PC: Personnel coaching exercise; SC: Subordinate counseling exercise; SE: Situational exercise; SME: Subject-matter expert

Consulting Strategy 1: Lend a Helping Hand

The company in this case, a small mortgage brokerage firm, was founded in 1997, is 100 percent woman-owned, and has well over two thousand clients in Florida. The firm handles mortgages for first homes, investment property, rehab or renovation loans, new construction loans, and government loans for veterans or first-time homeowners, as well as refinancing of loans. The firm also has automated underwriting and can close in five days or less, even though the normal process for closing on property is two weeks or more.

Problem/Situation

The president of a mortgage brokerage firm approached me and asked for a proposal to design a new hiring system for her firm. She had experienced a lot of turnover in the business and had decided to downsize the office staff temporarily until she moved into a building that was being purchased. Until such time, she wanted to ensure she had effective hiring processes. She admitted that she was used to hiring from "the seat of her pants," which often entailed hiring the first person she interviewed. This time around she wanted to invest the time and money in a more reliable hiring process to reduce future employee turnover.

Data Collection

The data collection process involved interviewing an incumbent loan processor (one of the SMEs) who had given his two-week notice. I spent about three and a half hours interviewing him to find out what his job tasks were, reviewing critical incidents he dealt with and how he handled the situations, and reviewing in detail the paperwork he processed. I only interviewed this one individual because, at the time, he was the only loan processor employed by the firm. The other positions were vacant, and the president had eliminated other positions in the company. This is not the best situation. However, considering that the other loan processor positions were vacant or had been eliminated and the president and current loan processor were very familiar with the work, they were the only two persons interviewed. Therefore, the competency model was based on his and the president's input only. I had also interviewed the president about the position.

Draft competency–based structured situational interview (CBSSI) questions and response standards were developed and reviewed and revised by the president and me. The process is summarized below.

I conducted interviews with the loan processor and president and reviewed organizational data and work samples. The interview process consisted of having the loan processor do the following:

1. Describe a typical day in terms of what tasks he completed and what his overall duties and responsibilities were;

2. Provide sample copies of the forms and papers a person must complete in order for the loan processor to review and process the loan;

3. Review and explain the important parts of each form (that is, why the loan applicant must provide the various types of information and so forth);

4. Describe critical incidents that had occurred on the job, how the incidents were handled, what actions were taken that were effective, and what should have been done to handle the situations more effectively; and

5. Identify the level of education and number of years of experience, knowledge, skills, abilities, and other characteristics necessary for successful performance in the position.

The above information was used to develop CBSSI questions and response standards. The same interview process was also conducted with the president. This is formally known as the critical incident method of job analysis.

Examples of some CBSSI questions are as follows:

- As you know, a loan processor must be able to multi-task, keep track of many simultaneous events and files, and ensure that all loan processes are completed in a timely and accurate manner right up to and through closing. Give us an overview of how you personally handle your many duties to ensure that nothing falls between the cracks.

- After working diligently with a borrower for months, the closing date for his residence finally arrived. You are sitting at your desk anticipating the next closing when you receive a call from his attorney informing you that, just before the final moments of closing, it is discovered that the borrower's PMI insurance is much higher than originally quoted. The borrower is so upset that he is ready to walk out.

  As luck would have it, there is no one to consult with, including the principal of your company. What might be the likely explanation and what are your options in order to still make this closing happen?

- Many people awaiting the purchase of homes often become anxious for many reasons. This could be due to credit report problems, delays in inspections, obtaining various paperwork or adequate insurance, slow title search, and a myriad of other snags and delays. Also, sometimes a closing just fails to happen. Discuss some of your own experiences in this regard and how you handled irate and upset clients.

As previously mentioned, each CBSSI question has pre-determined response standards that the president reviewed and approved. This was done to ensure that each question was job-related, focused on issues and problems that occur in her company, and to ensure that the sample response standards were what she expected.

The response standards were used as the benchmarks for rating how each candidate answers the questions in terms of how effective or ineffective a response is. We rated the candidate's responses on a 1 to 5 scale: 1 being the least effective and 5 being the most effective answer. The specific response standards were the prioritizing and planning and customer service behaviors.

Then a job description was written. The president reviewed it and made changes and reorganized the tasks in order of priority and importance. I also conducted research and obtained samples of loan processor newspaper ads and job descriptions from other companies. I used the job analysis information described above to draft a newspaper advertisement. Then, I provided training to the president on how to note take, the consensus process, how to establish rapport, and so on. We interviewed the eight candidates together.

Process Outcome

The new selection process was viewed very favorably by the president because she had several applicants to choose from, since the newspaper advertisement and online job posting were very specific and attracted candidates who had the desired education and work-related experience. She also learned not to select the first and only person she interviewed. Some of the candidates' answers to the questions substantiated that they were not qualified for the position even though they met the minimum qualifications, education, and work experience.

The president also learned that having a list of job-related CBSSI questions and a job description is very important. The newspaper advertisement and careful screening of the resumes and new job description were also very helpful. The customized CBSSI questions and work sample test also helped her determine very quickly whether or not each candidate had the technical job knowledge, despite what was stated in his or her resume. She communicated to me that she would continue to use the bank of questions and response standards and work sample test when she hires staff and will have a carefully written job description for each position.

Consulting Strategy 2: Listen to the Voice of the Customer

The regional bank was formed in 1952 with the opening of a single office. Now comprised of seventy-three branches, it is one of the largest and oldest financial institutions in the southeastern United States. It has invested more than half a century building its community branch network in many counties.

The bank is dedicated to serving its customers and community. Some of the convenient services it offers include, but are not limited to, seven-day branch banking, extended weekday hours, and a 24/7 customer service center.

The bank's approach to providing convenient customer service hinges strongly on anticipating and listening to the needs of the customer. The bank encourages feedback and takes seriously suggestions that can help it help its customers.

Problem/Situation

As one of the executive education professors for an executive development institute in the southeastern United States, I taught managers from various departments in the bank branches to develop CBSSI questions and response standards to reduce their hiring mistakes. Managers from the bank specifically expressed dissatisfaction with their hiring process and wanted to improve it. They engaged the services of the institute to assist them in this pursuit.

Generally, the executive development services offered at the Institute are generic, with some customization of program materials based on the client's needs and desires. The customized program I developed was designed to assist bank staff in assessing and selecting the best-qualified candidates to fill a few critical entry-level positions that were experiencing high turnover. The bank was having difficulty with the reliability of candidates who said during the interview process that they could work any hours required and then, once hired, reneged on their commitments.

For this bank, a four-hour management development module was delivered to management and supervisory personnel based on a generic model, part of which I designed. This four-hour workshop was part of a comprehensive, forty-hour management development program. The module is titled: Assessing, Selecting, and Hiring Employees. After the first presentation of the program, the human resources training and development staff asked the Institute to customize a program based on the bank's competency model. This was done for an additional fee. In this case, the Institute and the consultant listened to the voice of the customer, the bank, by revising the module to best meet its needs.

Data Collection and Process Design

The first step in the customization of the program was to meet with the manager of training and organization development and identify her needs. Prior to the meeting, I asked her to compile a packet of materials (competency model and competency definitions, hiring process procedures, forms job descriptions, etc.) and identify for me which bank positions had the highest turnover.

I reviewed the material and conducted an interview with her to find out exactly what the bank's assessment and selection processes entailed. This was an important part of the customization of the initial program, which was designed based on the use of panel interviews conducted by the bank staff.

The bank's current interview process did not require personnel to interview all candidates together and did not provide a list of competency-based questions and response standards that were asked of all candidates. At times, candidates were interviewed by more than one person. However, the questions were very generic and did not specifically tap into the competencies listed in the bank's competency model.

We also reviewed and discussed the feedback previous workshop participants had provided after the first workshop was delivered. The job descriptions were reviewed in order to develop some CBSSI questions and response standards that became part of the training program. All of this information was utilized to develop a new program for the bank.

The Bank's Competency Model

Figure 1 depicts the bank's core competency model. The bank developed the model based on the competencies it expected its employees to demonstrate to be successful on the job. The definitions of each competency were determined by the bank's human resources staff and were used when the employees who attended the training and I developed the CBSSI questions and response standards.

Some, but not all, of the competencies were already listed in the various job descriptions. Also, up until the time of the training session, the bank was neither using nor had developed a bank of questions that would tap into the competencies listed in the competency model. Additionally, the questions were generic, did not have response standards, and were not specific to the job.

The model was used as the framework to develop the sample questions and response standards and to teach the participants how to develop their own bank of questions based on the job descriptions and competencies from the model that pertained to each job description.

If the job descriptions require a person to provide "wow" customer service, then questions are developed that tap into the candidate's ability to demonstrate that competency. The definitions of the behavior are determined by the bank employees who are the subject-matter experts for each job and therefore know what "wow customer service" behaviors they are looking for.

Process Outcome

The assessing, selecting, and hiring module was considered the most valued of all of the management training modules, based on the surveys given to the employees who attended the training. Other anecdotal information was provided to the Institute by the manager, training and development, and shared with me. The survey results reflected 100 percent of the participants recommending the entire program to other bank managers. The program met or exceeded their expectations in terms of quality of course materials and activities. They strongly agreed that there was a good balance of theory and application.

As noted previously, the bank wanted the program to be customized and agreed to pay the additional cost for the customization. The survey results are a testimony to this. We were successful because we listened to the voice of the customer.

Consulting Strategy 3: Validate a Competency Model

As an elected constitutional officer, the clerk of the circuit is the public trustee for the judicial circuit and for a large county located in the southeastern United States. The clerk provides services to the public, the legal community, and the courts for both

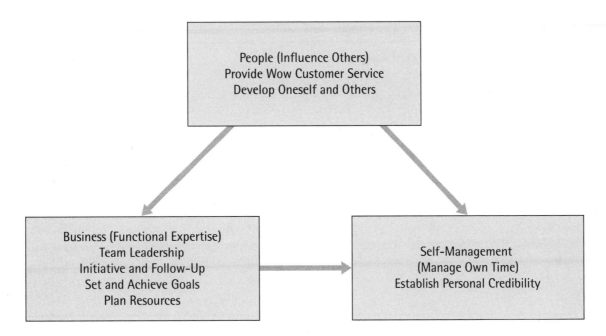

Figure 1. Bank Core Competency Model

the county and circuit criminal and civil court systems and is the custodian of court files and court-ordered payments. The clerk is also the chief financial officer to the Board of County Commissioners, custodian of all county funds, county auditor, county recorder, and custodian of the official record books. Each year, more than 4.3 million documents, 541,000 new cases, 800,000 walk-in customers, and 900,000 phone calls are processed through a variety of delivery systems. These include public service counters, public access computers, the Internet, telephone systems, mail, and interactive voice response (IVR). Each year, the approximately one hundred staff members process $151 million in payroll for 5,800 county employees and pre-audit more than 247,000 invoices totaling $514 million.

Problem/Situation

The clerk's human resources department did not have the resources or staff with the technical background to develop exercises for executive selection using assessment center methodology. The clerk was in the process of filling the chief deputy clerk of court services position and contracted with my firm to design and develop the process and train her human resources staff on how to administer and score the exercises.

Also, a comprehensive competency model was in place, but no competency-based type questions or exercises had ever been developed or used for executive selection. The process my firm developed validated the existing competency model for management personnel.

Exhibit 1.   Clerk of the Court Management Competencies and Sample Questions

Broad Competency: Environmental Awareness

Sub-Competency: Organizational Awareness

Is alert to events and trends within the organization and considers how they might influence the long-term performance of the organization. Can maneuver through complex political situations effectively and quietly. Keeps up on developments outside the organization that may have an impact on the business, such as trends in the industry, new technologies, and events in the larger economic and political environments.

Sample CBSSI Question: We assume that you understand the broad scope of the position's responsibilities, including five hundred direct and indirect reports, the importance of continuous smooth-running systems, the broad array of stakeholders, including customers, as well as the political ramifications of errors in judgment.

If you are selected, how would you acclimate yourself in your new job at the Clerk's office? Please be as specific as possible.

Broad Competency: Compelling Vision

Sub-Competency: Strategic Focus

Thinks strategically, creates an ongoing, dynamic strategic process, and communicates the organization's long-term direction.

Sample CBSSI Question: Tell us about a time when you seized the initiative when you became aware of an opportunity to "stay ahead of the curve" or saw the opportunity for a major enhancement to move the organization (or your department) forward in its function or mission—and how you accomplished it.

Process Design

Exhibit 1 depicts some of the competencies that each candidate was assessed on in the executive assessment process and some of the CBSSI questions that were asked of each candidate.

The job data, which included many critical incidents, was used to develop the job-related questions and response standards.

Now we will cover one of the competency-based exercises used in the process.

Personnel Coaching Exercise

The personnel coaching exercise (PC) requires the candidate to assume the role of chief deputy clerk of the circuit court, review some personnel file data, and prepare to answer some questions about a problem employee. The candidate is given background information about a problem employee and the contents of a personnel file. The in-

Exhibit 2.   Scenario for Personnel Coaching Exercise

Scenario: You are to assume that you are Chief Deputy Clerk Marjorie/Mike Brilliant, with Any County of the Circuit Court, Any County, U.S.A. You were recently promoted due to the sudden death of Chief Deputy Clerk Joanne Wizard. You do not know the personnel well. Your immediate supervisor is Clerk of the Circuit Court Marianne Ideas. You directly supervise nine managers and have five hundred employees working in the Court Services Division of the Clerk of the Circuit Court.

It is August 15, 2004, and Marianne Ideas, Clerk of Circuit Court, has requested your input regarding a situation so she has compiled some information for your review and evaluation. Unfortunately, your predecessor, Joanne Wizard, did not handle this personnel situation before her unexpected death. She was out ill for a few weeks before her death and was unable to complete many projects or deal with personnel issues. The clerk wants this situation handled before it's too late and she wants to know what your approach will be for handling the situation before you take any action. She has included four questions she wants you to answer. She and other members of her senior staff may also ask you some additional questions that are not included in your packet. The questions are located on page 12 of this exercise packet.

You have thirty minutes to review the information in this packet. You will then be escorted to a presentation room where you will have a maximum of ten minutes for your presentation to the rater panel. In your presentation to the raters, the clerk would like you to focus on what approach you will take, if any, to solve the problem(s). Be concise in describing your plan of action, if any, for handling the situation. Remember that you are Chief Deputy Clerk Marjorie/Mike Brilliant and are presenting to Marianne Ideas, Clerk of the Circuit Court, and some of her senior staff.

The specific questions are

1. What are the main issues/problems regarding this employee?

2. How would you go about dealing with the problems/situations, i.e., what strategies would you utilize?

3. How would you implement your plans? Please be specific.

4. What other actions would you take?

5. Please give us an experience where you took steps to develop a subordinate and how you generally went about it.

---

structions are very specific and detailed to ensure that there is no confusion and so each candidate clearly understands what is expected. The scenario is listed in Exhibit 2.

A complete sample of one of the competencies the candidate is assessed on is listed in Table 2. The behaviors are actually the response standards that tap into a candidate's ability to demonstrate the competencies.

The candidate is evaluated by the assessors in regard to what degree she or he demonstrated the behaviors listed in the assessor/rater guide. He or she is also given credit for other most effective behaviors or actions demonstrated. Each candidate is rated on a scale of 1 to 5 as follows:

5 = Highly desirable

4 = Desirable

3 = Somewhat desirable

2 = Would consider

1 = Would not consider

Table 2. Sample Competency Definitions and Behaviors

Judgment/Reasoning: Effectively diagnoses problems, identifies core issues,
exercises common sense, sees critical connections and ramifications, and analyzes alternatives.

Most Effective Judgment and Reasoning Behaviors/Actions	Least Effective Judgment and Reasoning Behaviors/Actions
1. Outlines general problems/issues with John Doe: his performance appraisal is due, the recent file data I just reviewed indicates both positive and negative feedback about him.	1. Just notes that this employee has some problems.
2. Identifies core issues, e.g., mixed feedback about him, commendation letter from clerk, citizen letter, staff complaints, performance appraisal is overdue, and performance issues do not seem to have improved since last year based on data at hand.	2. Is very vague on outlining the core issues.
3. Indicates s/he would review additional data (to include recent customer and employee survey results) in order to prepare a fair and accurate performance appraisal about employee before meeting with him.	3. Notes s/he would just prepare the review based on the data s/he has read; no other review of data noted would be done.
4. Would schedule a meeting with him to review and discuss his performance overall and the other information before preparing the performance appraisal document.	4. Would just prepare the review and/or a written warning without taking time to meet with him.
5. Recognizes that his recent nasty divorce, illness, and family medical problems may still be affecting his attitude and performance.	5. Does not recognize that there may be a connection between his performance and family problems, nasty divorce, injury.
6. Recognizes that staff complaints are same problems noted in his last performance appraisal.	6. Does not connect the recent staff complaints to what was documented in his last performance appraisal.
7. Indicates s/he would continue to keep clerk informed of situation.	7. S/he makes no mention of needing to keep the clerk informed.
8. Indicates s/he would start to prepare the performance appraisal based on this and other data, as the review is overdue and needs to be completed.	8. Makes no mention of the need to complete the performance appraisal.
9. Other most effective behaviors /actions.	9. Other least effective behaviors/actions.

Process Outcome

The clerk of the circuit court and her human resources director and other senior executive involved in the process were very pleased with the outcome. Their competency model was validated, and they were pleased that they had actively participated in the development of the process by serving as SMEs and providing me and my associate with valuable information about the position and with positive feedback about how satisfied they were with the process.

Consulting Strategy 4: Adapting to International Culture and Clientele

The resort hotel is a collection of eleven of some of the most idyllic beachfront resorts on earth, created exclusively for couples on several exotic islands. Each resort features a wide choice of gourmet dining experiences with free-flowing premium spirits. The resort also offers water sports, outside trips, on-site activities, and plenty of peace and quiet.

People from all over the world go to the resorts, and many return because of the first-class service offered and the warm and friendly hospitality. The resorts have also won numerous awards over the years.

Problem/Situation

The resort hotels on one of the islands rely on the company's training institute at corporate headquarters, which is located on another of the islands, to design and deliver many of the training and development programs for its staff. Resources were lacking on the nearby islands in terms of the availability of consultants with the expertise the resort chain needed to develop its personnel.

My firm was contracted to conduct strategic management and leadership competency development training. The course agenda for the eight-hour program is outlined in Exhibit 3.

Another problem was that the two programs needed to be delivered to all staff at all hotels on the island during the same two-week period with the least disruption of staff scheduling. I worked with the training manager for the three hotels to coordinate and schedule the training so as not to negatively impact operations.

Process Design

During the design of the process, I made sure that I became very familiar with the culture of the residents of the island as well as what some of their norms and values were. This also included finding out about managers who came from other countries to work for the resort. Also, during the training program, participants were asked to work on teams with people from different departments as well as different ethnic and racial backgrounds. The material was also designed and delivered such that it did not represent an American viewpoint. Not all principles and competencies apply to the island

Exhibit 3.   Program Agenda

I.   Introductions, Leadership Models, and Data and Group Exercise
  A.   Review of leadership models and study data exercises (half-hour)
  B.   Small-group exercise (1 hour)
    1.   What have you done as a leader to demonstrate what the gurus say is important?
    2.   What could you have done to improve?
  C.   Each group records each person's examples and discusses

II. Leadership/Competency Review/Discussion (1.5 hours)
  A.   Select three competencies most relevant to the hotel
    1.   Record what you have recently done that demonstrated selected competencies
    2.   Record how and why this has helped the hotel
    3.   Selection of most relevant competencies and their definitions
    4.   In small groups brainstorm other examples
  B.   Small-group exercise about competencies
    1.   Mistakes you have made?
    2.   What can you do to improve?
    3.   Final group discussion

III. Employee Coaching Exercise (1.5 hours)
  A.   Script review
  B.   Role assignments; supervisor (coach) and employee
  C.   Review of competencies assessed in exercise
  D.   Preparation/note taking
  E.   Conduct two role plays
  F.   Feedback and discussion

LUNCH

  G.   360-degree feedback (half-hour)
  H.   What is this tool? How is it used and why?
  I.   Peer, subordinate, boss or just one group
  J.   How to act on feedback obtained
  K.   Competency tie-in

IV. Staff Meeting Role Play (1 hour)
  A.   Script review
  B.   Role assignment
  C.   Review of competencies assessed
  D.   Preparation/note taking
  E.   Conduct one role play
  F.   Feedback and discussion

V.   Brainstorming Exercise (1.5 hours)
  A.   Small-group exercise—ways to improve in competencies
  B.   Individual action plans
  C.   Review sample action plans
    1.   When and how will you follow up?
    2.   Whom will you follow up with?
    3.   What about your staff?
  D.   Wrap-up and evaluations

culture, and this was stressed throughout the program. In other words, what is relevant in U.S. companies and resort hotels does not necessarily apply to the island country, even though the resort caters to similarly wealthy clientele.

Establishing rapport, showing respect and consideration for each participant's culture, not using technical jargon, and having them focus as much as possible on their experiences in the region of the world in which the hotel was located contributed to the success of the training program.

Process Outcome

The post-training survey results were very favorable. The majority of the ratings were either 4 or 5, and many favorable open-ended comments were provided by the participants. The training manager was so pleased with the results that, shortly after I returned to the United States, she asked me to conduct the same program at two other resort hotels in the region.

Conclusion

When working on projects for any client, no matter what the scope of the project, several summary points are worth noting. First, utilize a methodology that works and enables you to complete all aspects of the project. Second, standardize components when applicable. Third, focus on the strategy or strategies that will result in a successful project, even if the strategy selected is one where you decide to walk away from the contract. The major goal should not only be delivering the product to the client on time and within budget, but to complete a project that will be viewed very favorably by the client. Even though as a consultant you do not own the final product, you are still obligated to make sure that what the client invested in he or she is pleased with. This can only happen if you carefully select your methodologies and design and develop the products and strategies that ensure the success of the project.

My overall goal for any consulting project is to make a positive contribution to the organization that will have lasting results. Also if, at the end of the engagement, I retain that client I have also succeeded.

Strategy is critically important to completing any project and for success in consulting, business, or government. The consultant must be able to execute different strategies for successful implementation. At times, the needs of the client, organizational resources, personnel and budgetary issues, and other variables may and do change. When this occurs, the consultant must be adaptable and willing and able to modify his or her strategy in order to ensure successful completion of the project. The projects discussed in this paper pertain to competency-based assessment for personnel selection and leadership development, where each project conforms to generally accepted principles and practices and contains strategy components for successful consulting engagements. If you focus on the client and the strateg(ies) and their execution, the final project outcome will be positive and should have a lasting effect.

Dr. Linsey Craig-Willis, *SPHR, is president of L.J. Craig & Associates Inc., a management and organizational consulting firm specializing in the custom design of people management systems (written exams, assessment centers, interview processes), leadership training, organization development, and expert witness services. Dr. Willis is also on the adjunct faculty at Florida Atlantic University College of Business Administration, Barry University, Florida, and Lynn University School of Business and Management.*

Human Resource Management:
Lessons Learned from the U.S. Army
Jack L. Howard

Summary

All organizations face challenges when managing their human resources, and the U.S. military is no different. Like many organizations around the world, the U.S. military has downsized, focusing on technological advances as a competitive advantage. However, those leaders responsible for managing human resources, whether human resource planning or executing missions requiring human resources, have failed to effectively manage their human resources, particularly those from the Army's reserve components.

In this paper, several examples of how human resources were mismanaged will be presented. With a focus on human resource planning, possible solutions for future operations will be discussed, including the adoption of human resource management practices from both the private and public sectors.

Pursuing human resource planning is essential in order for organizations to maximize both their effectiveness and the effective use of their human resources. Regardless of the advantages that technology or other resources might provide to organizations, without people to effectively utilize that technology or other resources, the organizations will rarely, if ever, achieve their maximum potential. This is especially true of organizations that rely on human resources to exercise discretion in the conduct of their operations, such as the U.S. military.

In this article, human resource planning practices and issues are discussed, followed by an examination of activities that occurred during a recent military operation, with a focus on human resource planning. Finally, a discussion of recommendations to improve the human resource planning for military operations is presented.

Human Resource Planning

Human resource planning has been defined as "the process of assessing the organization's human resource needs in the light of organizational goals and changing conditions and making plans to ensure that a competent, stable work force is employed" (French, 2003, p. 140). This indicates the need for those in the position of planning for the effective use of human resources to take into account the organization's strategic plan, as well as scanning the environment for changes in technology and the conditions under which the organization is going to operate (French, 2003; Jackson & Schuler, 2003; Jarrell, 1993; Kudia, 1978; Thomas, 1980). While scanning the environment could involve a seemingly endless list of issues to address, one of the keys is to focus on the relationship between the organization's goals and the human resources needed to achieve these goals (Dessler, 2004; Fisher, Schoenfeldt, & Shaw, 2003).

When doing human resource planning, organizations should consider a variety of organizational plans. Certainly, the strategic plan should be considered as an overall guideline, but human resource planners should also consider tactical and operational plans as well (Jarrell, 1993). This allows for the refinement of human resource planning in order to address specific environmental factors facing all or part of the organization. By considering both tactical and operational plans while scanning the environment, appropriate forecasts for human resources can be made. These forecasts should focus on getting the right people with the right skills in the right place at the right time. This will ensure that human resources will be used effectively and efficiently, rather than having human resources that are underutilized.

A second consideration is the organizational structure, since this can influence how tasks and responsibilities among various organizational units are allocated (Jackson & Schuler, 2003). This is especially pertinent in military operations, as units as a whole are mobilized and deployed. This process is explained in more detail in the following sections. Additionally, the use of effective human resource planning can and does influence the ability of organizations to effectively recruit and retain quality employees (Jackson & Schuler, 2003). Organizations that consistently hire employees who are either over- or under-qualified for positions will face challenges, such as increased turnover and decreased morale and motivation.

Finally, when considering human resource planning, it is imperative to continue to link human resource plans to specific objectives. The most specific objectives in an organization's plans will be consistently found at the tactical and operational levels. The strategic plan provides the overall direction, while the tactical and operational plans focus on the issues at hand. As such, considering the issues at hand should lead to refined and more effective human resource plans, to include needs forecasts for the specific number of employees and the skills required of these employees.

Army System for Deployment

The U.S. Army has a system for selecting units for mobilization and deployment around the globe in support of various military operations. While the system is very complex, a brief examination of what should occur in a perfect world from a layman's perspective are presented. Three components are discussed in the next few paragraphs.

First, units have an *organizational structure,* including equipment, that the army planners have decided is best for the army's needs. This structure and equipment dictate the type of unit, as well as limit the types of missions that the unit should be assigned, given the skills of the personnel and the other resources at the unit's disposal. This is the most basic component of the three to be discussed, as the structure and equipment dictate the abilities and limits of the unit. For example, a variety of truck companies exist. One type of truck company hauls fuel, another type hauls general cargo, while still another type is designed to haul heavy equipment, such as tanks and mechanized artillery. The type of hauling equipment dictates the type of equipment or supply that the truck company is capable of moving. This is the case for both active duty and reserve component units.

Second, units, whether they are active duty or reserve component units, belong to a *larger, overarching organization.* Additionally, reserve component units belong to two different organizations. At times when the unit is not mobilized and deployed, reserve units belong to a peacetime command, comprising other reserve units. However, reserve units also belong to an organization, even during peacetime, that represents their wartime chain of command. This chain of command comprises both active duty and reserve component units. For reserve units, however, this chain of command approves the mission and related tasks that the reserve unit is supposed to train on in preparation for possible mobilization and deployment.

The wartime chain of command is an organizational structure, based on capabilities of units that should be able to conduct operations together to ensure mission success. For example, a Corps might be identified as an overall organization for an operation of a particular scale. That Corps then has Divisions assigned to it. Those Divisions have Brigades assigned to them. This carries on down to the Battalion, Company, and Detachment level. So if a Corps is tapped to do a mission, then the entire wartime chain of command, meaning all of its divisions and subordinate units, will be mobilized and deployed. If the decision is to tap a division, rather than a corps, to conduct a mission, then that division's wartime chain of command, meaning all subordinate brigades and lower will be mobilized, but the other divisions affiliated with the corps will not be mobilized.

It is important to note that reserve and National Guard units that typically work together within a peacetime chain of command often do not fall under the same wartime chain of command. Additionally, rarely do these units interact on a face-to-face basis, and more often it is the case that the determination and agreement on missions and related tasks are made through various communication channels, such as telephone and email. Nonetheless, this provides the highest level of command with information as to the number and types of units at its disposal so that exercises and operations can effectively be planned.

Finally, when units are mobilized and deployed, once a level of command is notified of the mobilization and pending deployment, all units that fall under its command structure are also notified. In other words, the entire organization that falls beneath that command is then mobilized and prepared for deployment. This provides the organization the advantage of knowing what assets should be on their way, as well as their capabilities and allows the organization to draw up operational plans in order to support its requirements.

Human Resource Plans in Action

During late 2002, the U.S. military was gearing up for major operations in Southwest Asia, due to increased tensions between the United States and Iraq. The plan was for most units to move to Iraq and Kuwait, but other locations, such as Turkey, Qatar, and Bahrain, were also being examined. Beyond the units that were already present in the region, additional units were sent to the region in preparation for the anticipated operations. Additionally, major commands had been identified and operations were being planned during this time, even though most units would not arrive in the region until early 2003. This information is critical to the following discussion, which represents one unit's experience during this operation.

Mobilization and Deployment Experience of One Unit

One reserve unit that fell under a major command that was tapped to conduct military operations during 2003 and 2004 had no inkling of its possible mobilization and deployment. The immediate higher peacetime command also had no information about such activity, as numerous conversations between the commander of the unit being examined and the next-higher-level commander occurred during the several months preceding the mobilization of this unit, and neither commander had any information about possibly being deployed. Additionally, the unit was scheduled for a typical fourteen-day annual training and was in the middle of this annual training when it was notified of its mobilization. As a leader within this unit, I had access to the details of what the unit experienced.

It is important to note that this unit, a detachment, is the lowest level of units in existence in the U.S. Army. Additionally, this unit works closely with a peacetime chain of command, which is in touch with the overall army system and must work through this system to identify and work with the wartime chain of command. A key fact is that the unit was never able to determine its wartime chain of command. Attempts to determine the wartime chain of command over a period of thirty months had resulted in no positive identification of this command. The peacetime chain of command consistently pointed to a unit that was not an appropriate or correct higher wartime headquarters, and this command indicated on numerous occasions that it was not the correct wartime chain of command.

Once notified, the unit immediately packed up its equipment and personnel and arranged for the transport of both to its reserve installation so that it could pack up and move to a mobilization station. This occurred in less than twenty-four hours. Once at the reserve installation, the unit had seventy-two hours to pack up its equipment for transport to the mobilization station, where the unit was to report for final preparations in support of its deployment to Southwest Asia.

Once at the mobilization station, the unit pursued necessary training in order to be properly prepared for its deployment. This training occurred over a fourteen-day period. During this time, it became apparent that the shortage of two key leader positions would need to be addressed, and the peacetime command intervened, identifying two soldiers to be sent to the unit to fill these vacancies. These two soldiers arrived twenty days after the unit had arrived at the mobilization station. Given this situation, these two soldiers had to complete necessary training over the next ten days.

Even though the unit was prepared for its mission within thirty days of arrival at the mobilization station, transportation was not available to the theater of operations for an additional forty-nine days, resulting in a total of seventy-nine days spent at the mobilization station. This additional time provided the opportunity for the unit to attempt to make contact with its higher headquarters. Several attempts to contact the planners to determine the immediate higher headquarters were unsuccessful. Calls and email messages went unanswered. When these attempts failed, the unit commander went to the commanding general's staff at the post where the unit was training to seek assistance from a higher level. Attempts on the part of the general's staff were also met with unanswered telephone and email messages.

Once the unit arrived in Southwest Asia, it became apparent at the reception station that there was no one there who knew who the unit was to report to. After a period of two days, the appropriate higher headquarters was identified. Once the unit reported to the higher headquarters, a message was sent by the overall command in the operation that the reserve unit was not to come to Southwest Asia; it was to remain in the United States and demobilize, meaning it was to be released from active duty and returned to reserve status. However, since the unit was already in Southwest Asia, it was not to be sent back to the United States.

After reporting to the higher command, it became apparent that the battalion did not have a plan on how to use the detachment, its assets, or capabilities. After approximately thirty days, the unit began to be dismantled, with the unit being broken into four major segments. Some soldiers were used to supplement the higher headquarters' administrative staff, assisting in the processing of personnel paperwork and activities, such as performance evaluations, processing soldiers' paperwork for leave, and ensuring that soldiers were paid correctly. Other soldiers were used to supplement the higher headquarters' operations staff. In this capacity, soldiers worked directly with the battalion staff, planning operations in order to meet the requirements of the operation. Essentially, these soldiers planned and monitored battalion operations to ensure the mission requirements were met successfully. Finally, the rest of the soldiers were broken into two major operations components at three different locations, a minimum of forty-five miles apart. Soldiers either controlled access points to various military locations, determining which vehicles and personnel could enter, or worked on transporting cargo via the use of a railroad system. As such, the unit was disbanded for the operation, only to be put back together to return to the United States.

Finally, it is important to point out that the tasks performed by the personnel in these four major components were not what the unit had trained for and were inconsistent with the mission and structure of the unit. As such, soldiers were learning on the job and were not used in their areas of expertise and strength. This led to low morale among soldiers, as well as inefficiencies while soldiers learned new tasks. It also led to confusion, as in many cases the assigned tasks changed several times prior to a unit being assigned a mission or task on a permanent basis.

The Army System Meets Reality

When one compares what is supposed to occur with the army's system and what did occur, some glaringly deficient areas are apparent. In the following paragraphs, I briefly summarize these major areas.

First, given that plans were being made for the unit's wartime chain of command in 2002, warning orders should have been given to the subordinate units about pending mobilization and deployment. Knowing now that these plans were being made, the unit being examined should not have gone to an annual training and instead should have been preparing for mobilization and deployment.

Second, the reserve unit being examined was unsuccessful over a period of thirty days in trying to contact its wartime chain of command. In fact, the higher headquarters that had been identified by the peacetime command was incorrect, and attempts to bring this to the attention of higher headquarters went unheard. Units did not know their appropriate chains of command due to unknown communication problems within the active and reserve components of the U.S. Army. This made it clear to the unit that the higher headquarters did not have accurate information from the larger army system about the wartime chain of command. It also made it clear that the higher peacetime headquarters, up three levels in this case, did not fully understand the capabilities and missions of all of its subordinate units. If it did understand these capabilities and missions, the headquarters could have easily identified that the movement control detachment did not logically report to a materiel management center. As a result of this problem, considerable confusion was experienced on the part of all units involved, resulting in the inability to contact higher headquarters and arrange to meet once in Southwest Asia.

Third, because the higher headquarters was not familiar with all of its subordinate units, this resulted in units being mobilized and deployed with a specific mission, when in fact the mission was inappropriate for the environment and operations to be pursued. This further resulted in employing soldiers in capacities other than what they had been trained for, resulting in low levels of morale and motivation. For example, the movement control team in question is designed to work in airports or seaports, assisting in the flow of cargo and personnel into and out of an area of operations. This is very different from assisting on the administrative and operations staffs, and certainly does not include work on rail transportation operations. In many cases, soldiers believed that they were being set up for failure, given the lack of experience and training for the tasks they were being required to perform.

Finally, it is important to note that while the situation that faced this unit is being presented, this situation was not unique to this unit. Conversations with many individuals from a wide variety of units revealed that this was an issue that many units faced. Based on my interaction with over forty different units, it became clear that at least ten of these units faced similar circumstances, representing units with a variety of structures and missions.

Recommendations

Any organization should examine its operations to determine what works well and what needs to be improved in order to better operate in the future. In terms of the military operation examined in this paper, some areas work well, such as mobilizing and deploying an entire wartime chain of command, while others need improvement, such as communication between the various levels of a wartime chain of command. Six specific recommendations are made in the following paragraphs.

First, while activating an entire command structure and all of its subordinate units did occur, improvements need to be made if this is the model that will continue to be used. First and foremost, the wartime chain of command needs to be accurate and communicate effectively down to the lowest levels. This can be accomplished by the wartime chain of command making contact with the subordinate units on a regular basis, in addition to the active duty, reserve, and National Guard commands working together to identify the correct chain of command for every unit in the U.S. Army system. By working on this from more than one perspective, all units would be identified as belonging to an overall wartime organization. To illustrate the problems, the unit under examination was consistently told a particular unit was their higher command for wartime scenarios. However, that was not the case. In fact, the supposed higher command is in an entirely different functional area than the subordinate unit, and there is no logical relationship between the two units. Not having the correct information led to delays for the unit being mobilized and deployed, as well as the correct higher command not being able to plan effectively for the use of the subordinate unit.

Communication within chains of command needs to occur and should require, at a minimum, semi-annual meetings within the chain of command. Commanders of all units should be required to meet with their higher headquarters as part of a conference, ensuring that the various units know the larger wartime organization to which they belong. While some might argue that this is an expensive venture, the fact is that these meetings would allow for the streamlining of information, in effect saving in the future, as transitions could be conducted on a more efficient basis. Thus, my first recommendation is as follows:

- *Recommendation 1:* The army needs to ensure that the wartime chain of command provided to subordinate units, particularly reserve and national guard units, is correct, and regular communications and meetings should be established.

The army does an outstanding job of determining its strategic plan and determining which units would best support that strategy. However, from a layman's perspective, it appears that when facing a specific situation, environmental scanning and tactical planning either do not occur or are largely ignored. If the U.S. Army conducted environmental scanning and tactical planning, changes could be made to best support the strategic plan (French, 2003; Jackson & Schuler, 2003; Jarrell, 1993; Kudia, 1978; Thomas, 1980). In the situation examined in this paper, this would have resulted in selecting the correct number of specific types of units for a specific mission, rather than selecting units that had no definite mission, resulting in the dismantling of the unit because there was not a specific mission for them. Essentially, this means that the army should consider the specific details of the mission from a tactical and operational planning perspective. This would effectively employ units and soldiers in a manner consistent with their training and mission, improving morale and motivation considerably.

My second recommendation is as follows:

- *Recommendation 2:* Mobilize and deploy units based on the tactical mission faced, as opposed to the overall wartime chain of command.

When units are dismantled for a specific operation, only to be brought back together in order to be sent home, any benefits of training as a unit, such as cohesiveness and synergies, are lost (Jackson & Schuler, 2003; Jarrell, 1993). Additionally, morale and motivation drop as well, as was the case in Southwest Asia with several units (Jarrell, 1993). Human resource management ensures that commanders and leaders determine how to use their resources, even if it is at an aggregate, unit level. The most valuable resource in the U.S. Army is its human resources, for without the human resources, all the technology in the world cannot be operated and is thus rendered useless. It became apparent that some higher-level commanders (higher than the line units) did not know how to effectively utilize their human resources. In many cases, not only were units dismantled to meet a variety of needs, but certain individuals were moved around constantly. Few, if any, attempts were made to determine the knowledge, skills, and abilities (KSAs) of the soldiers being placed in these situations. Knowing the KSAs of employees is imperative if an organization is to effectively employ its human resources in order to achieve its objectives (Jackson & Schuler, 2003). However, few, if any, conversations took place to determine what KSAs the soldiers brought to the table. This is particularly important in the case of working with reserve and national guard units, as these soldiers not only have military occupations, but they bring with them a wide array of KSAs from the civilian workforce. If these KSAs are ignored, the army may not be employing these soldiers in a way that best benefits the soldiers or the army, resulting in negative consequences such as low morale.

In order to address this issue, the following are recommended:

- *Recommendation 3:* All officers and senior non-commissioned officers (E-8 and above) should be required to receive human resource planning and management training.

- *Recommendation 4:* Resources (that is, units) should be used appropriately. Deploy units for a mission consistent with their mission and training.

- *Recommendation 5:* In the event that individual soldiers are pulled from units or units are dismantled to meet mission requirements, spend the time to determine the KSAs that the soldiers bring to the table in order to employ these soldiers in a manner that benefits both the organization and the individual.

Finally, in some areas within the military, units work in a field with related missions, but each is assigned a specific mission so that the unit can focus on a given area. For example, soldiers can work in an area called "movement control." While soldiers are all from the same occupational specialty, there are vastly different tasks and requirements depending on the type of movement control team to which a soldier is assigned. One area is highway regulation, which acts as a checkpoint to ensure that traffic is moving smoothly and that only authorized traffic is proceeding. Another area is area movement control, which regulates when units leave and enter an area of operations. Finally, there are port movement control teams, which focus on either airport or seaport operations. As such, there are very different tasks involved, and a soldier exposed to only one of these areas will not as easily be able to transition into a different area. This system results in units developing a level of skill and expertise, but also limits the flexibility of the military to mobilize and deploy units, which could result in selecting units that are not appropriate for a mission due to a shortage of units that are appropriate for the mission. In order to allow for increased flexibility, the army could examine its units and, rather than assign a specific mission to a unit, assemble multifunctional teams that are capable of performing a variety of related missions. By training in all areas, the units would essentially become multifunctional teams, providing increased flexibility for the U.S. Army. Thus, recommendation six is as follows:

- *Recommendation 6:* In cases where it is appropriate, use multifunctional teams rather than mission-specific teams in order to provide increased flexibility in operational environments.

What Business Can Learn from the U.S. Army Experience

Several lessons can be applied directly to business. First, when planning in business, strategic plans and operational plans are found on a regular basis, but tactical plans should also be developed and utilized (Jarrell, 1993). Even after these plans are developed, environmental scanning should continue, as changes in the environment may affect the resources, including human resources, that a business needs to consider in order to remain competitive. This in many cases will influence human resource forecasts, ensuring that the right people with the right skills are in the right place at the right time. Additionally, by including and continuing to refine the tactical plan, this might enhance the business's ability to effectively recruit and retain quality employees (Jackson & Schuler, 2003). Ultimately, however, it is important to continue to link these plans to the strategic plan, ensuring that long-term objectives are not forgotten.

A second lesson learned is that all employees in a supervisory or managerial position in business should receive training on human resource management issues. In many cases, these individuals are evaluating performance, recommending salary increases, making recommendations concerning training for employees, and making recommendations for promotion. These are all human resource management issues, and many supervisory and managerial employees may not have had the benefit of receiving training on human resource management. Given this, organizations should provide supervisory and managerial employees some training and/or education on human resource management issues, such as performance evaluation, training, and compensation.

Third, businesses should use their human resources appropriately. Employees bring to the business a wide variety of KSAs (Jackson & Schuler, 2003). Employees are typically hired for a particular job, but these same employees might also have other KSAs that are not being utilized. A potential solution is to incorporate human resource information systems where data on employees is stored. This data can include such information as education, positions held in the organization, foreign language knowledge, certifications, and specific skills. In addition to this system, a business should encourage employees to provide all information about the various KSAs and backgrounds they have, since some employees might provide only information that applies to their current jobs. By having this information, organizations can quickly identify employees who might be suitable for a wide variety of assignments within the organization.

Fourth, a business should examine its processes to determine whether it is possible with the present workforce, or with appropriate training, that multifunctional teams can be used in the workplace. While some might consider this to be an expensive venture in terms of training costs, the flexibility that a business might gain could result in increased productivity for the organization. For example, on a work team, each employee might have a particular job to do. If an employee with critical information or KSAs that others in the team do not possess is absent, progress might be inhibited. By having multifunctional teams, one employee's absence might not result in slower progress. This could provide many benefits for the organization, as well as enhancing the KSAs of the employees.

Conclusion

Clearly, the human resource planning practices of the military need to be improved. The strategic plan and alignment of units for missions appear to focus largely on an overall strategy—and from a line unit's perspective do not consider the tactical and operational situations faced by units, nor do they effectively consider various environmental factors. By seriously considering the recommendations made in this paper, human resource planning by the U.S. Army can be improved. By taking these actions, units and soldiers who have not been properly trained for a given mission will not be selected, and loss of motivation and morale will be reduced, improving not only the performance of the units and soldiers on the immediate mission, but also improving retention of quality soldiers.

It is imperative that leaders within the military learn, understand, and apply the basics of human resource management. Knowing what KSAs are and understanding how to best utilize the KSAs brought by the soldiers would provide an enormous opportunity for the military. Additionally, the present military struggles are anything but traditional military operations, so taking advantage of the diverse KSAs that reserve component soldiers bring to the battlefield could enhance future non-conventional operations.

By reconsidering how missions are assigned, the U.S. Army can increase its flexibility through the use of multifunctional teams. This would also provide the benefit of avoiding situations in which units and soldiers believe that they are being assigned missions inconsistent with their units' missions and training. This would assist in preventing situations where morale and motivation drop to very low levels. Additionally, this could potentially increase the effectiveness of the units, as units and their soldiers would receive training on a variety of potential missions, rather than focusing in on a single mission.

The lessons learned apply to businesses, which should ensure that human resources are utilized effectively and to their fullest. Knowing what KSAs employees bring provides the organization with increased flexibility when facing changing conditions in the workplace and the marketplace. Enhancing employees' skills can assist the business in developing this flexibility. By considering and implementing these lessons, business and their employees can both benefit.

References

Dessler, G. (2004). *A framework for human resource management* (3rd ed.). Upper Saddle River, NJ: Pearson Prentice Hall.

Fisher, C.D., Schoenfeldt, L.F., & Shaw, J.B. (2003). *Human resource management* (5th ed.). Boston, MA: Houghton Mifflin.

French, W.L. (2003). *Human resources management* (5th ed.). Boston, MA: Houghton Mifflin.

Jackson, S.E., & Schuler, R.S. (2003). *Managing human resources through strategic partnerships* (8th ed.). Cincinnati, OH: Thomson–SouthWestern.

Jarrell, D.W. (1993). *Human resource planning*. Englewood Cliffs, NJ: Prentice Hall.

Kudia, R.J. (1978). The components of strategic planning. *Long Range Planning, 11*(6), 48–52.

Thomas, P.S. (1980). Environmental scanning: The state of the art. *Long Range Planning, 13*(1), 20–28.

Jack L. Howard, *Ph.D., is an associate professor of human resource management at Illinois State University, Normal, Illinois, where he teaches and conducts research on human resource management issues. Additionally, he is a Major in the Army Reserve. He has written numerous articles on a variety of human resource management topics, including human resource management issues for small business, employee rights, workplace violence, and political influence in the workplace.*

Implementing a Human Resource Planning and Development System at Cape Cod Health Care

Richard P. Kropp

Summary

This paper describes how Cape Cod Health Care put in place a human resource planning and development system. Cape Cod built a three-stage model to distinguish themselves in the marketplace and address a series of business issues. They defined the major components of the project to ensure a single mindset on what was about to take place. This paper identifies the necessary components of the system as determined by environmental scans and the benefits of the system to managers and employees.

Cape Cod Health Care (CCHC) is a health care organization of approximately 5,500 employees that has three major business entities as well as several smaller but important units. In calendar year 2003 we initiated the process of developing a human resource planning and development (HRPD) system. We developed the plan in three stages.

During the first stage we assembled a team of human resource professionals and external resources to identify the needs of the organization, outline the essential elements of the HRPD system, and develop a model for the system development.

In stage two we used a similar team construct to develop the system to the point that it could be discussed with various senior executives in order to identify cultural and organizational needs that needed to be met, as well as determining the degree to which the executive team was ready to support implementation of such a comprehensive system.

When stage two was complete, we supplemented the existing team with additional resources and completed the development process. Tools to support the system were also developed for HR and executive staff. A comprehensive briefing was provided to all those who were involved in implementation.

Before moving on to the outline of the HRPD system, it is worthwhile looking at the rationale behind this initiative.

Reasons for Taking Action

This health care organization wants to be "best of breed" in all three basic functions of its business: quality/service management, financial management, and human resource management.

As its mission and vision state, this organization is in business to provide the best possible health care services in response to the current and future needs of its community. Its priorities will always be based on this service to the community. But, as a business, it will only be able to continue to provide those services—at the level it knows the community deserves—if it operates successfully as a business based on financial solvency, the quality of services, and the performance of its people.

Compelling business issues are associated with the commitment to best practices in human resource management. The organization wants to:

1. Prepare for the future, not the present. It needs to learn to better identify the competencies it and its clients will require in two or three years and develop these resources appropriately.

2. Reduce the costs associated with voluntary turnover, recruitment of outstanding employees, unfilled vacancies, and lost business and opportunities due to unmotivated or under-performing staff.

3. Be an employer of choice, using principles from the magnet hospital studies, and attract and retain the best and brightest health care professionals available from anywhere. Cape Cod would prefer to grow its own wherever and whenever possible and retain them by offering more desirable job and career opportunities than any other employment alternatives.

4. Reduce or eliminate employment-related practices liability exposures.

5. Improve the productivity and performance of all employees.

6. Reduce the costs associated with unfilled job openings.

7. Improve employee and customer satisfaction with CCHC.

8. Provide clear performance expectations for all employees (especially leader-managers) and the skills and resources required to exceed those expectations.

9. Grow our own talent in all functions and professions.

10. Better inventory our human assets and apply them where they will most benefit CCHC and the individuals involved.

The Development Process

In stage one, as mentioned earlier, the essential elements of the system were identified. At that time those elements were listed as talent acquisition, performance management, employee training and development, promotables management, high-potential management, succession and replacement planning, and reward and recognition systems. These elements, linked together in an HRPD system, provide a talent pipeline for the enterprise. Additional definition was developed as the process continued through stages two and three. This included a serious look at the process of human resource management.

What Is Human Resource Management?

Human resource management (HRM) refers to our organization's commitment to maximizing our investment in our most important assets: our human assets. HRM includes two basic components: HR planning and HR development. Each of these components is described in detail in subsequent sections.

For the purposes of our discussion about HRM, we use the following definitions:

1. *Human resource management* refers to the process that represents the organization's commitment to maximizing its investment in our most important asset: people. This includes the following responsibilities for every leader/ manager:

   - Anticipating the near- and long-term knowledge, skills, and abilities needed to provide the best possible health care services to the community and implement associated planning processes within the operation;

   - Recruiting, hiring, assimilating, and developing new employees in accordance with the organization's standards, policies, and procedures; this includes both outside and internal candidates;

   - Developing and communicating performance expectations for each employee;

- Monitoring performance periodically, and communicating perform-ance results with the employee (including—but not limited to—an annual performance evaluation);

- Working continuously with each employee to help improve his or her performance, including agreeing on an annual individual development plan; and

- Conducting an annual review of employee career interests and related CCHC career opportunities.

2. *Human resource planning* refers to the part of the human resource manage-ment process associated with the responsibility of every leader-manager to anticipate the near- and long-term knowledge, skills, and abilities needed to provide the best possible health care services to the community and to implement associated planning processes within their operations.

3. *Human resource development* refers to the part of the human resource man-agement process associated with the responsibility of every leader-manager to increase the value of human assets.

4. *Human Resources Department* refers to the organizational unit that is respon-sible for assisting the organization's leader-managers in performing their human resource management responsibilities.

5. *Human assets* refers to the employees of the health care system. (Please note: human assets are the only assets that can appreciate in value.)

6. *Leader-manager and management* refer to all employees of the organization who have primary hire/fire responsibilities for any other employees.

7. *Human resources department consultant* refers to individual employees of the Human Resources Department who are trained in human resource man-agement support skills and assigned to assist leader-leader-manager teams in all human resources functions.

The front-end work for any successful HRPD process is what we called *human resource planning.* It is what is necessary to identify current and future "people" and "organiza-tional" needs of the organization. It feeds the talent acquisition and the development sub-systems. We highlight that process, providing significant detail because of the im-portance we place on it, and then provide an overview of some of the other elements of the HRPD system.

Introduction to Human Resource Planning

Definition

Human resource planning is a process that helps the organization's leader-managers to identify our current and future human resource needs. These needs include:

- Identifying the appropriate number of employees needed and in which positions;

- Projecting the competencies (knowledge, skills, and abilities) expected to be needed to achieve strategic goals and objectives;

- Anticipating and filling staffing gaps; and

- Aligning human resources strategies with the organization's strategic goals and objectives.

A comprehensive human resource plan identifies and addresses each department's strategic human resource issues as it plan its operations to achieve quality/service, financial, and human resource management goals.

All department leader-managers at the health care system will be asked to submit a departmental human resource plan that includes and supports the organization's human resource plan. Each department will also report on mid-year and year-end results for the annual budget cycle year.

Key Action Steps in Human Resource Planning

Some key steps at the individual level are

- Understand the strategic direction of the organization and your pieces of it;

- Conduct an internal and external environmental scan;

- Determine local staffing needs over the next three years;

- Create an action plan to ensure that staffing needs are met; and

- Measure and report on progress and results.

Each of these action steps is described in detail in the remainder of this section. Among the programs necessary to complete the action steps described above are

- Identify succession plans for all key positions in the department;

- Develop competencies for clinical, technical, professional, and support positions within the department and related career development programs;

- Continuously solicit and use employee recommendations associated with improving working conditions;

- Ensure that all employees have career development plans in their personnel files;

- Implement annual workplace diversity work plans with attainable quantitative and qualitative goals;

- Determine staffing requirements, considering financial, operational/clinical, and human resource management goals;

- Survey and identify talent within the department/organization;

- Know the training and development requirements for each employee; and

- Ensure follow-through on planning and action items.

The Benefits of Human Resource Planning

Good human resource planning benefits patients/customers, employees, managers, and the health care system as a whole.

Benefits to Patients, Customers, and the Community

Customers and patients of the health care system need and deserve the best possible health care services. We all understand that meeting (at least) or exceeding these expectations is a part of our collective responsibility. Good human resource planning ensures that qualified caregivers and support staff are available and perform at their best when customers/patients need them.

Benefits to Employees

Employees want to work in an environment that:

- Clearly identifies their jobs;

- Specifies performance expectations;

- Provides training, tools, and resources needed to do the job well;

- Encourages continuous improvement;

- Recognizes good performance;

- Provides constructive performance feedback;

- Allows them to do the job; and

- Reduces undesirable "surprises" (e.g., being alone on a three-person shift).

Good human resource planning (and implementation) helps provide the kind of environment in which working for and with us is far more attractive than any alternatives. Adequate staffing, the availability of required skills, and professional management are all direct results of good human resource planning.

Benefits to Managers

Leader-managers have the responsibility for assisting employees in developing their potential and making the best use of their abilities and are also responsible for ensuring that the organization provides the services the community requires.

Human resource planning is all about ensuring that the organization has the right people for the right jobs at the right time. It reduces uncertainty and increases the manager's ability to do his or her job. And managers, as employees, also benefit, as described above.

More specific benefits to leader-managers include:

- Reduced stress associated with inadequate staffing;

- More control over outcomes;

- Increased ability to delegate work;

- Improved multidisciplinary and unit teamwork resulting from collective participation in the planning process;

- The opportunity to advocate resource needs; and

- Improving own career development opportunities by growing potential replacements.

Core Components of Human Resource Planning

This section outlines the core components that are essential for an effective human resource plan. A sample outline is provided, along with tools to assist in developing a human resource plan.

An effective human resource plan includes the following elements:

Introduction

This is an overview of your department and its key partners. The purpose of this section is to provide some high-level information on the department, including what it does and who its key partners are. It should provide readers with a general understanding of the department. The following information should be included: description of the department's reason for existence; high-level information on the programs and services delivered; and identification of key partners required to deliver on the plan.

Strategic Direction of the Department

This is a summary of where the department is headed over the next one to three years and what action steps it intends to take to get there. Based on what factors, how are they measured, and in whose judgment? To what business needs/goals are they connected?

Environmental Scan

This scan includes a brief summary of the key human resource issues and trends arising out of an internal and external environmental scan. This identification and analysis of the key human resource issues and implications includes both the external and internal environments (that is, economic climate, legislation, technology, social factors, organizational climate, etc.). Most of this information should be contained in summary format when the environmental scan is completed.

An *internal* environmental scan answers some of the following questions:

1. Are there any key forces affecting the department's operations (collective agreements, staffing issues, cultural issues, work/life balance, demographics, technology requirements, budget issues, expectation of clients)?

2. What knowledge, skills, abilities, and capabilities does the department have?

3. What is the department's current internal environment?

4. What elements support the department's strategic direction?

5. What elements deter the department from reaching its goals?

6. How has the department changed its organizational structure?

7. How is it likely to change in the future?

8. How has the department changed with respect to the type and amount of work the department does and how is it likely to change in the future?

9. How has the department changed regarding the use of technology and how will it change in the future?

10. How has the department changed with respect to the way people are recruited?

11. What is the public's perception of the quality of the department's products, programs, and/or services? What is being done well? What can be done better?

12. Are current programs, processes, or services contributing to the achievement of specific departmental goals?

13. What do the employee opinion survey results tell me about my department? What influencing factors can I improve?

An *external* environmental scan answers some of the following questions:

1. What is the current external health care environment like?

2. What elements of the current external environment are relevant to the department (legislative, technology, managed care, etc.)?

3. Which external factors are likely to inhibit or deter my department from reaching its goals?

4. What is the impact of regional trends on the department (demographic, economic, political, intergovernmental, cultural, technology, etc.)?

5. Are there comparable, competitive organizations in this region that provide a similar service, and how do they impact what we do? How might that change? How would that affect the department?

6. Who are my patients/customers? How might that change? How would it affect the department?

7. What forces might change the external environment? What implications will this have for my department?

8. How is my department's work funded? How might that change and how would it affect my department?

Workforce Analysis

This section highlights a department's current workforce composition, future supply and demand needs related to workforce needs, competencies, and so on. The workforce analysis is a critical component in the human resource planning process. Workforce analysis considers information such as occupations, retirement eligibility, diversity, separation rates, competencies, and other issues. The workforce analysis will assess the current workforce and forecast the potential internal employee supply available for the next one-to-three-year time line. The analysis will also identify the critical competency developmental needs of a department in the future.

There are two steps in analyzing your workforce: supply analysis and gap analysis.

Supply analysis projects future supply of needed staff based on the assessment of the department's current workforce and employee movement into, through, and out of the department. The analysis of the current workforce includes number of employees, age, occupation, level, location, retirement trends, separation rates, diversity, hiring patterns, and other issues.

Internal supply refers to current employees who can be retrained, promoted, or moved to fill anticipated requirements. The ability to meet human resource demand through internal sources is dependent on the size of the current workforce and the levels of ability to perform certain jobs.

External supply refers to potential employees who may currently be undergoing training (i.e., interns, students), be working elsewhere, or not yet be in the workforce. It is difficult to determine the potential external supply due to variables involved in recruiting external candidates to the department, many of which depend on how human resource policies are perceived by potential employees (for example, compensation packages and recruiting strategies).

In a *gap analysis,* you compare your supply of employees with your current and future demand to determine future shortages and excesses in the number of employees needed, types of occupations, and competencies.

Summary of Identified Staffing Issues

After completing an internal and external environmental scan, describe the major environmental trends that have significant impact on the department's human resources. Identify three to five high-priority staffing issues with associated risks.

Action Planning

The last step is to create an action plan to close the gap between supply and demand. You want to make sure your department human resource plan aligns with Cape Cod Health Care's corporate human resources plan.

Measuring and Reporting

The final component in human resource planning is measuring and reporting. Measuring, monitoring, and reporting performance against established goals will assist in measuring progress, setting targets, and most importantly, integrating performance result information into decision-making processes.

The corporate human resource plan includes measures to examine the effectiveness of corporate human resource activities in relation to attaining corporate goals and objectives. This will assist all department managers in prioritizing activities and allocating resources (financial and people).

Monitoring and measuring should occur throughout the year, with departments providing progress reports regularly on key actions and respective performance measures. This report might include:

- An explanation of the activities taken under each key action;

- Documented results and accomplishments for each key action;

- Available performance measurement results and data; and

- A brief description of any factors affecting the department's completion of the action plan, either positively or negatively.

Summary

The human resource planning model includes the components of the human resource planning process we have just discussed. The model is shown in Figure 1.

Succession Planning

In the ever-changing and competitive business environment of health care services, succession planning is an important part of every manager's business plan. We, as managers, have the responsibility to identify the key positions in our organizations and to create a back-up plan to fill vacancies, both expected and unexpected. In addition, we have the responsibility to ensure that our best performers are given opportunities to grow professionally, both in our own departments as well as in other areas of the organization. This ensures a continuous flow of our most talented people into available positions to ensure that we meet the business performance objectives of the health care system and its business units efficiently and effectively.

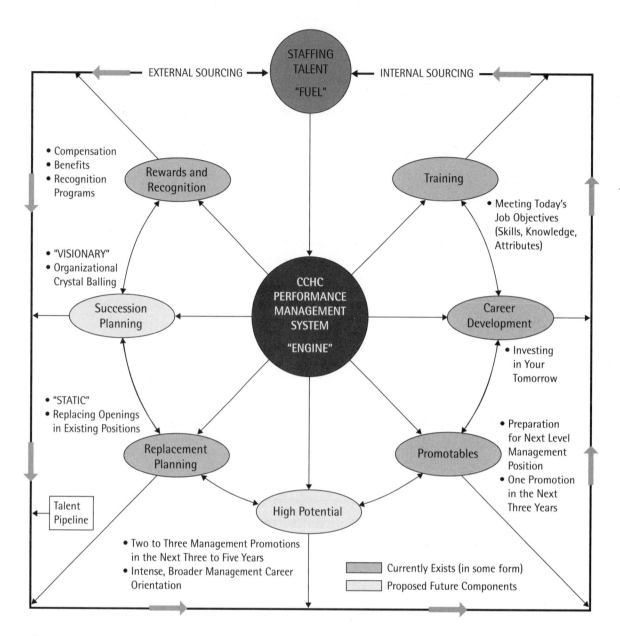

Figure 1.   CCHC Human Resources Planning and Development

Executives/managers in charge of leading businesses tend to have the following eight common characteristics:

1. The top executive is personally committed to, and involved in, the system.

2. All executives/managers in the hierarchy care for, and are held accountable for, the development of direct reporting employees.

3. It is recognized that producing an internal, upward flow of competent executives/managers is a continuous and long-term proposition.

4. Executives/managers are promoted on the basis of performance and achievement.

5. Vertical growth to the top levels of the hierarchy is attainable.

6. The system had been designed and tailored to meet the needs of the company and reflects its uniqueness.

7. It is recognized that executives/managers develop primarily on the job, and thus jobs are utilized developmentally.

8. Unique staff contributions are required to make the system function properly.

The term "system" is applied to this process of succession planning because it is an orderly way of handling necessary decisions with respect to appointing people to jobs in a way that serves the developmental needs of employees and departments. If data is gathered in an orderly, efficient, and systematic way and the pieces (that is, performance appraisal, appraisal of potential, salary classifications of jobs, and organizational structure of the business itself) are interrelated and produce an orderly understanding, the process can be considered a system. As a system, succession planning provides a foundation for establishing assistance to the organization's leader-managers in the form of a well-organized staff group.

Objectives of Succession Planning

Some of the main objectives of those doing succession planning in an organization are listed here:

- Filling key positions in an efficient and effective manner through an ongoing, broad candidate search, preferably internally or, if necessary, externally for short-term and long term successors;

- Active development of longer-term successors, ensuring their career progress and designing the range of work experiences they need for future positions;

- Auditing the "talent pipeline," influencing, in a positive way, acquisition and development strategies and activities;

- Fostering a corporate culture through the development of a cadre of leader-managers who are perceived as a corporate resource and who share key skills, experiences, and values;

- Encourages a "grow our own" approach to executive/management development rather than recruiting outside the organization when vacancies, planned or unplanned, occur;

- Ensures the attainment of diversity goals through the systematic development of a diverse workforce;

- Shortens the learning curve for future executives/managers to meet a complex, rapidly changing health care environment;

- Increases commitment and loyalty within the employee base;

- Shifts employee focus from job progression to job progression, job expansion, and job enrichment;

- Promotes a learning organization; and

- Recognizes that increasingly demanding and escalating competencies are required to manage our complex business.

Obstacles to Succession Planning

If this succession planning process is so simple, why then are there so few companies that really do it well? Research (Rothwell, 1998; Schein, 1985, 1997; Sullivan, 2004) indicates there are several reasons why:

1. Senior management is not personally committed and willing to take the time to become involved or involve the management team in a full-planning system for selection of personnel to fill key positions.

2. The accumulation and dissemination of data in a timely and orderly fashion is vital. This can be a challenging administrative task. It is clear that an executive/management development or executive/management succession planning system cannot be started unless certain administrative details are in place.

3. It is very difficult to do succession planning unless there is an orderly salary classification system in place corporate-wide so that there is some way of identifying and codifying the relative value of positions in order to plan promotions and other moves.

Knowing these obstacles can provide us with the knowledge necessary to plan for a successful transition to formalize succession planning at Cape Cod Health Care.

Succession planning has three components: (1) key position backup; (2) key personnel identification; and (3) selections for key positions.

Key position backup is the process of defining key executive/management positions within your department/unit and establishing criteria for these positions.

Key personnel identification is the process of identifying internal candidates who would successfully meet the competency requirements of the position. This includes identifying both key employees already identified as key back-ups and key employees who should be candidates for other jobs beyond the business unit. The information is appropriately shared with executives/managers from other parts of the organization where opportunities for key personnel may exist.

Selections for key positions is the process for filling existing vacancies within Cape Cod Health Care's executive/management team with the most qualified internal candidates, if available, prior to going external to recruit. These candidates may be identified back-ups (if ready) or other qualified key personnel who will be identified through an in-depth interviewing process.

Succession Planning Process Summary

In summary, here is the list of steps for succession planning:

1. Identify Key Positions

2. Establish Criteria for Key Positions

3. Identify Potential Candidates

4. Assign Mentors

5. Create Candidate Development Plans

6. Provide for Candidate Review/Tracking

The Role of the Human Resource Consultant in the Human Resource Planning Process

Career Ladders.   Career ladders is a process for creating and using career paths in the organization. Classic career pathing methods were used and now assist individuals in their career journeys. The HRC's role is to serve as a guide to the organization in the development of these ladders and to the individuals as they climb them.

Communication Vehicles, Including Newsletters and Email.   The HRC's role is to use a wide variety of communication vehicles to ensure that the employees can become intelligent consumers of the process.

Recognition Programs, Including Employee of the Month, Annual Recognition Receptions/Dinners. Each of these classic methods, as well as many more, should be used to supplement other activities to aid employees in their career journeys. The HRC's role is to facilitate the selection and use of the best methods given the culture of the organization.

HR Development

HR development (or career development) refers to the investment in an employee for his or her future. It delivers a message to employees who are valued by the organization beyond their current work assignments.

Career development is a responsibility shared by managers and employees. By utilizing an evaluation tool that compares an employee's potential across multiple job skill sets, employees can focus on their desired career directions. In this way it differs from pre-employment assessment, which is done on a single, specific position within our company.

A career development assessment presents an employee with the formal opportunity to identify a general career direction, such as whether one should be in a clinical setting or possibly in management. It then focuses on his or her strongest opportunities within the proper career direction, since his or her strengths may cover more than one particular position. Specific coaching suggestions are included for building on strengths in addition to overcoming weaknesses.

Career development is for all employees, not just those who are ambitious or those who want a "career." Career development activities will not always be upwardly focused, nor will they necessarily lead to salary increases. Other relevant activities could include job redesign and/or enrichment or the broadening of current roles, as well as exploratory and/or permanent movements downward, laterally, or to options outside of the local facility.

The implementation of career development will need a strong commitment from both employees and managers. A corporate commitment to career development for all employees creates a priority for planned activities so that employees will not need to apply for isolated opportunities. Career development plans will need to be regularly updated and reviewed, with managers and colleagues providing input, evaluation, and feedback.

Other personnel policies in areas such as staff development, evaluation, conditions of employment, and promotion and reward should be consistent with and supportive of career development.

Career development has two dimensions: career planning and career management.

In *career planning,* individuals analyze their own aptitudes, skills, qualifications, interests, and values and plan accordingly.

In *career management,* management supports and assists both planning and achievement through management and system support. This will require an organized, planned effort by the staff member and the leader-manager to regularly define, develop, and refine his or her career goals, skills, aptitudes, attributes, and responsibilities.

The career development system will integrate agreed-on employees' career development plans with opportunities realistically available to them in terms of the needs, requirements, and strategic directions of the organization and their locations or departments within it. The success of career planning for all employees at Cape Cod Health Care involves everyone.

Summary and Final Thoughts

Human resource planning and development is an effort to integrate a wide array of traditional human resource practices in an effort to provide the organization with an effective, efficient, and productive approach to workforce planning and to offer the employee a process for creating a roadmap to career and competence growth.

The effort takes a willingness on the part of management to identify career paths and competency models, as well as a willingness to follow through. An organization can offer many programs, but they will all be hollow if the organization is not willing to use them. A major talent review effort will become just an exercise if, the first time an opening occurs, the hire is someone not identified by the system or if someone from the outside is hired without a first look inside.

The effort takes willingness on the part of the employees as well. They must trust the system and place faith in its inherent equity.

In the end, this system will work. It will produce a highly competent workforce and it will produce a highly motivated employee group.

References

Rothwell, W.J., Sanders, E. and Soper, J. (1999). *ASTD models for workplace learning and performance: roles, competencies, outputs.* Alexandria, VA: The American Society for Training and Development.

Schein, E.H. (1985). *Organizational culture and leadership.* San Francisco, CA: Jossey-Bass.

Sullivan, J. (2004). *Rethinking strategic HR.* Chicago, IL: CCH Inc.

Richard P. Kropp, *Ed.D. is the vice president of human resources at Cape Cod Health. He has been in HRD and HRM as a practitioner, consultant, and university professor. He is the co-author of* 50 Activities for Team Building *(Volumes 1 and 2) and has published numerous articles in HRM and HRD.*

Getting a Grip on Stress:
What HR Managers Must Do to Prevent Burnout and Turnover
Bob Losyk

Summary

This article takes a look at the devastating impact stress is having on the American workplace. It makes the case for the critical need for HR managers to create interventions to lower the levels of stress in employees, which is a significant causal factor of burnout and turnover. It then discusses what HR managers can do to make changes within their organizations. The implementation of a stress audit or questionnaire is discussed. This is followed by discussion of such interventions as stress management training and the creation of a health and wellness program. Numerous other successful, proven ideas are given that are cost-effective in reducing stress in any organization.

The American workplace is sick. Fear, anxiety, anger, depression, and burnout run rampant in stressed-filled companies. Desk rage, phone rage, rudeness, and violent acts in the workplace make HR professionals shudder and sometimes wonder if their own job description has been reinvented to include being a psychologist. Loss of jobs, outsourcing, jobless recovery, plus world events such as war and terrorism, are all making workers more anxious, tense, and depressed. Many employees have been forced to do the work of two or three people due to reductions in force. People take this stress home with them, where it has a negative impact on their family and friends.

The stress encountered by today's employees runs unabated and is creating some disturbing trends. The American Institute of Stress states that illnesses related to stress cost more than $300 billion per year (Job Stress, www.stress.org/job.htm, 2005). The Marlin Company, a Connecticut-based workplace communication firm, conducts a yearly survey on employee attitudes. Its 2003 survey found that employee stress levels from the workplace continue to rise. The survey also states that employees have observed an increase in stress-related illnesses and emotional problems and well as lower morale compared to one year ago.

Stress takes its toll in many ways, detracting from a company's profitability and ability to grow. No organization, whether non-profit or for profit, is immune from its dire impact. Uncertainty and insecurity create fear and apprehension in people. If employees are always worried, they cannot fully focus on their jobs. They become disengaged; they are present, but not focused. They may work more hours, but are less productive and more prone to mistakes. Process improvement is an afterthought. Safety goes down, and injuries and illnesses go up.

Decreased performance, less teamwork, low morale, increased health costs and workers' compensation claims, lawsuits, lateness and absenteeism, theft, and sabotage are all results of out-of-control stress levels in workers. Eventually, many employees begin to feel that the high stress levels are not worth the paycheck. They become burned out and begin to look for other employment. Stress and burnout are two of the greatest reasons for employee turnover, but, surprisingly, they are not often mentioned in exit interviews.

What HR Managers Can Do

HR managers have a vested interest in managing stress. In addition to the humanitarian costs, there are the business costs and the costs due to lost opportunities. The more you prevent stress from getting out of control, the more savings. Healthy workers are happy workers. When they are unhappy, health care and other costs rise.

The amount of job stress has a great impact on an employee's decision to stay with a company. The more you contribute to your employees' health and well-being, the less turnover. When employees leave, companies lose their knowledge, skills, and abilities and incur the costs to replace them. When potential new employees contemplate taking a job at your organization, they also look at the number of hours they will work and the amount of stress they will have to endure. You can't afford the loss of intellectual capital and the negative impact on the bottom line that stress generates.

Find and Reduce the Stressors

Look at any stress-reduction program as a two-pronged attack: first, reduce the workplace stressors through organizational change and, second, help people to cope and reduce their levels of stress, both during and after work. In order to create an intervention strategy that decreases work stress, you must get to the root causes of the stressors. Start by creating and/or administering a stress audit or questionnaire. Numerous diagnostic surveys are available in the marketplace. Unfortunately, many of them are not related specifically to the workplace. You may want to consider creating your own in order to measure the specific factors causing stress at your work environment as well as the degree of stress.

Investigate the main factors that create stress in your workplace and where employees perceive they originate from. Determine what effects the stress has on your people. A stress audit should attempt to quantify the costs of stress as it relates to decreased productivity, sickness, depression, absenteeism, and health care costs. Once you have this information, you can show senior management that stress is a huge business issue, with high costs that prevents growth and profitability. Then you can successfully make the case for a stress-reduction/employee wellness program.

Any such survey should first determine whether people are physically and mentally satisfied in the work environment. Begin by looking at environmental factors such as temperature, lighting, air quality, safety, noise, crowding, and dangerous materials. Does the environment make people feel safe and comfortable? Many work environments have been created with the employees as an afterthought, with the belief that people have to fit in, no matter how uncomfortable their surroundings are.

The remainder of the audit should deal with all those social and mental factors that create a productive work environment. They can all lead to stress, burnout, and turnover. The areas mentioned are not all-inclusive.

First, determine whether workloads, work schedules, overtime requirements, and time pressures are overwhelming. Do employees have too much to do and not enough time and/or resources to accomplish the work? Is the amount of work beyond their capabilities? Remember that employees will often not complain about the extra demands or overload, at least not to management. They are afraid to admit they need help for fear of looking like they cannot handle the job; all the while, the stress is building within them.

Find out if and what barriers block the way of employee productivity. Determine whether there are management systems and policies in place that stand in the way of success. Is the job designed so that a certain amount of failure is inevitable? Evaluate the amount of boredom and repetition existing in certain jobs, because the people who are assigned to them tend to quit as soon as something more exciting becomes available. Obtain employee input to find ways to do a job more effectively so there is higher job satisfaction. Involve them in decisions that impact their jobs.

Check the training at your firm to determine whether it improves performance. See whether there are any areas that people need training in that they have not received yet. Look at career paths for your people. Are many employees stuck in the same repetitive work each day with no upward mobility? Lack of growth and development leads to boredom, burnout, and turnover.

Survey the management style of your organization. Does it lead to conflict, anxiety, anger, and fear? Determine whether your management staff respects people and treats them as associates with common goals. Valuing each person as an individual is critical to performance. If you have toxic, intimidating managers, then they are destroying people's morale and job satisfaction. This only leads to more stress and burnout. Eventually people leave an organization that is good because of a supervisor or manager who is bad.

Determine whether there is conflict or ambiguity within work roles. Confusion only adds to stress. Find out whether employees have a clear understanding of all policies and procedures. Do they know exactly what they should be doing and how to do it? Be sure each person knows how he or she fits into the big picture.

This is where communication becomes especially important. Communication must be open, continuous, and in all directions. Information must be shared openly and freely. People cannot feel valued if information is kept from them. When communication flows openly, it reduces uncertainty. The informal grapevine that is often filled with misinformation is prevented from taking root.

What kind of feedback systems are in place? People must receive constructive feedback that fits, on a timely basis. Destructive, accusatory feedback only destroys trust and creates hostility. Many supervisors find it easier to blame than to correct or retrain. The feedback must fit the situation, be frequent, and be given at the right time. It should be given in private. It cannot be judgmental, labeling, or exaggerated. Poor quality feedback is a great stressor.

Examine the reward systems that are in place to determine whether people receive the proper incentives and recognition for excellent performance. What behaviors or skills are being rewarded or ignored? Ignoring positive behaviors leads to lower morale. A fair system must be based on performance and merit, where those who are the best get the most. Determine whether your best people are properly rewarded and recognized when they go above and beyond.

Finally, examine the personal relationships and interactions at your workplace. People who spend eight or more hours a day together must be compatible. They must be able to work together as a team. Yet in so many organizations, people are increasingly experiencing more gossiping, turf protection, and back-stabbing than ever before. Many workers claim it is harder than ever to get along with their co-workers. Incompatibility has become a real source of stress in many firms. This all impacts productivity and the ability for organizations to stay competitive.

Implement Stress-Reduction Programs

Implementing a comprehensive stress-reduction program does work, and it gives a concrete return on investment. What employees learn and implement carries over into their personal lives and families. They tend to live healthier lifestyles. It also brings employees closer as a team, as they tend to work together as buddies and groups to help one another achieve and maintain their stress-reduction goals, so a program can only benefit your organization.

I am not suggesting that you can eliminate all the stressors at your organization or all the stress within your people, because that would be impossible. Nor do I suggest that you have the time and resources to implement all of the following interventions to reduce stress. However, you can bring it to acceptable levels, so that people are healthy and can function and be productive.

Stress-Management Training

Stress-management training is relatively inexpensive and easy to implement. Any stress-management training program must be developed from the data provided by a stress audit, questionnaire, or needs analysis. In order to create the learning objectives, analyze the data from the audit and ask the following questions:

- What are the major sources and root causes of stress in our organization?

- What impacts do they have on our people?

- What do our people already know about stress management, and what do they need to know?

- What are the main objectives of the training?

- How will we create and deliver the training?

- How can we ensure transfer of training?

- How will we evaluate the training program afterward?

Stress-management training should be conducted for all employees, regardless of the position, even if they state that they have little or no stress. The training must focus on knowledge acquisition and changes in beliefs, attitudes, habits, and behaviors. Managers should also undergo training on how to deal with stressed-out employees and how to be better at supervising their staffs during tough times. Managers must also learn to facilitate meetings with employees after the training to discuss stress-related problems.

Any stress-management training should begin with discussions of what stress is and how it impacts people. Most people are only aware of how stressed they are when it reaches the critical stages. They don't realize that stress impacts their lives on a daily basis, taking its toll on their minds, bodies, and spirits. The training must address ways to rejuvenate all three elements on a daily basis.

People must realize what their biggest stressors are and the ways they react to them. Self-awareness and analysis questionnaires, case studies, and group discussions are all good methods to create an understanding of individual stress levels and reactions. Trainers can then teach people ways to mentally and emotionally react during stressful situations. These methods include positive self-talk, affirmations, and visualizations.

Fitness programs are probably the most important components of stress reduction and wellness programs. A main key to success is getting employees to make a time and energy commitment to the program. Before beginning one, it is best to have everyone undergo a physical exam and fitness screening to determine whether it is safe for them to exercise. This includes blood pressure testing and blood screening for cholesterol levels before they start.

Bring in an exercise expert who can discuss light, moderate, and advanced exercises that give everyone a chance to be involved, depending on health and ability. The training must cover the major ways of de-stressing, such as walking, stretching, aerobics, weight training, and yoga.

Other methods of de-stressing include meditation, breath counting, T'ai Chi, and Chigong. There are many myths and fictions associated with these practices. Again, bring in an expert to teach these areas if there is interest. These ancient forms of exercise and relaxation date back over two thousand years. They are widely accepted in Eastern medicine, where one cannot separate the mind from the body. Millions of people practice these methods because they work. Yet these practices are still sometimes looked at with distrust or cynicism in the West. When they are brought into American organizations, these practices have such great health benefits that the return on investment far outweighs the costs.

Create a Comprehensive Health and Wellness Education Program

Health and wellness programs have existed in U.S. organizations since the late 1970s. They can be defined as any programs designed to improve an employee's health or eliminate negative health habits. Stress management is a major component and a driver of health and wellness programs, but there are other activities that aid in improving employee health and overall employee well-being. Contact groups such as the American Red Cross, the American Heart Association, and the National Wellness Council, all of whom offer free information and services.

Again, many of these activities are cost-effective, easy to implement, and have a return on investment that is very high. For example, you can set up a health and wellness information station that continually trains people on issues important to them. Include in your stress audit or survey questions about specific areas and health issues employees need and want to know about. Have a different health theme for each month, with specific information related to that theme. Hold short seminars and mini-discussion groups related to the theme.

Bring in a diet specialist or a person from Weight Watchers® to discuss diet, nutrition, and weight loss. When people are stressed, they often eat more. Many of the foods they ingest are the wrong types of foods, filled with sugar, carbohydrates, and fats. Food can act as a tranquilizer for a while, but the wrong kinds of food take a toll. Caffeine can actually stimulate the release of stress hormones, making us even more stressed out. People must have the opportunity to learn about better health alternatives and lifestyle habits, including smoking cessation programs and other addictions.

Some organizations bring in masseurs and acupuncturists to help relieve stress. We see these practices increasing in use for one simple reason: they work. Massage is an effective therapy for combating anxiety, tension, and stress. It helps people to relax and become more mentally alert. Massage is also effective in eliminating muscle tightness, stiffness, and pain associated with sitting or standing in one position all day. Contact the American Massage Therapy Association at www.amtamassage.org to find out what to expect during a massage and to locate qualified therapists in your area.

Acupuncture and acupressure date back thousands of years to the practices of ancient Chinese medicine. Acupuncture makes use of very thin needles placed at specific points in the body, which stimulate the flow of energy. Acupressure is a form of acupuncture that uses the hands instead of needles to stimulate certain points of the body. Each practice has been proven effective to increase relaxation and healing, while decreasing pain and stress.

Healthy Marriage/Relationship Seminars

When people come home from a tough day on the job, they bring the stress right along with them. This often spills over into family life and relationships through anger, fighting, lack of communication, and isolation. Bringing in a marriage counselor or expert on relationships to discuss these issues can be very helpful in allowing families to function better during tough times. Healthy marriages and relationships make healthier employees.

Time-Management Training

Getting a grip on stress and getting a grip on time are inexorably linked. Many people are under great stress due to their lack of organizational skills. Bad habits learned early in life become ingrained in people. With the proper training, these habits can be changed, and people can become more productive and less stressed.

Time-management training must focus on both the knowledge needed to make change and the actual skills involved. People must leave the training with solid action plans that they can implement immediately. In order to create a list of training objectives, refer back to the questions previously asked about stress management training. A good time-management training program has the following objectives:

- Learning to track your time and determine your biggest time wasters;

- Establishing priorities based on what is urgent and/or important;

- Organizing information and being able to retrieve information quickly;

- Overcoming procrastination and getting things done;

- Dealing with interruptions;

- Knowing how and when to say no;

- Cutting clutter and paperwork; and

- Learning how to run effective meetings.

Redesign Job Descriptions

Job descriptions are often vague, meaningless, and useless. Redesign them so they are more specific and enable employees to share the overload. Get people involved in redesigning their jobs. Rotate jobs that are repetitive, routine, and boring.

Encourage Breaks

Be sure that people take lunch and breaks. Encourage them to get away from the work site and breathe some fresh air. People must be able to get away for a few minutes to de-stress or relax. Eating meals at their desks or work stations while working is unhealthy and leads to burnout.

Financial Training

This is one area management often overlooks that brings great results. Many businesses have found they can ask a financial planner or accountant to come in and speak for free with the hopes of obtaining new business. Helping people to plan their financial futures through retirement plans, IRAs, pensions, or investing is well worth the time. Some employees have maxed out their credit cards and can't make ends meet. Others are just not savvy about the best way to obtain a car loan, mortgage, or financing in general. Assisting your employees to function financially and helping them to stay out of financial debt sends a very powerful message about how your company values its people. This also lessens everyday stress and improves worker and family relationships.

Be Family Supportive

Organizations that are highly family supportive have less stressed employees and lower turnover. Flexible scheduling, compressed work weeks, job sharing, family leave, dependent care, and telecommuting all have a direct impact on employee well-being. Work schedules and benefits that are compatible with people's lives and responsibilities at home make a tremendous positive impact on stress levels. These practices can counteract the tension and anxiety from a difficult commute or the stress of a tough family situation.

Many workers have problems with family obligations such as getting the children to school and elder care. Single moms are under almost unimaginable stress. Surveys of mothers tell us that the most important priority to them is to be able to get the proper care for a sick child during the work day and to be able to get to school for an important meeting or event, such as a school play. Once again, allowing time for these practices send out the message that we value our people.

Have a Violence/Harassment Policy

With so many more people under stress, the frequency of arguments, anger, rage, and violent behavior has accelerated. Unfortunately, no one can know when someone may just "lose it." However, this is one kind of extra added stress that you cannot tolerate. People must know what is acceptable behavior and what is not.

Establish a policy in writing that everyone must sign. It must clearly state that rudeness, aggression, threats, harassment, or acts of violence will not be tolerated. Describe the behaviors that are considered improper, harassing, and/or violent. Require your employees to report any such behavior immediately, because violence can rapidly escalate. Investigate the situation and take appropriate action right away. Implementing a zero tolerance policy in this area sends a message that your company cares about employees' safety and security.

Establish Employee Assistance Programs

Many people need assistance and counseling that is beyond the scope of human resources. An employee assistance program (EAP) that offers private and confidential counseling can be very effective in helping employees deal with stress, burnout, addictions, marital problems, parenting concerns, bereavement, and other personal issues. If you have a program in place, encourage people to make use of it. Many HR managers are concerned about the costs, but companies actually save money because they get back increased productivity, less absenteeism, fewer mistakes, and reduced turnover. Compare a plan based on fee-for-service versus a plan based on the number of employees to determine which is more cost-effective. Those companies that have wisely invested in EAPs have seen a return on investment with a drop in health care and workers' compensation costs.

Measure Your Success

Since creating interventions that produce positive change is the goal, you must have some mechanism for measuring their effectiveness. You can easily track people's health care costs, productivity, absenteeism, sickness, and turnover. Gather anecdotal evidence through employee interviews and group discussions. Get their perceptions to see whether the programs are working. You can also link all this information to the bottom line in such areas as increased sales, better service, and fewer errors or defects. You can show upper management that lowered stress levels are directly connected to business success. This enables you to justify your costs and obtain increased funding for more training and interventions.

Conclusion

Creating a stress-management and wellness program at your organization has such an enormously positive impact that human resources and top management cannot afford to ignore it. Employees who are stressed cannot care about excellence, innovation, profitability, and the competitive edge. Employees who feel they work for an organization that invests money in order to make them healthy and happy will stay with that employer much longer and thrive in that environment. If you invest wisely in the health of your people, you will become known as an employer of choice, while your competition who chooses not to invest will continue to lose profits and keep struggling to recruit, hire, and retain the best and the brightest.

Bob Losyk, *M.Ed., MBA, is an author and certified speaking professional who has spoken to over 1,500 audiences. He is the founder and president of Innovative Training Solutions, a consulting firm specializing in stress and workforce issues. A prolific writer, Bob has written over 150 articles on management topics. He is the author of the highly successful books,* Get a Grip! Overcoming Stress & Thriving in the Workplace, *and* Managing a Changing Workforce: Achieving Outstanding Service with Today's Employees. *Losyk has appeared on national TV shows and many nationally syndicated radio shows. His opinion has been sought for the* Wall Street Journal, USA Today, *and a variety of newspaper and magazine interviews.*

The Aging Workforce:
Best Practices in Recruiting and Retaining Older Workers at Publix

Bahaudin G. Mujtaba and Jim Rhodes

Summary

Many of the best firms in the world are in search of wisdom, more specifically the type of wisdom that comes with age and experience. It is estimated that about 43 percent of the civilian labor force will be eligible for retirement within the next ten years (Mujtaba, 2004). As such, there will be a shortage of talented and skilled professionals.

Many excellent practices exist for attracting and hiring senior citizens, and it often starts with the elimination of behaviors stemming from one of the most common barriers—traditional biases and stereotypes toward older workers in the United States.

The Society for Human Resource Management (SHRM, 2002) states that the education system in the United States has failed to deliver graduates who are perceived to be qualified to successfully enter and meet the demands of today's labor market. As such, more and more organizations are trying to retain, recruit and hire senior citizens because of their skill, professional expertise, and accumulated knowledge.

Reality of an Older Workforce

Elderly professionals are often fairly healthy, wealthy, and choosy in terms of what they would like to do in their later years. As a result of their years of productive work in society, they tend to live in better neighborhoods and often have hobbies or community roles. As such, one barrier for attracting the elderly is that they can be selective in determining where they would like to work. Often, they would like flexible hours with options to come and go to pursue their hobbies and personal community obligations.

An "older worker" in the United States is a worker that is forty years of age or older. Unfortunately, there have been many firms that have shown patterns of discriminating against "older workers." When such discrimination becomes an "unseen" part of the culture, it can hinder the organization's morale and productivity and may possibly cause many legal problems for the firm. Creating an effective organizational culture that avoids age discrimination requires long-term commitment and resources, since there are no panaceas.

Organizational leaders and managers must be concerned about age discrimination because an increasingly larger percentage of the workforce is coming and will continue to come from the older population as Baby Boomers continue to age. According to the United States Census Bureau and the Administration on Aging (2001), the number of Americans who are sixty-five years of age or older has increased by a factor of twelve since the early 1900s. The unparalleled growth of this age group in the workforce will continue.

In contrast to intentional age discrimination, most discrimination against older employees seems to be subtler in nature, and human resource managers should be aware of such discrimination. Further research has revealed that unintentional code words are often used during the interview process, such as "We're looking for go-getters" and people who are "with it" to describe desirable employees. Generally, buzzwords seem not to apply to people who are seasoned and experienced.

According to a *U.S. News* article (Clark, 2003) titled "Judgment Day," about two-thirds of all U.S. companies use performance as at least one factor when deciding whom to lay off during tough economic times. Some firms use the forced ranking systems, which executives like because they seem to be the "fairest and easiest way to downsize." Regardless of the method used, "older workers" seem to get the worst of it as larger portions of them lose their jobs, possibly because they earn higher income and benefits compared to their younger counterparts. For example, in 1999, Ford wanted to increase diversity in its work environment and change Ford's culture to be more change oriented while embracing new technology and new markets. As such, Ford created a new performance appraisal process for its 18,000 salaried, white-collar employees in which supervisors were required to give a yearly grade to each of their subordinates of A, B, or C (Jones & George, 2002). If an employee received a C, that employee could not receive a pay increase; and if this happened two years in a row, the employee was either demoted or fired. In 2000 management told the supervisors to give only 10 percent A's, 80 percent B's, and 10 percent C's in their overall performance appraisals. The following year it was the same, except 5 percent was moved from C to B, which was now 85 percent. The new process supposedly negatively affected some older managers. It has been a very negative experience, with forty-two employees filing two class action lawsuits against Ford, claiming that the new process was used to terminate older managers. Their attorney had suggested that Ford stereotypically assumed that older workers were slow to change or learn new things and so tried to diminish their numbers.

Changing the Traditional Paradigm of Aging

The United States has a diverse population of about 290 million people. The perspective on aging in the United States can be seen from the high level of discrimination against older workers due to biases and stereotypes against older workers (Mujtaba, 2004).

It may not always be obvious to some people how important older workers are to the economy and businesses, but older workers contribute immensely to the success of not only the United States, but to other countries of the world. In a national survey, older workers were found to possess the following qualities: functioning well in crisis; possessing basic skills in writing, reading, and arithmetic; loyalty; solid performance; and good interpersonal skills (Harvey & Allard, 2002).

The presence of more "older workers" in the workforce presents many challenges and opportunities for organizations. The challenges are stereotypes and age discrimination that are widespread in the American workforce. Organizations must effectively transcend such challenges and proactively take advantage of the experienced workforce as they attempt to be globally competitive.

Managers must remember that older workers are one of the desired categories of employees because they are stable, experienced, and consistent. Companies have recognized that older workers value stability and quality in their work. Khan (2003), from the retail industry, said, "We are now targeting and hiring alternate profiles. . . . Our industry is customer service driven, and older people are sensitive to customer needs." It is clear that some companies are tapping into the advantages of having highly skilled older workers within their organizations. Another example of a company that has utilized older employers while still exploring better ways of managing older employees is McDonald's. Michael O'Shaughnessy, employee relations director, McDonald's Australia, said fast food chains regularly target older employees (Comtex, 2003).

Seniors and Job Opportunities

In most cases, the jobs offered to older workers are of the nature that requires mature, experienced, and knowledgeable individuals, says Renee Ward (*Senior Journal*, 2004), founder of www.Seniors4Hire.org, a website that provides a list of companies that recruit and hire older workers. This is an online career center geared to promote businesses that value a diverse workforce and actively recruit and hire those who fall in the category of "older workers." According to the *Senior Journal*, there are at least seventy small businesses that are good places for older workers to be employed, and some of the firms recently added to the list are Regal Entertainment Group, Mayo Clinic-Jacksonville, and General Nutrition Centers.

Hiring seniors for project assignments or on a part-time basis saves on health care costs. According to a survey conducted by Thomas Regional, of the nearly 2,500 industrial small businesses owners surveyed nationwide, 63 percent stated that health care coverage is their biggest challenge. Hiring seniors to work part-time or on temporary assignments in most cases saves health care benefits costs (Recruiting Seniors, 2004).

Senior Skills

A 2003 survey from the Society for Human Resource Management (SHRM) indicated that 68 percent of organizations employ older workers; however, only 41 percent specifically target older workers in their recruitment efforts. The survey also indicated that reasons for hiring older workers included their willingness to work a flexible schedule, their ability to serve as mentors, and their invaluable experience. Of course, other important reasons included the reliability and strong work ethic that often comes with older workers. Generally, firms recruit and hire older or retired workers because they offer:

- Leadership and coaching skills for younger or new employees;

- Superior customer service experience;

- Stability;

- Ability to initiate sales and transaction dependability;

- Eagerness to provide support and guidance;

- Superior communication skills;

- Varied work experience;

- Better ability to work with a mature clientele; and

- An old-fashioned work ethic.

Overall, a mature employee's greatest assets (compared to younger demographics) are likely to be lower absenteeism, punctuality, less likelihood of changing jobs, commitment to quality, superior customer service skills, better people skills, eagerness to learn new skills, a positive attitude, and the willingness to speak their minds and to point out the flaws of the organization.

Companies hire older workers because they have certain characteristics that other generations of employees may not always have. The following are some general elements associated with older workers:

- Older workers thrive on quality and hard work. They believe in putting in a full day's work for a full day's pay.

- Older workers are loyal. They appreciate the opportunity to work and stick with those who give them a chance to perform and produce.

- Older workers take great pride in their accomplishments. They care about doing a good job.

- Older workers are dependable.

- Older workers do not always get involved in politics. They don't play political games, have hidden agendas, or harbor secret ambitions.

- Older workers have more than their share of "emotional maturity" and common sense.

Retaining Older Workers

With a skilled worker shortage in some American firms and industries, companies need to do more to attract skilled older workers and retain skilled employees as they age. Many companies are finding themselves in the same position of needing more skilled employees and resort to the international labor pool or move the jobs abroad (to China, India, and other developing nations). Among the benefits offered by employers to recruit older workers are

- *Financial Services*—Most companies offer some sort of retirement plan, but the best ones provide workshops, seminars, and counseling.

- *Health Benefits*—Many employers offer not only basic benefits such as prescription drugs and health, vision, and dental care, but long-term-care insurance and short- and long-term disability insurance. Some even offer wellness programs.

- *Training Opportunities*—These include everything from skill development to career counseling.

- *Mentoring*—Ideally it works two ways: (1) experienced employees help train younger workers and (2) older workers return to the company and receive mentors to help re-train them.

- *Flexible Schedules*—Forget the punch clock: 28.8 percent of American workers now have flexible schedules, nearly twice as many as ten years ago.

- *Phased Retirement*—Rather than quit cold turkey, many employees prefer to ease into retirement.

- *Welcome Back Policies*—Some companies allow retirees to return to work after they have left the job.

In many cases, a company's attitude toward older workers has a lot to do with the industry. Age bias is especially pronounced in youth-oriented sectors like advertising, technology, and securities. The entertainment industry is notorious for its youth obsession. In a company like a dot-com with predominantly younger workers and very little training on cultural competency and diversity issues, one tends to find more age bias. Inexperienced young managers often have a difficult time supervising older workers due to their own incompetence and lack of effective management and leadership skills.

Many firms attempt to differentiate themselves from their competitors through quality service by treating customers with respect and dignity. These firms are finding that an older workforce has the experience to treat customers like kings and queens while taking care of them with pleasure. As such, firms like Wal-Mart, Publix, Target, Wegmans, Stu Leonard, and many others target older workers to help them create cultures of satisfying and delighting customers. More important than formally recruiting older workers is the organizational culture of these firms, as they focus on only serving quality products, offering excellent service, providing flexible hours and benefits to part-time employees (mothers, fathers, older workers, individuals with disabilities, etc.), being involved in the community, and making charitable contributions. This type of an organizational culture makes employees proud of their firms and tends to not only attract but also retain older workers, since they too would like to be involved in such activities in the community. As such, Publix is successful because it has created an organizational culture that attracts and retains older workers.

Publix: Where Working Is a Pleasure

Publix employs about 125,000 employees in the states of Florida, Georgia, South Carolina, Alabama, and Tennessee. It generated $16.8 billion in sales during 2003, and this number is expected to grow at a rate of about 10 percent annually.

At Publix, the goal is go above and "beyond the norm" to create extraordinary "shopping experiences" that shine in the industry. Customer service is about providing consistent, high-quality attention to the customers who come to the stores for some sort of service and/or product. The aim is to satisfy the customers all the time through a culture of customer intimacy and an experienced workforce. Because of its stellar performance through an experienced workforce and a culture that is focused on customer intimacy, it has had excellent performance, even during a bad economy. Such success starts at the top from the vision and mission of an organization. The mission at Publix is to be "the premier quality food retailer in the world. . . . To that end we commit to be Passionately focused on Customer Value; Intolerant of Waste; Dedicated to the Dignity, Value, and Employment Security of our Associates; Devoted to the highest standards of stewardship for our Stockholders; and Involved as Responsible Citizens in our Communities."

The authors, one-time retail managers, had hired many seniors in their departments because they brought a focus on quality and service. They also make great team players and are able to treat customers as they would like to be treated. Hiring seniors can attract other seniors and bring in more local customers, since older workers tend to be very involved in the community. As such, when older workers are treated with dignity and respect, their word-of-mouth advertising can then generate more candidates for prospective positions.

Recently, for the sixth year in a row, Publix was named one of the country's best places to work by *Fortune* magazine. Publix ranked eighty-seventh on *Fortune*'s annual list of the "100 Best Companies to Work For." The ranking was determined from formal responses from randomly selected employees, evaluating trust in management, camaraderie, and pride in the company. Furthermore, each company is required to complete a questionnaire on its benefits and practices offered to employees. Publix CEO Charlie Jenkins, Jr., said, "I'm proud that our associates continue to consider Publix to be one of the best companies to work for in America. They are the reason we're one of the best." Publix associates go above and beyond the call of duty to make sure a customer's shopping experience is a pleasure while he or she is at one of their stores. More information about the survey and how companies were ranked can found at *Fortune*'s website (www.fortune.com/bestcompanies). Publix has also received national recognition for being one of the country's Top Employers of Older Workers; this award was presented to them in September 2002 in Washington, D.C. through the Experience Works Prime Time Awards Program.

For years, Publix has attempted to differentiate itself by offering "an environment where working and shopping is a pleasure." Publix leaders have achieved this goal partially by attracting, recruiting, and retaining older workers, since they require little training with regard to customer service. Also, older workers are likely to effectively interact and communicate with customers more often than younger employees, who can become too focused on getting tasks done. Older workers tend to be great listeners when customers have specific desires, requests, or complaints. Also, older workers tend to know some of their customers on a first-name basis, since they may be involved in community activities, politics, and other committees impacting their city.

Conclusion

Over thirty-three years after Congress enacted the Age Discrimination in Employment Act, some employers feel as though they have solid economic reasons for not wanting to hire and train employees who may soon be retiring. Furthermore, others rationalize that people do "slip" with age. Some writers have stated that reasoning skills may decline with age. While some of these myths/opinions might have been based on a few occurrences with some individuals, they are not representative of an individual's ability to successfully complete a task based on his or her age.

As more and more companies downsize, merge, and are bought out because of economic reasons, layoffs and cutbacks are inevitable. These changes are likely to significantly impact the employment of older workers. Unless biases about age are brought to the fore, the authors think that many more employers are going to focus on a more youthful workforce when the economy is slow, rather than one that is mature and more experienced because of the stereotypes, myths, and costs associated with "older workers." It has been true over the past several years that as older individuals have lost their jobs because of layoffs, they may well have wondered whether age was a factor in the decision. Many of these people have years invested in their organizations, but were dismissed regardless of their seniority. The authors have observed that younger workers have consistently been brought into organizations at higher rates than older workers, and this makes one wonder "Why?"

We believe that managers should consciously decide to increase their knowledge in human resources and age discrimination issues in order to become more aware of the laws governing unfair employment practices, in hopes of making a positive difference in the lives of many experienced, honest, loyal, able, knowledgeable, and willing workers in order to recruit and retain them.

References

Administration on Aging. (2001). Department of Health and Human Services. [Online]. Retreived November 13, 2003, from www.aoa.dhhs.gov/

Clark, K. (2003). *Judgment day.* Money & Business. U.S.News.com. Retrieved January 13, 2003, from www.usnews.com/usnews/biztech/articles/030113/13performancehtm

Comtex. (2003). *McDonald's targets older workers.* Retrieved October 30, 2003, from Infotrac.

Harvard Business Review. (2001). *HBR on managing diversity.* Cambridge, MA: Harvard Business School Publications.

Harvey, C.P., & Allard, M.J. (2002). *Understanding and managing diversity: Readings cases and exercises* (2nd ed.). Englewood Cliffs, NJ: Prentice Hall.

Jones, G., & George, J. (2002) *Contemporary management* (3rd ed.). New York: McGraw-Hill/Irwin.

Khan, S.Y. (2003) *Desperately seeking older employees.* Retrieved October 1, 2003, from Infotrac.

Mujtaba, B., Hinds, R.M., & Oskal, C. (2004). Cultural perspectives of age discrimination and unearned privileges associated with age. *Applied Business Research Conference (ABR) Proceedings.*

Mujtaba, B., Richardson, W., & Blount, P. (2003). Age discrimination and means of avoiding it in the workplace. *SAM International Conference Proceedings on Trust, Responsibility, and Business."*

Publix. (2004). *Publix news release.* Retrieved August 20, 2004, from www.publix.com/about/newsroom/NewsReleaseItem.do

Publix awards. (2004). Retrieved August 20, 2004, from www.publix.com/about/Awards.do

Publix careers. (2004). Retrieved August 18, 2004, from www.publix.com/about/careers/Careers.do

Recruiting Seniors. (2004). Why hire seniors and retirees? Retrieved August 19, 2004, from www.recruitersnetwork.com/articles/seniors.htm

Senior Journal. (2004). Website helping seniors find jobs adds 12 new employers. Retrieved on August 8, 2004, from www.seniorjournal.com/NEWS/WebsWeLike/4–02–09Jobs.htm

SHRM. (2002). *School-to-work program survey.* Alexandria, VA: Author.

SHRM. (2003). *Survey of employers targeting older workers.* Alexandria, VA: Author.

U.S. Bureau of the Census. (1996). *Current population reports,* p. 25–1130, Population projections of the United States, by age, sex, and Hispanic origin: 1995 to 2050, February 1996; and U.S. population estimates, by age, sex, race, and Hispanic origin: 1990 to 1994.

Bahaudin Mujtaba *is an assistant professor of human resources and international management. He is also the director of institutional relations, planning, and accreditation for Nova Southeastern University's H. Wayne Huizenga School of Business and Entrepreneurship. Mr. Mujtaba has worked as a trainer and educator, as well as in retail management, for over twenty years. His current research and focus are in the areas of outcomes assessment and diversity in higher education.*

Jim Rhodes *is vice president of compliance in human resources at Publix Super Markets Inc. Mr. Rhodes has worked as vice president of human resources at Publix for many years and has previously worked as a trainer, mentor, director, manager, and internal consultant.*

Request for Proposal (RFP):
A Process That Really Works

Linda M. Raudenbush

Summary

Although often characterized as cumbersome to use, the request for proposal (RFP) process, when carefully implemented, can result in obtaining a vendor qualified to provide specific, high-quality products and services in a timely manner. This article presents a streamlined version of the RFP process, using a proven five-step method: (1) prepare; (2) write the statement of work (SOW); (3) solicit proposals; (4) analyze proposals; and (5) select vendor. The method is illustrated by a case taken from the National Agricultural Statistics Service (NASS). When the five-step RFP process is led by competent and knowledgeable HR staff, it results in identifying, selecting, and hiring the most appropriate consultants and vendors.

Organizations are increasingly challenged to meet and exceed performance and productivity standards with diminishing resources of time, money, materials, and staff. Government agencies and corporations alike need to operate in an ever-increasing climate of efficiency, effectiveness, and timeliness. It is not unusual for organizations to turn to outside vendors for assistance in providing products and services to their employees. Therefore, human resource managers often find themselves in a position of identifying, selecting, and hiring consultants and vendors through the request for proposal (RFP) process.

Any RFP process is complex and can be cumbersome and confusing to implement. The five-step process presented here is rigorous yet straightforward and has been proven through experience to yield the desired results: a vendor qualified to provide specific, high-quality products and services in a timely manner.

In 2001, the National Agricultural Statistics Service (NASS) of the U.S. Department of Agriculture (USDA) began an extensive RFP process for the purposes of designing and implementing a fundamental leadership course for its professional staff. An agency with eleven hundred employees, NASS conducts surveys and prepares reports covering virtually every aspect of U.S. agriculture, including production and supplies of food, farm costs, and other key aspects of farming in the U.S. This case study describes the design, implementation, results, and assessment of the RFP process for its Leadership Academy Program (LAP). The process was successful and resulted in a well-designed and appropriately delivered leadership course. The RFP process is presented in this article in a generic, step-by-step way so that it can be applied to the selection of consultants or vendors in any private or public organization.

Step One: Prepare

In order to prepare for the RFP process, the human resource development function, which resides in the Training and Career Development Office (TCDO) at NASS, conducted a thorough needs assessment. The results of the training data collection and analysis enabled the TCDO trainers to document critical course details for LAP, including goals, objectives, modules, and participants.

In addition to clarifying essential course information, TCDO trainers produced a timeline of critical milestones, including:

- A deadline for vendor proposals;
- Proposal review by NASS;
- Interviews of top vendors;
- Vendor selection;
- Contracting with selected vendor; and
- Service delivery.

Finally, TCDO trainers established a list of weighted criteria that USDA NASS would use to prioritize and select a vendor, including:

Proposed content will meet NASS' objectives (Instructional Systems Design or ISD integrity)	20 percent
Proposed content meets competencies described in NASS RFP	15 percent
Course consistently adheres to adult learning principles in delivery	15 percent

Prior federal government, USDA, or NASS experience	10 percent
Time/length of course meets NASS' needs	10 percent
Proposal is price competitive	10 percent
Feedback from vendor's references	10 percent
Vendor is easy to communicate and work with	5 percent
Best value to government	5 percent
	100 percent

In summary, Step One of the RFP process is to thoroughly prepare, by describing specific details about the desired products or services, outlining an estimated time frame for the RFP, and identifying weighted criteria for evaluating the proposals.

Step Two: Write the Statement of Work (SOW)

Federal procurement guidelines require agencies to write detailed statements of work (SOW) prior to requesting or soliciting proposals. In order to create such a document, key stakeholders were consulted, including financial and procurement experts. Together with the TCDO trainers, they determined the required and optional sections for the NASS Statement of Work. This collaboration resulted in a comprehensive SOW that met federal requirements and contained considerations that were important to the agency seeking a vendor, including:

- Organizational description;

- General description of the requirement;

- Relationship of the requirement to other projects;

- Background;

- Purpose and objectives of the acquisition;

- Derivation of program: needs assessment results;

- Overall program/project objectives: workshop goals;

- Specific objectives of this requirement: module objectives and draft course outline;

- Participant description;

- Contractor requirements: proposal due date, deliverables, review process and decision criteria, terms and conditions, invoicing for contractor payment and payment schedule;

- Appendix 1: Needs assessment results; and

- Appendix 2: Other training currently provided by NASS.

In summary, Step Two of the RFP process is to collaborate with key stakeholders to produce a detailed statement of work fully describing all important issues related to the anticipated vendor products and services.

Step Three: Solicit Proposals

The goal of this step is twofold: (1) identify vendors that could provide the appropriate products and services and (2) inform selected vendors of the organization's specific needs, requesting a proposal.

Many approaches can be used to identify vendors, including:

- Browse websites to identify providers of products/services;

- Network with other professionals and organizations that have similar needs;

- Make a list of vendors your organization has used and been satisfied with in the past;

- Read professional publications, brochures, and other print media for advertisements of specific products/services;

- Contact local, regional, national, or international organizations that provide information on the specific products/services of interest, such as Better Business Bureaus, professional membership associations, and small business consortiums; and

- Government organizations have approved vendor sources, such as the General Services Administration's (GSA) approved Management, Organizational, and Business Improvement Schedule (MOBIS) list.

Exploring one or more of these resources usually yields an abundance of prospective sources that might be able to meet your organizational needs. Next, take some time to prioritize and reduce your list of vendors. A useful rule of thumb is to decide how many proposals you want to receive and then to contact twice the number of vendors (since, in most cases, all vendors you contact will not submit proposals).

Use a straightforward cover letter and the SOW to inform and invite vendors to submit proposals. The short cover letter should contain key pieces of information, including:

- General description of needed products/services;

- General description of application and users of needed products/services;

- Clear request to submit a proposal;

- Specified deadline for proposal submission; and

- Contact name and number for questions.

The cover letter and SOW can be mailed, e-mailed, or faxed to vendors, or posted on your organization's website for access by selected vendors. It is critical that all vendors receive the complete information at approximately the same time in order to assure a relatively equal playing field for preparing proposals.

In summary, Step Three of the RFP process is to identify a range of possible vendors and inform selected vendors of the organization's specific needs, using a cover letter and the statement of work to solicit vendor proposals.

Step Four: Analyze Proposals

In the case of NASS's LAP, twenty-five vendors were contacted and invited to submit proposals for the SOW; twelve complete proposals were received. The TCDO trainers, during the needs assessment of Step One and the SOW documentation process of Step Two, contacted many users and other stakeholders prior to requesting or soliciting proposals. In Step 4, the TCDO trainers invited some of these key stakeholders to form a Review and Analysis Committee.

The role of the Review and Analysis Committee was decisional, with the goal of reading and rating all vendor proposal materials and choosing the top three vendors. This group consisted of internal and external trainers, managers, and a facilitator. Each committee member was contacted personally and given a full explanation of the group's role, responsibilities, and deadlines. When an individual agreed to join the Review and Analysis Committee, he or she received a list of three proposals to be reviewed and a package of information containing the SOW, a complete list of vendors submitting proposals, and an evaluation form with requirements and evaluation criteria and space for evaluator's comments (see the sample form in Exhibit 1).

In total, there were nine members of the Review and Analysis Committee; three reviewed all vendor proposals, and the other six each reviewed three proposals. Each

Exhibit 1.   Checkoff List and Evaluation Form

Vendor Name: _____

Your Name: _____

Checkoff List

Using the table below, begin by reviewing the proposal to make sure it includes all required elements.

Requirement	Check If Met	Comments
1. Proposal met due date		
2. Course/module matrix		
3. Proposal mapped modules to required competencies		
4. Learning objectives		
5. Course outline		
6. Module description, including instructional methodology, how topic will be presented, and what exercises/activities will be used to allow participants to practice topical skills		
7. Sample course evaluation		
8. A/V that will be used (should be variety, such as slide show, charts, job aids)		
9. Developer and instructor biographies		
10. Sample pre-course assignment with explanation of how it will be used in module		
11. Complete example of instructor guide, a/v, and student materials for any previously developed and delivered management/leadership course		
12. Company history		
13. Three prior customers (within the last two years), with names and contact numbers as references		

Evaluation Criteria

Instructions: Using the table below, award points indicating your evaluation of how well the vendor's proposal met each criterion. Note the strengths, weaknesses, and any comments regarding the vendor's proposal for each criterion. Add up the total points for each vendor's proposal. Finally, make any overall remarks concerning the vendor's proposal.

In addition to the previously established criteria, keep in mind the following:

- Additional consideration will be given to any vendor who provides competitive benefits to NASS for using a vendor "package" of course registration, materials, instructor fees, and lodging and food. However, awarding this contract is not contingent on a vendor's ability to give NASS competitive rates on lodging and food.

- Because NASS course participants come from all states, the course must be taught in a location with economic and convenient air travel.

- NASS participants must be lodged in the equivalent of three-star or better accommodations at or below government hotel and per diem rates.

- Some vendors have chosen to include additional optional features for consideration. These items are noted at the end of the table.

Criterion	Points (Max/Rating)	Strengths	Weaknesses	Comments
1. Proposed content meets its objectives (instructional systems design integrity)	max = 20 points rating =			
2. Proposed content meets competencies described in SOW	max = 15 points rating =			
3. Proposed course consistently adheres to adult learning principles in delivery	max = 15 points rating =			
4. Vendor has prior experience with federal government, USDA, or NASS	max = 10 points rating =			
5. The time/length of proposed course meets NASS needs	max = 10 points rating =			
6. Vendor's proposal is price competitive	max = 10 points rating =			
7. Feedback from vendor's references is favorable	max = 10 points rating =			
8. Vendor is easy to communicate with and work with	max = 5 points rating =			

continued on the next page

Exhibit 1.   Checkoff List and Evaluation Form, *continued*

Criterion	Points (Max/Rating)	Strengths	Weaknesses	Comments
9. Proposal gives best value to the government	max = 5 points rating =			
10. Optional package with accommodations, food, etc., economic, convenient	max = 5 points rating =			
11. Vendor's Option 1	max = 5 points rating =			
12. Vendor's Option 2	max = 5 points rating =			
Total Points				
Remarks:				

vendor proposal was rated by at least four group members, and most proposals were reviewed by more members because all were encouraged to review more than their required three proposals. To facilitate proposal review, a library room was designated where all proposals were exhibited. Materials could be read in that room or signed out. After the designated review period, committee members submitted their vendor rating sheets to the facilitator, who summarized them in preparation for the selection of the top three vendors. A sample of an overall ranking sheet is shown in Exhibit 2.

The final part of this step was the convening of all members of the Review and Analysis Committee for a facilitated decision-making meeting. The purpose of the meeting was to thoroughly discuss each proposal and its ratings by each committee member and to reach a consensus on the top three vendors. Due to the large number of proposals (twelve) and reviewers (nine), the meeting was scheduled for six hours and adhered to the following agenda:

- Introduction: Purpose of meeting
- Data clarification

Exhibit 2.   Overall Vendor Ranking Sheet

Criteria	Vendor 1	Vendor 2	etc.
1. Content meets objectives—ISD (20)			
2. Meets competencies in SOW (15)			
3. Adheres to adult learning principles—delivery (15)			
4. Prior experience with Federal government, USDA, NASS (10)			
5. Time/length meets NASS requirements (10)			
6. Price competitive (10)			
7. Feedback from references is favorable (10)			
8. Easy to communicate and work with (5)			
9. Best value to government (5)			
Subtotal (100)			
Optional package (lodging, food) (5)			
Vendor option 1 (5)			
Vendor option 2 (5)			
Subtotal for Options (15)			
Grand Total (115)			
Remarks			

- Summary of all reviewer ratings

- Discussion of general trends and wide variations

- Vendor proposal discussion
  Three-minute discussion by each reviewer of each proposal
  Fifteen minutes of general discussion and Q&A on each proposal

- Nominal voting: each reviewer casts votes for top three vendors

- Result: prioritized list of vendor proposals

- Next steps and close

Despite the rigorous nature and duration of the meeting, all Review and Analysis Committee members attended and fully participated in the entire decision-making meeting. The final results were definite and gratifying: by consensus, the group identified the top three vendors.

In summary, Step Four of the RFP process is to thoroughly review and analyze all vendor proposals in order to determine the top three vendors. This is a rigorous analytical process best accomplished by a group of project stakeholders with clear responsibilities and goals. It is imperative that the weighted evaluation criteria, as stated in the SOW, be applied equitably in evaluating each proposal. The final decision-making meeting was critical. The thorough review of the individual analyses fostered synergistic collaboration among the group of stakeholders and enabled them to make the final decision by consensus.

Step Five: Select Vendor

The goals of this step are to discern differences among the top three vendors and then select the one that best meets the organizational needs according to the SOW. There are several approaches that can be taken to determine the unique capabilities of each vendor, such as telephone or in-person interviews, individually or with a panel of all three vendors together.

NASS invited each vendor to meet face-to-face with all available members of the Review and Analysis Committee. The purpose of each meeting was to thoroughly discuss how the SOW would be implemented by the vendor. This series of three meetings accomplished three purposes: (1) it afforded NASS the opportunity to determine organizational compatibility with each vendor; (2) it gave both buyer and seller the opportunity to discuss specific implementation plans; and (3) it enabled each vendor to bring to life its specific proposals, highlighting distinctive aspects.

The three meetings demonstrated clear differences among the three top vendors and provided sufficient information for the NASS decision makers to unanimously agree on selecting the most suitable vendor.

In summary, Step Five of the RFP process is to identify the differences among the top vendors and to select the vendor that best meets the organizational needs. The key to success for this step is obtaining a clear understanding of exactly how each vendor proposes to fulfill the SOW. As shades of differences appear among vendors, you will be able to select the vendor most capable of meeting your organizational needs and most compatible with your organization's working style.

Conclusion

In the near future, your organization might be challenged to supplement its resources by using outside vendors for assistance in providing products and services to employees. As a human resource professional, you will be in a stronger position for identifying, selecting, and hiring consultants and vendors by using the five-step request for proposals (RFP) process. You will know exactly how to proceed successfully through this complex process, obtaining the desired results: a vendor qualified to provided specific, high-quality products and services in a timely manner to your organization. This is the process you will successfully lead your organization through:

- Step One—Prepare

- Step Two—Write the Statement of Work (SOW)

- Step Three—Solicit Proposals

- Step Four—Analyze Proposals

- Step Five—Select a Vendor

There are a few final points to keep in mind about the five-step RFP process:

1. The RFP process provides an opportunity for synergistic collaboration among various parts of an organization.

2. The RFP process, by including stakeholders from varied functional areas, builds support for a new initiative, thus contributing to its organizational acceptance.

3. The RFP process is very flexible and adaptable for public and private sector organizations alike.

4. The RFP process provides HR professionals with another opportunity to lead their organizations in partnering with outside vendors to obtain vital products and services.

The NASS case study has proven that the five-step RFP process, when led by competent and knowledgeable HR staff, results in identifying, selecting, and hiring the most appropriate consultants and vendors. In conclusion, the five-step request for proposal (RFP) process really works!

Linda M. Raudenbush, *Ed.D., has more than twenty-five years of human resource development (HRD) and organization development (OD) experience in both the private and public sectors. She is employed by the U.S. Department of Agriculture (USDA) in the National Agricultural Statistics Service (NASS) as an HRD/OD specialist and coach. She is also an adjunct professor at the University of Maryland, Baltimore County (UMBC), where she has taught undergraduate and graduate courses for more than twelve years. Dr. Raudenbush was a judge for the 2003 HR Leadership and Scholarship Awards of Greater Washington, D.C.*

Performance Management:
Helping an Organization Improve Its Process
Roslyn Vargas

Summary

Performance management is a set of activities that ensure goals are consistently being met in an effective manner. Performance management systems focus on performance of the organization, its departments, and most importantly, its employees. A performance management system includes the development of clear job descriptions through a job analysis, an appropriate selection process, established performance standards, outcomes, and measurements, to name a few. A misaligned performance management system not only fails to add value, but also creates high costs in employee turnover and misdirected behavior. This article provides insight on how an organization's performance management system is being realigned.

For an HR professional, walking into an organization for the first time brings about many challenges. First, there is the desire to get acquainted with the corporate culture and the employees at all levels. This is a good time to learn the business goals of the organization, which help you in understanding whether or not the performance appraisals are strategically aligned with the business goals of the organization. A good way to get acquainted with the employees is to review past performance appraisals. This gives insight as to where the employees are currently assigned, whether they have worked in other areas of the organization, whether they have been promoted during their tenure, what skills they currently possess, and what goals the employees may have listed. The performance appraisals not only tell something about the employee's being evaluated, but they also reveal quite a bit about the evaluator.

Employee Documentation System

In the organization that I will be highlighting the employees each had three different file folders assigned to them. One folder was for medical files, one for miscellaneous forms, and then a main file folder for performance evaluations and payroll information, including changes in wages or transfers. Since the files were not organized in any particular manner, it was difficult to find things for a particular rating period. Therefore, a manager getting ready to do a performance appraisal would have to pull out all of these papers from within the folder and try to get them in order by date. It appeared that the paperwork was not put back into the folder in chronological order, leaving confusion for the following year.

Observations

As I looked through the employees' evaluations from the past several years, I began to notice a pattern. The vast majority of the employees had overall ratings of "exceeds standards." I also observed that the section where "significant strengths" are to be listed was usually left blank. However, when strengths were listed, there were no specific explanations or "back-up" documentation provided to show what the significant strengths really were and how the employees' performance affected the organization.

In the section titled "Describe Any Weaknesses," I consistently found "none" or "none observed," or the section was left blank. I concluded that either there was no observation by the evaluator, or the most perfect employees worked for the same organization. According to the performance appraisals reviewed, it appeared that there had never been any need for improvement for any of the employees because that section also was usually left blank. In the section where there are quite a few lines for goals and objectives to be listed, again I found this entire section left blank.

Another observation I made was that the managers' appraisals were not that different. It appeared as though the managers were following the same patterns used for their own appraisals by senior executives.

I also noted that the performance appraisals were not done consistently within a year of the previous appraisals. The time range varied across the board. It almost appeared as though the performance appraisal was done as an afterthought, when an employee may have inquired about an increase in salary. (This is one of the reasons that salary increases and the actual performance appraisal should be done separately.)

There did not appear to be any indication that performance was discussed with any of these employees except at the time of the evaluation, which was not even done on an annual basis. Some employees had not had a performance evaluation for anywhere from one and one-half years to two years.

Another observation I made was that the section for the employee to make a comment was always left blank. There was absolutely no indication as to how the employee felt about his or her performance appraisal. The questions thus became (1) Are the managers just telling the employees to sign on the dotted line without input? and (2) Are the employees made to feel that they cannot or should not make comments?

Why Make a Change?

Giving the employees a performance appraisal whenever someone gets around to it clearly diminishes the value of the appraisal process. How is the employee to know whether or not his or her performance is up to par? If it isn't, how does the employee improve? How are the managers evaluating whether employees need further training or re-training in order to perform their tasks at acceptable levels? Most importantly, how are the managers or senior executives determining who will be promoted? Are the promotions in the organization done because an employee has been able to perform his or her duties in an acceptable manner? Or are the promotions because of tenure within the organization or because of personal biases? Some of these are the very reasons organizations find themselves in litigation.

The performance of each employee is critical to the overall performance of the organization. Therefore, the performance appraisal should be looked at as a necessity in the organization and should be a part of the managers' day-to-day operations.

As I inquired about the performance management system in the organization, it was apparent that the system might have become "broken" due to changes in the organization's structure. Now was a good time to improve and make changes to the system that had once been in place. Knowing the importance of performance appraisals and the reasons why performance appraisals are needed, I began to speak to the managers about the current system and tried to get their "buy-in" for a better system.

I began by inquiring about their feeling on doing performance appraisals for the employees and found that the unanimous number one reason for not doing the appraisals more frequently was "I don't have the time" or "I am too busy." In order to show the managers what the employees may be feeling when the employee evaluations are delayed, the managers were asked how they felt about not getting their own performance appraisals on time. Most replied, "I don't think I should go more than a year without getting an increase." Notice that the managers' responses were tied to their salaries, and not to their performance. The purpose of asking the managers about their own evaluations was to show the managers that, just as they do not like waiting for their evaluations, neither do their subordinates. Another purpose was to try to show the managers there should be a separation between performance evaluations and annual increases.

Tying the salary increase to performance was the corporate culture. This being the case, one has to wonder how many employees probably felt that their performance was just "good" or felt their performance didn't really matter since they had to wait for an increase anyway. This was the perfect opportunity to help managers understand that managing their staff's performance was a significant aspect of the job.

Further inquiries resulted in determining that the managers had never been trained in doing performance appraisals. As a matter of fact, managers for the most part had not had any managerial training. As in most companies, these managers had been promoted because of their knowledge about and ability to do particular tasks. One of the reasons the managers "don't have time" or are "too busy" to do performance appraisals is that managers are still doing work the staff should be handling. Delegation of work to the staff was never accomplished. Managers needed to learn to delegate more of their work to the staff so that they had time to manage the staff's performance and develop the staff so that the managers, too, could be promoted.

Another reason for the change is to show managers how easy it really is to do performance appraisals. As in many companies, managers lack skills in writing and conducting performance appraisals, and the performance appraisal form itself is too general for all the different types of positions in the organization. Providing managers with a chance to improve these skills and creating more job-specific appraisal forms makes the managers' job of conducting performance appraisals much easier.

The Bottom Line

The objective here is to develop and implement job-specific performance appraisal forms and train the managers in how to write effective performance appraisals and properly conduct performance reviews. The completed project will have an impact on management and employee development. Since litigation can adversely affect the "bottom line," managers need to become aware of legal issues that could arise if performance is not tracked and properly documented in the performance evaluation. Job-specific performance appraisal forms will help managers write better performance appraisals and conduct good appraisal meetings. In turn, this will help employees in receiving objective reviews, setting goals with their evaluators, and working on competencies and will eventually affect the bottom line for the organization.

Initiating Change

Getting "buy-in" from the managers and senior executives was the most challenging aspect of the project. Although the managers and senior executives knew that a change was needed, all were skeptical about how the changes would affect them in terms of "time." In the insurance industry, production is the foremost aspect of the job. It was time to show the managerial staff how production could improve through the proper management of performance. The managerial staff needed to learn that measuring an employee's performance correctly and developing employees would help tremendously in the area of production.

The managers as well as the senior executives complained about the evaluation form currently being used. The complaints were that the forms were too lengthy and had no relevance to certain positions within the organization. Change was needed, and change was about to take place.

Phase I: User-Friendly Documentation

The first step in changing the performance management system in the organization was to set up the employees' files differently. As mentioned earlier, there were three file folders for each employee: medical, miscellaneous, and the main pocket folder. Paperwork was put into the folders, but sometimes not in any particular order. The files were not "user friendly" when attempting to do an appraisal and look for documentation.

In order to make the process of looking for documentation for a performance appraisal easier and less time-consuming, we set up the files in a six-part folder. The tabs on the folders were labeled as follows: hiring packet, payroll information sheets, performance appraisals, commendations/discipline, education/training, and miscellaneous. The files are now organized in easy-to-find sections, and each section is filed in chronological order, the most recent on top. This makes it easy for the managers to find documentation for a particular rating period. This also reduces the possibility of documentation being missed due to lack of time and desire to look through every page in a file.

Phase II: Training

The second step was to facilitate a training session entitled "Documentation," which focused on the critical importance of documentation. It was important to let the managers and supervisors know that employers basically no longer had an option of whether to document employee-related matters and regularly maintain employee files. More than ever, when an employee files a wrongful discharge or discrimination claim, the employer's documentation of the entire employment relationship is critical. It can literally make the difference between winning and losing a lawsuit. More importantly, good documentation can prevent a lawsuit from being filed in the first place. Waiting to document an issue leaves room for error. Important facts may be forgotten or overlooked. Dates and times may be recorded in error. Thus, the best way to record incidents is at the time of occurrence.

If documentation is done immediately often enough, it will become second nature. Managers and supervisors must be made to understand the essential nature of documentation. Although writing something down will take longer than orally communicating it, the written word will have much more impact in a courtroom than will the remembrance of something that was said. In addition, documentation is important because it assists the supervisor or manager in refreshing his or her recollection as to the facts and circumstances surrounding a particular employment action.

A "For the Record" form was designed and developed to help the managers and supervisors in documenting incidents immediately. The "For the Record" forms are used for all incidents, whether to reinforce positive behavior or to change less-than-optimal behavior. The form was intended to also help the managers and supervisors when preparing to write performance appraisals.

Phase III: Job Analysis

The third step of the process was to do a job analysis of each position in the company. The purpose of the job analysis was twofold. First, it was to get a better understanding of employees' responsibilities within their positions and, second, to assist in the writing of job descriptions. Employees from different departments were interviewed as to what tasks or functions they performed in order to determine the knowledge, skills, and abilities required for their positions.

Once the job analyses were completed, it was time to write job descriptions. Although there were some job descriptions on file, after interviewing employees as well as managers, it appeared that the staff and management had never viewed the job descriptions. Managers, supervisors, and even group leaders were involved in the process of getting job descriptions written. It should be clear that employees must understand what is expected of them to perform their jobs in an effective and efficient manner. There must also be clarification of performance expectations and goals for the employees.

Phase IV: Preparing for Appraisal

Changing how managers and supervisors prepare for performance appraisals was the key to their success in meeting the performance appraisal due date. Therefore, an action plan had to be put in place. Managers had to be reminded that the performance appraisal was not just based on the last couple of weeks before the appraisal was due.

The performance appraisal had to be based on the entire rating period for an effective result.

The manager had to ensure that the appraisal was an honest and accurate evaluation of the employee's specific job duties. The manager should be evaluating, through some type of measurement, the employee's job knowledge, productivity, and behaviors related to the job. It is important to ensure that managers and supervisors not provide superficial appraisals or group most employees in the "exceeds standards" category without specific recommendations. Although rating all employees with such favorable appraisals may make the managers and supervisors look good, doing so will merely cause problems for the employee and possibly the employer if a claim of wrongful discharge is filed at a later time.

Another point brought up to the managers and supervisors was to beware of providing much better appraisals than what are deserved to what might appear to be their "favorite" employees. Writing appraisals of this nature causes problems with morale and could result in a decrease in productivity.

Phase V: Time Map

The fifth step taken was to begin notifying managers, as well as senior executives, one month in advance, about whose performance evaluations were due and to give a due date for each. The notification to the evaluator comes from the human resources department. At this point the evaluator requests the employee's files from human resources, which then gives the employee file to the manager, along with an attendance report for the corresponding rating period. The manager is then required to sign for the documents. This process makes the evaluator accountable for the timeliness of the appraisal. Giving the managers a one-month advance notice also helps the managers with their time management. It also has become the responsibility of the human resources department to check with managers and supervisors if a performance appraisal is not received on the due date. Again, managers and supervisors are held accountable for the timeliness of the appraisals.

Phase VI: Finalizing the Form

This phase of the process has been the most difficult. Developing a "job-specific" performance appraisal form was a huge task to take on. The company currently has fifty-three different positions, each with its own job description. However, after reviewing the positions, it was determined that it was not necessary to have a "job-specific" performance appraisal for each position. There were a few positions where the same appraisal could be used. The desire for "job-specific" appraisals came about because, during the observation phase of this project, it was difficult to see how an underwriter could possibly be evaluated the same way as a receptionist. Although personality trait type questions on the appraisal could be used for everyone, the evaluation of performance for specific competencies could not. Several meetings with supervisors and managers were required to obtain the necessary information on how the different appraisals could be developed and what specifically was to be evaluated. For example, the technical knowledge needed by the underwriters to underwrite policies is quite different from the skills required for the position of customer service representative.

Conclusion

According to Weatherly (2004), there are twelve critical success factors of performance management:

1. Mirror your corporate culture and values;
2. Design development and planning phase;
3. Focus on the right company performance measures;
4. Link job descriptions to the performance management system;
5. Differentiate performance fairly and objectively;
6. Train managers in performance management;
7. Link compensation to the performance management system;
8. Differentiate linkage to total rewards system;
9. Hold managers accountable for the communication process;
10. Set clear expectations for employee development;
11. Track effectiveness of performance management system; and
12. Adjust performance management system as required.

Eight of the twelve factors were used in this process of changing the performance management system, and two more of these factors will be ongoing.

The effectiveness of this performance management system will be tracked in the coming year. This process will be carried out through interviewing supervisors and managers and reviewing the performance appraisals written under the new guidelines. It will be the responsibility of the human resources department to make any necessary adjustments to the system. These changes will include continuous job analyses and updating job descriptions as deemed necessary. More training will be conducted for middle management in the area of goal setting and meeting objectives within the departments and with individual employees. This too will be an ongoing process in an effort to maintain a performance management system that will meet the goals of the company and the overall performance of the organization.

Resources

Boswell, W.R., & Boudreau, J.W. (2002). Separating the developmental and evaluative performance appraisal uses. *Journal of Business and Psychology, 16*(3), 391–412.

Camardella, M.J. (2003). Effective management of the performance appraisal process. *Employment Relations Today, 30*(1), 103–107.

Diggins, C. (2004). Emotional intelligence: The key to effective performance. *Human Resource Management International Digest, 12*(1), 33–35.

Findley, H.M., & Amsler, G. (2003). *Setting performance expectations: Return to the basics.* Society for Human Resource Management white paper [Online]. Available: www.shrm.org/hrresources/whitepapers_published/CMS_003969.asp

Greene, R.J. (2003). *Contributing to organizational success through effective performance appraisal.* Society for Human Resource Management white paper [Online]. Available: www.shrm.org/hrresources/whitepapers_published/CMS_005421.asp

Heinen, J.S., & O'Neill, C. (2004). Managing talent to maximize performance. *Employment Relations Today, 31*(2), 67–82.

Jamrog, J.J., & Overholt, M.H. (2004). Measuring HR and organizational effectiveness. *Employment Relations Today, 31*(2), 33–45.

Laumeyer, J.A. (1997). *Performance management systems: What do we want to accomplish?* Society for Human Resource Management white paper [Online]. Available: www.shrm.org/hrresources/whitepapers_published/CMS_000107.asp

Neary, D.B. (2002). Creating a company-wide, on-line, performance management system: A case study at TRW Inc. *Human Resource Management International Digest, 41*(4), 491–498.

Pritchard, K.H. (1997). *Introduction to competencies.* Society for Human Resource Management white paper [Online]. Available: www.shrm.org/hrresources/whitepapers_published/CMS_000428.asp

Stainton, A. (2004). Performance-management and pay reforms keep staff in loop. *Human Resource Management International Digest, 12*(2), 17–19.

Taylor, M.S., Masterson, S.S., Renard, M.K., & Tracy, K.B. (1998). Managers' reactions to procedurally just performance management systems. *Academy of Management Journal, 41*(5), 568–579.

Weatherly, L.A. (2004, March). Performance management: Getting it right from the start. *SHRM Research Quarterly.*

Roslyn Vargas *is currently an HR manager in the insurance industry. She has over eighteen years of experience in management, ten of those years in HR. Ms. Vargas has earned a bachelor of arts degree in sociology from Florida Atlantic University, a master of science degree in human resource management from Nova Southeastern University, and is currently seeking a doctor of business administration degree with a specialization in human resource management.*

Telling It How It *Really* Is?
Life in Organizations Revealed Using Heideggerian Phenomenology

Margaret H. Vickers and Melissa A. Parris

Summary

Heideggerian phenomenology is expounded here as a qualitative methodology of value in researching "how things really are" in organizational life. It is a methodology, and a philosophy, that recognizes *a priori* the value of the subjective, lived experience of the individual, and the physical, sociological, and psychological phenomena that come together to create a life-world. In this paper, the authors present three cases where this methodology successfully revealed the employee's reality. Stories about working in teams, being downsized, and having an unseen chronic illness at work are shared to demonstrate the ability of Heideggerian phenomenology to reveal how life really is in organizations. The benefit for HR practitioners and managers is an increased understanding of and, hence, ability to address these sensitive and often unspoken aspects of organizational life.

One of the difficulties researchers face when exploring organizational life is finding methodological approaches that do the job. This paper highlights the use of a qualitative methodology that is profoundly helpful in elucidating what is "really" going on for employees in organizations. We argue that knowing what is going on means finding out about people's lived experience, sharing and understanding their perspectives, and looking through their eyes at the situations they encounter in organizational life.

Three cases depicting unexplored aspects of life in organizations are presented: the dissonant experiences of working in teams; being "disposed of" from one's job; and the often silently endured experiences of working with an unseen chronic illness. These cases spotlight this methodology as one eminently suited to exploring what is not normally known about people's experiences in organizational life—but should be. It has been particularly useful in enabling the authors to challenge or extend the boundaries of knowledge in these three relatively unknown and little-understood experiences in organizational life. The methodology shared is Heideggerian phenomenology.

Heideggerian Phenomenology as Philosophy and Methodology

The term "phenomenology" is derived from two Greek words: *phainomenon* and *logos* (Stewart & Mickunas, 1990). *Phainomenon* is defined as "appearance" (Spinelli, 1989), anything that shows itself (Heidegger, 1927, 1962), without involving "any sense of the strange or spectacular" (Hammond, Howarth, & Keat, 1991, p. 1). *Logos*, meaning "reason" or "word," helps us to understand phenomenology as "a reasoned inquiry which discovers the inherent essences of appearances" (Stewart & Mickunas, 1990, p. 3). Through the use of phenomenology, we seek to understand what is *really* happening for employees at work.

Use of phenomenology should be a philosophical and a methodological approach (Street, 1996). Phenomenology is used to capture personal experiences and to bring them to awareness (Barritt, Beekman, Bleeker, & Mulderij, 1984). It recognizes that the question is not whether one research methodology is better than the other; nor is it about their respective merits or deficiencies. Phenomenology is about which methodology is *most suitable* for the project (Sarantakos, 1993).

Heidegger's expression of phenomenology focused on the "situatedness" of human existence in the world (Heidegger, 1927, 1962). To understand an employee's experience, we must recognize his or her world and the meaning he or she gives it. Thus, Heideggerian phenomenology attempts to interpret and makes sense of these subjective experiences. The task of the researcher is to explain what life is like for employees—to share their life experiences in a way that enables them to become very clear to the reader.

It is this essence of Heideggerian phenomenology that lends itself so well to the exploration of organizational life: the need to capture the subjective experiences of employees as interpreted by them (Taylor, 1993); an emphasis on the empathic understanding of human behavior as it is internally experienced and socially constructed (Sarantakos, 1993); and the attempt to describe lived experience (Oiler, 1982) and the meaning it holds for the individual concerned (Drew, 1989). Phenomenology illuminates the richness of individual experience. The only legitimate source of data is the individuals who have lived the reality being investigated (Baker, Wuest, & Stern, 1992). The importance, and value, of the individual's reality and the need for the researcher to share that reality with others is underscored (Swanson-Kauffman, 1986). Phenomenological research has a reverence for lived experience and attempts to describe human experience as it is lived (Oiler, 1982).

The method of hermeneutic analysis proposed by Heidegger (1927, 1962) is a method for the study of texts (in these cases, the texts were interview transcripts). Hermeneutic analysis also recognizes that the researcher will always bring a pre-understanding, a story, to the project that is not always rationalizable (Benner, 1985). Heidegger articulated the position that presuppositions should *not* be eliminated or suspended (bracketed), but are what constitute the possibility of intelligibility or meaning (Ray, 1994). There was, deliberately, no attempt to "bracket" researcher beliefs in any of the cases presented here (Koch, 1995; Schutz, 1932, 1967; Vickers, 2001) on the basis that the interpreter's experiences and orientations were deemed relevant to the analysis. These cannot be bracketed during the process of interpretation (Walters, 1996). Indeed, the interpreter should be aware of his or her prejudices through the process of self-reflection (Heidegger, 1927, 1962; Walters, 1996).

In the cases presented here, our respective backgrounds were grounded in our own organizational and life experiences and supported by relevant literature. Thus, our interpretations were influenced by past and present circumstances (Taylor, 1993) and knowledge. Heidegger states that nothing can be encountered without reference to the person's background understanding (Heidegger, 1927, 1962) and utilizing an awareness of the past to assist in understanding the present (Maggs-Rapport, 2001). Understanding the experiences of each individual on his or her own terms is the fundamental objective of phenomenological inquiry. Sociological factors cannot be separated from the individual's life. Understanding, for Heidegger, involved constant correction and modification based on the individual's own past experiences, understanding, reflections, and interpretations.

In sum, Heidegger's hermeneutical phenomenology is relevant to studies of organizations as a methodology and philosophy that supports a rejection of purely rational and objective approaches in favor of a focus on the individual's own subjective reality and how that might be artfully and thoughtfully presented by a researcher that acknowledges his or her own experiences and reality also. It is hoped that this provides a means to reveal what people actually experience in organizational life. In studies that value the subjective, the authentic, and the personal, it is Heidegger's methodological and philosophical maxim—"to the things themselves" (Heidegger, 1927, 1962, p. 50)—that was seen as so helpful.

Specifics of Method

In selecting participants for a phenomenological study, the key criterion is that they have experienced the particular phenomenon being studied (Creswell, 1998). Watters and Biernacki's (1989) *Modified Chain Referral Technique* was employed to recruit potential participants in each of the cases reported. "Intermediaries" (colleagues or friends of the researchers) were asked whether they knew anyone who might be a likely candidate for participation, based on the determined requirements for recruitment. The considered advantages of approaching potential participants in the studies were many: unpressured choice for employees to participate; employee privacy; trust established through the introduction of the researcher and his or her background via the intermediary; increased researcher safety levels; employees participating who were not previously known to the interviewer; and volunteers to participate in the respective studies becoming available quickly and in abundance.

Intermediaries asked potential volunteer employees for agreement, in principle, to participate in the study and for permission for the researcher to contact them to further explain the study and participation requirements (Vickers, 2001). Potential interviewees, who had agreed in principle to participate, were contacted directly by telephone by researchers to explain the project and to judge their suitability for inclusion in the study (Parris, 2002b; Vickers, 2001). Volunteer employees were included in the study if they met the set selection criteria for each study.[1]

In each of the cases reported here, one or more in-depth interviews were conducted with each employee who participated. The aim was to understand, through interview, the employee's point of view and his or her interpretations and the meaning of his or her experiences. Utilization of in-depth interviews allowed the researchers to listen to what employees said, including their views and opinions, in their own words (Kvale, 1996). "Hunches" and focus areas were developed prior to the interviews to guide the research process. These focus areas formed a starting point for discussions with employees interviewed and a guide to ensuring that key points were discussed with all participants in each study (Kvale, 1996). Additionally, due to the exploratory nature of each of these studies, new areas of concern were also raised during the course of the interviews and were then explored during subsequent interviews. In all cases, interviews were transcribed verbatim (Swanson-Kauffman & Schonwald, 1988), rather than summarizing the information from interview notes taken or a tape recording (Sandelowski, 1994).

When analyzing employee experiences, the identification of themes is an essential component of Heideggerian phenomenology (Leonard, 1994). Themes are patterns in the data (Taylor & Bogdan, 1998) that convey meaning (Benner, 1994). The analysis endeavored also to interpret concealed meanings. Transcripts were read, first, to get a "global" perspective of themes, before being revisited in detail to select passages of interest that depicted themes and required interpretation and consideration. The phenomenological model thus emerged, comprising all the themes identified and sharing

---

[1]Of course, the details of each case differ, such as the number of participants, the selection criteria, and the rationale and objectives of the study. Interested readers are provided with references to relevant published outcomes, including information about the specific research design and outcomes of each case. The purpose of this article is to demonstrate the transferability and capacity of this methodology as a useful window to organizational life.

the lived experience of employees at work and the meaning these experiences held for them. The following discussion presents some of the experiences that were shared.

Three Cases of How It *Really* Is in Organizational Life

The Individual's Experience Within a Work Team[2]

The use of teams in organizations has increased over the last twenty-five years (Guzzo, 1996), with a corresponding increase in research focus on teams. Katzenbach and Smith (1993) provide a useful definition of work teams of relevance to this study: a small number of people with complementary skills who are committed to a common purpose, performance goals, and approach for which they hold themselves mutually accountable (p. 45).

This definition incorporates many of the characteristics that shape the prevalent understanding of teams in the workplace and that were challenged in this study. One routinely noted characteristic of teams is having a common purpose, performance goals, and approach. The common goals are described as needing to be specific (Larson & LaFasto, 1989), achievable (Gmelch, 1984), and agreed to by all team members (Yammarino & Naughton, 1992). The common *purpose* or *approach* is considered separately from team goals (Moxon, 1993); it involves more than a task orientation and requires, instead, a supportive and participative process (Gmelch, 1984). Secondly, Katzenbach and Smith's (1993) definition incorporates *mutual accountability.* This requires coordination of activity among team members (Larson & LaFasto, 1989), in that team members "must engage in teamwork in order to accomplish team goals" (Weaver, Bowers, Salas, & Cannon-Bowers, 1997, p.169).

Much of the research on work teams has also looked at various aspects of team performance, such as effectiveness (Tannenbaum & Cannon-Bowers, 1996), productivity (Hallam & Campbell, 1997), and overall interaction (Hartley, 1996). Some researchers have looked at the importance of motivation, particularly with regard to resistance to the introduction and utilization of teams within the organization (Graham, 1991). Other studies have focused on individual team members with respect to job satisfaction (Cordery, Mueller, & Smith, 1991). However, until recently, little research has examined how working within a team impacts the individual employee (Knights & McCabe, 2000, 2003). Furthermore, much of the literature is underpinned by the assumption that employees working in teams are more effective than employees working as individuals. Few authors challenge this premise, preferring, instead, to focus on ways to further improve

---

[2]For the study on individuals in work teams, interested readers are referred to Parris (2001, 2002a, 2002b, 2003) for more details.

team functioning. Similarly, there is little attention given to the experiences of individuals within these teams, thus not allowing the voices of team members to be heard. As a result of this knowledge, the focus areas initially developed for the early interviews concentrated deliberately on issues relevant to the individual experience in the team, such as individuals' interactions with other team members, how effective they believed the team to be, whether they knew what the team's goals were, and the personal and career impacts for them of working in a team.

It was found that the stories of these employees were at odds with what is frequently reported in the literature. Remembering that the literature focuses so closely on the importance of team goals, even defining team membership in terms of their use, the stories depicted—unexpectedly—employees being very uncertain about their team's goals. In fact, not one respondent knew what they were. Readers are reminded that recruitment of volunteers for this study was made via individuals agreeing that their teams were working on one or more tasks for which the team had collective responsibility. All participants agreed that this described their teams. Further, during the interviews, most participants also described a team as a group working toward a common goal. However, when I [Parris] asked these employees what their team's goals or objectives were, none could define them. For example, Michelle demonstrates her difficulty in trying to articulate her team's goal. She remained uncertain at the end:

> *Michelle:* Yeah, there's no verbal—there's no written goal at all. We're
> just lucky that, um, we think the same way. [slight pause] Like, our
> goal, our *unspoken* goal would be—actually, our goal would be the
> customer services goals, it would be the same thing. But we would—
> I suppose our goal would be to—deliver really good service to our
> customers, and our customers are the people who work here in the
> building. That would probably be our goal: to make sure that the information we give is correct, to make sure that—we're professional
> and our standard is high. I'd say that is probably our goal.

Here, Michelle's uncertainty was very apparent in her hesitancy and confusion surrounding the team goal. This uncertainty over team goals or objectives appears strikingly at odds with the current thinking on teams in general. The literature on teams is axiomatic in its reliance on the premise that the team has a common aim (Adair, 1986) or a common purpose (Margerison & McCann, 1990). However, in the quote above, Michelle's description of what "would probably be" her team's goal shows that it was not clear to her. This lack of clarity about goals may find team members working at cross-purposes and also brings into question one of the major assumptions about teamwork in organizations—the common goal.

The second story considers the expectation for organizational support that employees have when working within teams. Many researchers have emphasized the importance of support from senior management wishing to adopt certain organizational structures, methods of working, and change (for example, Patrickson, Bamber, & Bamber, 1995). Only when employees believe support for their team is present will they embrace the team as a positive method of working. However, Karen's story indicates the presence of mixed messages regarding support. It also indicates the presence of organizational rhetoric. When considering her story, it is important to consider the role of organizational rhetoric in shaping individuals' meaning and understanding of work teams. Organizational rhetoric involves the expression of arguments in such a manner as to make them attractive to the listeners (Grant, 1999) and to persuade others of their validity (Watson, 1995):

> *Karen:* Well, that's the thing. They say they want people to [work cohesively]—and I think they think people do—but then there are examples like I said about the team-building weekend just being cancelled [Karen previously noted "this was the first thing to go" as part of cost-cutting], and actually at the last team-building weekend, the marketing manager had just been sacked . . . and there were quite a few people, particularly in the marketing area, who were really unclear of . . . what was the structure of the marketing department now and what was going to happen. It just hadn't been communicated, and yet, our CEO stood up and said that, you know, it was the best team and then after saying that at that team meeting, three more people got sacked. And he actually made the comment on the team building, "And I'm looking forward to seeing you all here at the next team-building thing." And then a couple of weeks later, three people were gone. So it's kind of, like, although they say that, you don't . . . it's a bit hard to believe.

Here, the use of rhetoric to persuade and influence is evident. Karen's CEO referred to a team-building weekend (in itself, a rhetorical term) to tell everyone in the organization that the marketing team was "the best team," no doubt with the aim of giving a feeling of comfort to those team members. Yet, following this meeting, three people were fired from this team—an emotionally unsettling and dissonant experience for Karen. How did she relate this action to the previous comments of the CEO? If that was "the best team" and team members were fired, what did that mean for *her* position and *her team*? Karen's closing comments highlight her sense of disillusionment: "Although they say that [people should work cohesively] . . . it's a bit hard to believe."

Other employees in the study also used phrases like "We're all in this together" and "We're all part of a bigger team" to encourage work within teams. The intended message for individuals was that all organizational members were working together for a common good, to provide benefits to both the organization and the individuals within it. However, Karen's experience also included a story of the disparity in the level of support given to different teams across the organization:

> *Karen:* And actually, there's one little part of our team—three of us, Robert, Lincoln [pseudonyms], and I—were put together, because at the company meeting each month a different team presents. But the IBS [Internal Business Support] team's a bit big, so we break up into IT [information technology] team or smaller groups. And Robert, Lincoln, and I were considered to not really fit in anywhere, even though we're supposedly in this team, so when the thing came around, with the different people, groups, or teams who will be the company meeting presentation, next to our names, we were called the "odds and sods"—*that was lovely.* So that's our team. We were just the scum of the earth odds-and-sods team.

It is interesting to see here a result of the pervasive concept of "teams" in this organization. Karen had said earlier: "You're all meant to be part of the same bigger team," a point emphasized by an organization structure grouped around different layers of teams, where each grouping had to also be called a team. But what was the impact for individuals being labeled "odds and sods"? What was the implied meaning for the individuals involved? Karen portrayed what it meant for her: "We were just the *scum of the earth* odds-and-sods team" [author emphasis]. Asking employees specifically about the experiences of working in the team revealed this sense of separation from the rest of the organization, as well as a feeling of being undervalued, alienated, and marginalized. This sense of isolation is in stark contrast to the "cohesion" and "togetherness" that team membership is professed to provide.

The two stories highlighted here indicate a reality of team member experience that is strikingly at odds with the prevailing understanding of teams. In contrast to sharing common goals and having cohesion in their teams, these employees experienced uncertainty, isolation, and alienation. Using Heideggerian phenomenology enabled a focus on the individual's experience and the meaning it held for the individual. It became clear when learning about what it is like to work in a team that many of the assumptions about working in teams are not equal to what is experienced by individual employees.

Human resource (HR) practitioners and managers in organizations can benefit from this kind of learning to improve practice. We have seen, for example, that it might be more productive and beneficial for both the individual worker, and for the organization, if workers are not always expected to work in a team. Restricting team membership and performance outcomes to situations in which teamwork can actually be demonstrated to enhance outcomes and efficiency would be a useful path forward. Where teams are in place and their performance is being undermined by the negative experiences of individual members within those teams, it may be that closer scrutiny of the reality of team processes and management expectations could prove fruitful, rather than blaming individuals for not being "team players." It cannot be assumed that team members will automatically know the team's common purpose, nor that the effectiveness, productivity, and communication skills of individuals will always be axiomatically enhanced through being a member of a team. Consideration of these issues will enhance the ability of management to direct its efforts for performance management in the right areas.

Being "Downsized"[3]

Whether you agree that the phenomenon of downsizing is still increasing (Downs, 1995) or now decreasing (Applebaum, Lavigne-Schmidt, Peytchev, & Shapiro, 1999), there is little question that downsizing has had, and will continue to have, an enormous impact on the lives of those affected. It is an activity argued to be applicable to both declining and growing organizations (Cascio, 1993; Palmer, Kabanoff, & Dunford, 1997) and is typically portrayed as a means of lowering overhead, simplifying bureaucracy, speeding decision making, facilitating communication, enhancing entrepreneurship, and increasing productivity (Cascio, 1993; Palmer, Kabanoff, & Dunford, 1997)—an inevitable outcome of living in a global world (Kets de Vries & Balazs, 1997). However, there has been insufficient addressing of the personal and subjective experiences of those who are "disposed of" during the downsizing process.

Downsizing is a phenomenon that has affected millions of workers since the late 1980s (Cascio, 1993). As a result of downsizing, employees have been slashed, cut, eliminated, excessed, rightsized, and surplused. Others have been severed, trimmed, reengineered, pared down, terminated, chopped, given early retirement, and put out to pasture (Laabs, 1999). Still more are downsized, separated, unassigned, and proactively outplaced (Micklethwait & Wooldridge, 1996). The rationale behind these thousands of terminations and the seeking of a more "flexible" workforce is that organizations will become more productive by terminating employees who are chronically unproductive, mismatched to their jobs, or in positions that are superfluous (Brammer & Humberger, 1984). However, downsizing is not supposed to include the discharge of staff for cause

---

[3]Interested readers are directed to Vickers (2002) for more details on this particular case study.

or for less than "rational" reasons, such as political agendas, power struggles, senior executive whims, or the uncritical propagation of management theory "fads." Downsizing should also have nothing to do with the health of the person being made redundant.

Thousands upon thousands of jobs have been lost and a great deal of unacknowledged pain and stress has been experienced. Most of the downsizing that has now become operating procedure for corporate America is not necessarily in response to actual, or even anticipated, business downturns or national economic conditions. Dugan (1996) argues (while reviewing Downs' [1995] work, *Corporate Executions*) that recent studies suggest that fewer than half of the organizations in which downsizing occurred actually reduced costs as expected. Nelson (1998) expresses similar concerns, indicating that a study conducted by the American Management Association found that fewer than half of the firms downsized since 1988 had increased profits since the layoffs. Only one-third reported an increase in productivity. Whatever the reason, downsizing is now considered normal practice by the wider business community (Orlando, 1999). Unfortunately, downsizing not only fails to deliver the promised economic benefits to employers, but results in a range of other problems, such as lowered staff morale, lost commitment, and reduced productivity (Cascio, 1993; Palmer, Kabanoff, & Dunford, 1997). Staff left behind are "bruised" by the process (Laabs, 1999, p. 35).

Most of the studies to date tend to focus on employer concerns only. For example, there are those who extol the costs and benefits of downsizing (e.g., Cascio, 1993; Mathews & Duran, 1999; Pollock, Dunnigan, Gaffney, Price, & Shaoul, 1999). Others consider the performance of those who are left (e.g., Braun, 1997; Layden & Harrington, 1998; Wright & Barling, 1998) and the likelihood that some downsizing approaches may be more effective than others (Mathews & Duran, 1999). Few consider the dignity of employees affected and the pain caused by unnecessary or thoughtlessly imposed layoffs. There has not been enough written about the countless numbers of former employees who have simply faded into obscurity (Applebaum, Lavigne-Schmidt, Peytchev, & Shapiro, 1999). Here, one worker's tragic experience with being "disposed of" is shared. At the commencement of the interview, Adrian showed me [Vickers] a small, pocket-sized card. It read [edited version]:

The Perfume Products Vision

Our Creed

People First. *Always.*

Our Mission

Above all else, we work to be known as *"The people company."*

I [Vickers] knew that the main reason that Adrian joined "Perfume Products" was because he related to the values espoused by the organization and, in particular, the managing director. Adrian reported to me the problems in the organization, including falling sales and staff being laid off as the organization restructured in response to this downturn. Alongside his concerns for the organization, Adrian suddenly learned he needed open-heart surgery. After taking time off work to have his surgery and recuperate, Adrian told me that he called in to the office, after visiting the doctor, to execute his return to work. He showed up at the office confident, expectant, and anxious to get back into life and work:

> *Adrian:* So looking for the surgeon, six weeks out. Went and spoke
> to him. He said, "Do you want to go back to work?" I said "Yep."
> And he said, "Well, it's going to be a bit of a mental drain on you."
> I said, "Sure, I'm ready for it though." So I went to work that day.
> Got stopped at the reception. Bob, the guy who was managing my
> group, came and spoke to me. So I went around to [Bob's] office,
> because I just wanted to debrief, to catch up and then tell him my
> plan, not expecting them to say no to any of that, you know. . . .
> So consequently to that, we're chat chat chat. We're talking about
> small stuff, you know, "How were the new people?" You know,
> "Good." Dah dah dah. Yes. He gets up, shuts the door. "Oh, OK,
> we're going to get into the sensitive stuff. Tell us what's happening."
> The sensitive stuff was about me! So, "Adrian, there's been a corpo-
> rate restructure and [pause] they've decided. . . ." "Who's decided?"
> "The Executives decided." I said, "OK". No one particularly, just "the
> executive's decided," "that your position's redundant." [pause]
> So that's what happened [emotion clearly heard in Adrian's voice
> now]. And I said, "Well, when does this happen? When do you
> want me to . . . when can I be redundant from?" thinking that,
> "Oh well, are they going to make it the end of the month, which
> was the end of July, or the end of August?" So he said, "We don't
> want you to start."

Adrian was clearly not expecting to have been made redundant after his illness and sick leave. He reported feeling very angry and shocked by the news of his "disposal." Note the use of the term "corporate restructure" to mask the probable real reason for his sudden departure. Adrian was feeling especially betrayed and reported specifically the disparity between the *espoused values* at his workplace (note on the corporate mission card presented to me at the commencement of our interview) and the *enacted values* (his termination, couched in terms of concern for his recovery, but directly co-inciding with his return from extended sick leave)—a particularly cruel juxtaposition. He continued:

> *Adrian:* But the whole thing that makes it nasty for me is not the re-dundancy, it is the timing of the redundancy on top of the heart, the heart problem, you know, the heart surgery, you know? Because once you look at some of the underlying beliefs of the company, you find there's a gap between what they say and what they do. . . . They [the "executive"] also indicated that this would help my re-covery, by the way.
>
> *MV:* Yes, yes. What did he say about that?
>
> *Adrian:* Well, he said, "We thought, the executive thought that, you know, this would also allow you to recover fully."
>
> *MV:* And what did you feel?
>
> *Adrian:* I felt, "Well, that's *bullshit*! That's *bullshit!*" You know? "You, you, you don't know me at all. You don't know how much I love *working*." You know, "You don't know how much I'm aligned to the philosophies here and also, serving the customer, you know?"
>
> *MV:* How did you feel walking out of his [Bob's] office?
>
> *Adrian:* Oh, it was bloody terrible! Because what I had to do after that, it was everyone wanted to see me! This was my first day. *Everyone* wanted to see me. So I had to go and do the rounds! And then the phone was ringing, my staff were ringing the phones and saying, "Oh, Mary upstairs, don't leave the building without seeing Mary." They [management] wanted me to leave straight away. I wasn't ready, in my own mind, to tell my own staff straight away [Adrian's emo-tions rising] . . . You know, I thought, you know, "What a lot of crap about. . . ." I was right, really into their belief systems. You know, "This is bloody disgusting. I've just had this heart operation, you know. How could they treat me like this? I've really been dedicated to them" . . . But it just wasn't . . . you know, they wanted me to go.

What I [Vickers] sought to do here was to encourage Adrian, through careful ques-tioning, to share what he was feeling and thinking on that fateful day. I asked him how he was feeling as he went through his ordeal, what his colleagues had said and done, and what his reactions were. Adrian shared very openly and candidly how he was feeling. The reader of his narrative is left with little doubt about his feelings and what had happened. Cartwright and Cooper (1994) describe the acute problem of coping with redundancy. They describe, importantly, "the extreme misery and sense of rejection that many people experience following job loss, and the importance and meaning which work gives to an individual's life" (Cartwright & Cooper, 1994, p. 149). What this methodology has done is to allow us to see directly how terms like "misery" and "rejection" are actually experienced.

We know that the anxiety of unemployment is known to lead to psychological symptoms such as depression, crime, violence, child abuse, and alcohol and substance abuse (Orlando, 1999). Being made redundant is also intuitively recognized as a painful experience for employees. However, there has been little exploration of how it feels to be made redundant, especially with a seemingly callous connection to a serious health condition. This methodology has enabled readers to see what a serious and painful experience this was for Adrian. More objective studies would have recounted him as another number in the list, and there would be no record of what he actually went through. It also allows us to see what is unsaid in the statistics of those made redundant, for example, what has been left unsaid about why Adrian might have been chosen as a candidate for redundancy and how that choice and its timing magnified his pain. Here we see the human and personal side of his experience—important for those who might not be experienced with undertaking such a role or who are looking for ways it might be improved. Being made redundant has been likened elsewhere to an experience of bereavement, with grief reactions of denial, anger, depression, and readjustment (Brammer & Humberger, 1984; Cartwright & Cooper, 1994; Horsted & Doherty, 1994). However, few have recorded the painful stories and been able to look through the eyes of the employee affected to reveal how such an experience is lived.

It is important for both line managers and HR practitioners to understand the effects on employees who are made redundant, from a perspective of justice and humanity, but also to protect the organization. Adrian's story demonstrates how thoughtless and callous handling of the situation at Perfume Products served to magnify the loss and grief that Adrian experienced. There was a clear sense of betrayal in Adrian's story, making his experience of rejection so much more acute. Further, the issue of exposing the organization legally, as was evident in Adrian's case, cannot be ignored, although for the most part, organizations seem to be more alert to such issues than Adrian's employers appeared to be. Finally, there is the question of the continuing morale of "survivors" of redundancy. Adrian has demonstrated that he had close personal ties with many of the staff at Perfume Products. Not only was he feeling shocked, angry, hurt, and betrayed, but it is reasonable to assume that many of his colleagues would also have been similarly affected—and fearing for their own futures. Any loyalty cultivated by this organization would have been rapidly eroded by its handling of Adrian's redundancy.

Living and Working with an Unseen Chronic Illness[4]

This final case also reports the experiences of one worker. Here, Heideggerian phenomenology serves to reveal experiences usually invisible and often unspoken in organizational life. Elsewhere, I [Vickers] have written about the experiences of those with unseen chronic illness in the workplace (Vickers, 1998, 1999, 2000, 2001), in particular, what a traumatic and turbulent journey life can be with an ongoing illness that your colleagues cannot see or understand. Below is a previously unpublished incident.

Maryanne has endometriosis and interstitial cystitis. Interstitial cystitis, the condition being referred to in the following extract, is a chronic, non-bacterial inflammation of the bladder of unknown cause (Martin, 1990). It is an extremely painful and uncommon bladder condition, often producing very disabling symptoms, including severe frequency, dysuria (pain, burning, or stinging during urination), and lower abdominal and urethral pain. The importance of using this methodology is clear: without it, there would have been no mention by this employee of what happened to her; it would have been easily avoided, and it is not usually talked about. Maryanne shares an especially embarrassing episode she experienced at work:

> *MV:* What's the worst thing that's happened to you related to your
>   work in having these chronic conditions?
>
> *Maryanne:* The worst thing that I always think, and the most embar-
>   rassing, which I've only ever spoken to one other person about, was
>   when I was working this job part-time. I also picked up some work
>   doing enrollments for an evening college in a school at Parramatta.
>   But one night, they kept, I kept asking where the loo [toilet] was,
>   and they kept saying, "Up there. Up there." And I couldn't find it.
>   And I literally, when I left, went out into the street, found an alley
>   and had to urinate into the street. [Maryanne is visibly upset by
>   this.] And that was pretty . . . I was only . . . How old was I? I was
>   only twenty-five. And that was just so traumatic for me . . . But it
>   was, I had no control. I had to, then, just go up and get a taxi . . .
>   it was just, it's so horrific. I can talk about it now . . . but it was
>   really, really traumatic to me. I didn't know about continence pads.
>   I didn't know about anything like that. That probably made my
>   attitude really bad, after having to do that.

---

[4]For those unfamiliar with the notion of unseen chronic illness, a chronic illness is an illness that is ongoing and may include physical, emotional, or cognitive problems. An unseen chronic illness is one that entails all the above characteristics while also being a condition that is not perceptible, not noticeable, not evident to others. In short, a condition that is "unseen" by others. Examples include chronic fatigue syndrome, HIV infection, multiple sclerosis, arthritis, epilepsy, depression, heart disease, and cancer (Vickers, 2001). Details of the full study, including demographic details of other participants, pseudonyms used, illness details, and where and when the study was conducted are detailed in Vickers (2001). However, the incident reported here has not been previously published and depicts the essential unspoken, silent quality of the experience.

Clearly, Maryanne has experienced a hugely traumatic event. By asking her what the worst thing that had happened to her was, I [Vickers] managed to uncover a story that had not been shared widely. At work, we are unlikely to share problems of excretion. It is certainly the kind of incident that few in organizations would ever hear about or know about—which is precisely the reason why it is important for it to be uncovered. By using this methodology, in addition to learning of the incident, I was also able to deduce meaning from her language—the repeated and direct use of the word "trauma" and the disjointed, rushed manner in which she recounted her story. The vignette portrays her embarrassment, not just in her difficulty in being able to discuss the event that had transpired many years earlier, but by her admission that she had been unable to talk to anyone (except one other individual) other than the researcher about her experience. It seemed especially poignant that Maryanne has credited her "change in attitude" to this particular incident.

"Invisible" problems—such as embarrassment and humiliation—tend to be trivialized, especially in our workplaces. After all, Maryanne was still alive, wasn't she? Tal (1996) reports that, when an individual is traumatized by an event, it displaces his or her preconceived notions about the world. Tal (1996) also subsequently reports that trauma is outside the bounds of "normal" human experience. In Maryanne's case, her Western cultural socialization makes her experience traumatic—outside the bounds of her "normal" experience. Her recollections might be characterized as the emotional or social dimensions of her trauma (Shearer & Davidhizar, 1995)—"post-traumatic" memories inflicting invisible scars that continue unabated (Lawson, 1987; Shearer & Davidhizar, 1995). If her colleagues had been more sensitive to her needs, they might have taken a moment to show her where the lavatory was located, especially if they had understood more closely the necessity for Maryanne to find it immediately. If management knew that Maryanne and other casual workers might be affected, they might take some time to consider posting signs to the toilet facilities more carefully. Unfortunately for Maryanne, she appeared perfectly healthy and was not comfortable explaining her health circumstances to others. The result for her was a very unpleasant workplace-related outcome. The result for the organization is that Maryanne never worked there again.

HR managers need to be especially vigilant about the concerns of workers with invisible symptoms of chronic illness or invisible disabilities. This is not always an easy task. Concerns, such as those Maryanne has raised, are unlikely to be forthcoming from workers, especially if they are related to embarrassing or "taboo" disabilities. Workers in a managerialist environment are unlikely to feel inclined to share such things. However, the development and promotion of HR policies that recognize the seriousness of invisible and unseen problems that relate to illness and disability in the workplace can assist. Such policies might provide for a secure and confidential environment where workers who have such concerns can discuss their needs or any accommodations they require in a sensitive, non-threatening environment. For example, a simple and inexpensive resolution to Maryanne's difficulties would have been to make sure she was located close to toilet facilities. Such an approach could serve both the individual and the organization by reducing the likelihood of a valuable staff member's skills being lost and by reducing the distraction and discomfort of the staff member concerned, which, in turn, may increase the productivity and loyalty of the affected staff member and those around him or her. Understanding personal, invisible, illness- and disability-related issues is important. Facilitating an environment where HR managers can get the information they need to respond appropriately and sensitively is essential.

Heidegger's Methodological Conception to Learn About Life in Organizations

Presented above is a Heideggerian phenomenology, a methodology showcased here as it was successfully utilized in three different research projects that were excavating the experiences of the individual employees in organizational life. There was an attempt on the part of the researchers to "truly know" (Gergen, 1991) what life at work is like for the employees who participated in these three projects.

We argue that Heideggerian phenomenology is *essential* to knowledge development of organizational life. Heideggerian phenomenology has been successfully utilized in the nursing and health sciences, as have other, often innovative, qualitative, reflexive, methodological combinations utilizing phenomenology and other qualitative approaches (Vickers, 2001). The use of Heideggerian phenomenology employs a critical and reflexive methodological approach ripe for use in uncovering the subjective, personal, painful, and, frequently, the unspoken in organizational life. Whether the experiences being investigated are about working in a team, being made redundant, or having an illness that others don't see or understand, or whether they are about one of a myriad of other experiences that employees routinely face in organizational life, Heideggerian phenomenology offers a sensitive approach to the investigation of the life experiences of employees at work.

It is hoped that these three cases have demonstrated the need for the use of more sensitive approaches to data gathering in organizational life. Investigating the experiences of individuals might extend to a myriad of events, outcomes, and processes in organizational life that are still not well understood, for example, bullying, violence, stress, staff turnover, leadership, followership, values, managing work-family balance, and career planning. HR managers can benefit from this kind of increased understanding in their organizations, so that the sensitive and the often unspoken in organizational life can be spoken about, better understood, and practically and productively addressed.

Heideggerian phenomenology provides a useful tool for managers who want to find out *how it really is* in their organization, so they can do something about it.

References

Adair, J. (1986). *Effective team building.* London: Gower.

Appelbaum, S.H., Lavigne-Schmidt, S., Peytchev, M., & Shapiro, B. (1999). Downsizing: Measuring the costs of failure. *Journal of Management Development, 18,* 436–463.

Baker, C., Wuest, J., & Stern, P.N. (1992). Method slurring: The grounded theory/phenomenology example. *Journal of Advanced Nursing, 17,* 1355–1360.

Barritt, L., Beekman, T., Bleeker, H., & Mulderij, K. (1984). Analyzing phenomenological descriptions. *Phenomenology and Pedagogy, 2*(1), 1–17.

Benner, P. (1985). Quality of life: A phenomenological perspective on explanation, prediction, and understanding in nursing science. *Advances in Nursing Science, 8*(1), 1–14.

Benner, P. (1994). The tradition and skill of interpretive phenomenology in studying health, illness, and caring practices. In P. Benner (Ed.), *Interpretive phenomenology: Embodiment, caring and ethics in health and illness* (pp. 99–127). Thousand Oaks, CA: Sage.

Brammer, L.M., & Humberger, F.E. (1984). *Outplacement and inplacement counseling.* Englewood Cliffs, NJ: Prentice Hall.

Braun, C. (1997). Organizational infidelity: How violations of trust affect the employee-employer relationship. *Academy of Management Executive, 11*(4), 94–95.

Cartwright, S., & Cooper, C.L. (1994). The human effects of mergers and acquisitions. In C.L. Cooper & D.M. Rousseau (Eds.), *Trends in organizational behavior* (pp. 47–61). Chichester, UK: John Wiley & Sons.

Cascio, W.F. (1993). Downsizing: What do we know? What have we learned? *Academy of Management Executive, 7*(1), 95–104.

Cordery, J.L., Mueller, W.S., & Smith, L.M. (1991). Attitudinal and behavioural effects of autonomous group working: A longitudinal field study. *Academy of Management Journal, 34,* 464–476.

Creswell, J.W. (1998). *Qualitative inquiry and research design: Choosing among five traditions.* Thousand Oaks, CA: Sage.

Downs, A. (1995). *Corporate executions.* New York: American Management Association.

Drew, N. (1989). The interviewer's experience as data in phenomenological research. *Western Journal of Nursing Research, 11,* 431–439.

Dugan, R.D. (1996). Corporate executions: The ugly truth about layoffs—How corporate greed is shattering lives, companies and communities, a book review of the work by Alan Downs. *Personnel Psychology, 49,* 998–1001.

Gergen, K.J. (1991). *The saturated self: Dilemmas of identity in contemporary life.* New York: Basic Books.

Gmelch, W.H. (1984). *Productivity teams: Beyond quality circles.* Hoboken, NJ: John Wiley & Sons.

Graham, J.W. (1991). Servant-leadership in organizations: Inspirational and motivational. *The Leadership Quarterly, 2*(2), 105–119.

Grant, D. (1999). HRM, rhetoric and the psychological contract: A case of "easier said than done." *The International Journal of Human Resource Management, 10*, 327–350.

Guzzo, R.A. (1996). Fundamental considerations about work groups. In M.A. West (Ed.), *Handbook of workgroup psychology* (pp. 3–21). London: John Wiley & Sons.

Hallam, G., & Campbell, D. (1997). The measurement of team performance with a standardized survey. In M.T. Brannick, E. Salas, & C. Prince (Eds.), *Team performance assessment and measurement* (pp. 155–172). Mahwah, NJ: Lawrence Erlbaum Associates.

Hammond, M.A., Howarth, J.M., & Keat, R.N. (1991). *Understanding phenomenology.* Oxford: Basil Blackwell.

Hartley, J.F. (1996). Intergroup relations in organizations. In M.A. West (Ed.), *Handbook of workgroup psychology* (pp. 397–422). London: John Wiley & Sons.

Heidegger, M. (1927/1962). *Being and time.* New York: Harper & Row.

Horsted, J., & Doherty, N. (1994). Poles apart? Integrating business process redesign and human resource management. *Business Change & Re-engineering, 1*(3), 49–56.

Katzenbach, J.R., & Smith, D.K. (1993). *The wisdom of teams: Creating the high-performance organization.* Boston, MA: McKinsey.

Kets de Vries, M.F.R., & Balazs, K. (1997). The downside of downsizing. *Human Relations, 50*, 11–50.

Knights, D., & McCabe, D. (2000). Bewitched, bothered and bewildered: The meaning and experience of team working for employees in an automobile company. *Human Relations, 53*, 1481–1517.

Knights, D., & McCabe, D. (2003). Governing through teamwork: Reconstituting subjectivity in a call centre. *Journal of Management Studies, 40*, 1587–1619.

Koch, T. (1995). Interpretive approaches in nursing research: The influence of Husserl and Heidegger. *Journal of Advanced Nursing, 21*, 827–836.

Kvale, S. (1996). *Interviews: An introduction to qualitative research interviewing.* Thousand Oaks, CA: Sage.

Laabs, J. (1999). Has downsizing missed its mark? *Workforce, 78*(4), 30–34.

Larson, C.E., & LaFasto, F.M.J. (1989). *Teamwork: What must go right/what can go wrong.* Thousands Oaks, CA: Sage.

Lawson, B.Z. (1987). Work-related post-traumatic stress reactions: The hidden dimension. *Health and Social Work, 12*(4), 250–258.

Layden, D.R., & Harrington, L.K. (1998). Downsizing, organizational justice, and the risk of workplace violence. *Proceedings of the Annual Conference of the Association on Employment Practices and Principles* (pp. 123–127). San Francisco, California.

Leonard, V.W. (1994). A Heideggerian phenomenological perspective on the concept of person. In P. Benner (Ed.), *Interpretive phenomenology: Embodiment, caring, and ethics in health and illness* (pp. 43–63). Thousand Oaks, CA: Sage.

Maggs-Rapport, F. (2001). "Best research practice": In pursuit of methodological rigour. *Journal of Advanced Nursing, 35*, 373–383.

Margerison, C., & McCann, D. (1990). *Team management.* London: Mercury.

Martin, E.A. (Ed.). (1990). *Oxford reference concise medical dictionary* (3rd ed.). Oxford: Oxford University Press.

Mathews, V.E., & Duran, C.A. (1999). Market memo: Some downsizing approaches more effective than others. *Health Care Strategic Management, 17*(9), 21–25.

Micklethwait, J., & Wooldridge, A. (1996). *The witch doctors: What the management gurus are saying, why it matters and how to make sense of it.* London: Mandarin.

Moxon, P. (1993). *Building a better team: A handbook for managers and facilitators.* London: Gower.

Nelson, B. (1998). The care of the un-downsized. *Public Management Review, 80*(4), 20–22.

Oiler, C. (1982). The phenomenological approach in nursing research. *Nursing Research, 31*(3), 178–181.

Orlando, J. (1999). The fourth wave: The ethics of corporate downsizing. *Business Ethics Quarterly, 9*(2), 295–314.

Palmer, I., Kabanoff, B., & Dunford, R. (1997). Managerial accounts of downsizing. *Journal of Organizational Behavior, 18*, 623–639.

Parris, M.A. (2001). *The individual experience within a work team: Early findings of a phenomenological study.* Paper presented at the 15th Conference of the Australian and New Zealand Academy of Management (ANZAM), Auckland, New Zealand, 5–8 December 2001.

Parris, M.A. (2002a). *Organisational support for work teams: Experiences of dissonance and discord.* Paper presented at the 16th Conference of the Australian and New Zealand Academy of Management (ANZAM), Victoria, Australia, 4–6 December 2002.

Parris, M.A. (2002b). *The individual experience within a work team.* M.Com (Hons) Thesis, University of Western Sydney, Sydney, New South Wales, Australia.

Parris, M.A. (2003). Work teams: Perceptions of a ready-made support system? *Employee Responsibilities and Rights Journal, 15*, 71–83.

Patrickson, M., Bamber, V., & Bamber, G.J. (1995). *Organisational change strategies.* Sydney: Longman.

Pollock, A.M., Dunnigan, M.G., Gaffney, D., Price, D., & Shaoul, J. (1999). Planning the "new" NHS: Downsizing for the 21st century. *British Medical Journal, 319*(7203), 179–184.

Ray, M.A. (1994). The richness of phenomenology: Philosophic, theoretic, and methodologic concerns. In J.M. Morse (Ed.), *Critical issues in qualitative research methods* (pp. 117–133). Thousand Oaks, CA: Sage.

Sandelowski, M. (1994). Focus on qualitative methods: Notes on transcription. *Research in Nursing and Health, 17*, 311–314.

Sarantakos, S. (1993). *Social research.* South Melbourne: MacMillan.

Schutz, A. (1932/1967). *The phenomenology of the social world.* New York: Northwestern University Press.

Shearer, R., & Davidhizar, R. (1995). Hidden scars: Posttraumatic stress disorder. *Nursing Connections, 8*(1), 55–63.

Spinelli, E. (1989). *The interpreted world: An introduction to phenomenological psychology.* London: Sage.

Stewart, D., & Mickunas, A. (1990). *Exploring phenomenology: A guide to the field and its literature* (2nd ed.). Athens, OH: Ohio University Press.

Street, A. (1996). Editorial 2: Reflections on doing and writing interpretive research. *Contemporary Nurse, 5*(2), 48–53.

Swanson-Kauffman, K., & Schonwald, E. (1988). Phenomenology. In B. Sarter (Ed.), *Paths to knowledge: Innovative research methods for nursing* (pp. 97–105). New York: National League for Nursing.

Swanson-Kauffman, K.M. (1986). A combined qualitative methodology for nursing research. *Advances in Nursing Science, 8*(3), 58–69.

Tal, K. (1996). *Worlds of hurt: Reading the literatures of trauma.* Cambridge: Cambridge University Press.

Tannenbaum, S.I., & Cannon-Bowers, J.A. (1996). Promoting team effectiveness. In M.A. West (Ed.), *Handbook of workgroup psychology* (pp. 503–529). London: John Wiley & Sons.

Taylor, B. (1993). Phenomenology: One way to understand nursing practice. *International Journal of Nursing Studies, 30*(2), 171–179.

Taylor, S.J., & Bogdan, E. (1998). *Introduction to qualitative research methods: A guidebook and resource* (3rd ed.). Hoboken, NJ: John Wiley & Sons.

Vickers, M.H. (1998). Life at work with "invisible" chronic illness (ICI): A passage of trauma—turbulent, random, poignant. *Administrative Theory and Praxis, 20,* 196–218.

Vickers, M.H. (1999). "Sick organizations," "rabid managerialism": Work-life narratives from people with "invisible" chronic illness. *Public Voices, 4*(2), 59–82.

Vickers, M.H. (2000). The "invisibly" chronically ill as unexamined organizational fringe-dwellers: Voices of ambiguity, confusion and uncertainty. In R. Hodson (Ed.), *Marginality* (pp. 3–21). Greenwich, CT: JAI Press.

Vickers, M.H. (2001). *Work and unseen chronic illness: Silent voices.* London: Routledge.

Vickers, M.H. (2002). "People first—always": Euphemism and rhetoric as troublesome influences in organizational sense-making—a downsizing case study. *Employee Responsibilities and Rights Journal, 14,* 105–118.

Walters, A.J. (1996). Nursing research methodology: Transcending Cartesianism. *Nursing Inquiry, 3,* 91–100.

Watson, T.J. (1995). Rhetoric, discourse and argument in organizational sense making: A reflexive tale. *Organization Studies, 16,* 805–821.

Watters, J.K., & Biernacki, P. (1989). Targeted sampling: Options for the study of hidden populations. *Social Problems, 36,* 416–430.

Weaver, J.L., Bowers, C.A., Salas, E., & Cannon-Bowers, J.A. (1997). Motivation in teams. *Advances in Interdisciplinary Studies of Work Teams, 4,* 167–191.

Wright, B., & Barling, J. (1998). "The executioner's song": Listening to downsizers reflect on their experiences. *Canadian Journal of Administrative Sciences, 15,* 339–355.

Yammarino, F.J., & Naughton, T.J. (1992). Individualized and group-based views of participation in decision making. *Group and Organization Management, 17,* 398–413.

Margaret H. Vickers, *Ph.D., is an associate professor at the School of Management, University of Western Sydney. She has published in excess of fifty international refereed articles and book chapters, in addition to dozens of international conference papers. Her research focuses on traumatic experiences in the workplace and includes projects such as Bullying in the Workplace; Living and Working with Multiple Sclerosis; Experiences of Redundancy; Experiences of Parents Who Work and Care for a Child with Chronic Illness; and Living and Working with Unseen Chronic Illness. Her research monograph* Work and Unseen Chronic Illness: Silent Voices *(2001) has had international acclaim, and she is on the editorial boards of* Review of Disability Studies: An International Journal *and* Journal of Qualitative Research in Management and Organizations. *Professor Vickers is associate editor of the* Employee Responsibilities and Rights Journal.

Melissa Parris *is a Ph.D. candidate at the School of Management, University of Western Sydney. Ms. Parris' research is concerned with the perspective of the individual at work. Her Ph.D. research, currently underway, is focusing on the work-home interface for middle managers. A previous research project led by Ms. Parris examined the experience of individuals working in teams in organizations. Ms. Parris' work on these two projects, and others related to concerns for individuals in organizational life, have resulted in several international conference papers and presentations and international journal articles being published.*

Introduction
to Insights and Perspectives

Everyone has an opinion on HR. Most people think they know how to carry out solutions to HR problems. Opinions are great because they focus attention and create an interchange of ideas. Everyone enjoys a free-flowing discussion as a forum to present their knowledge and experience. Solutions, though, have to be the result of a process with laser-like focus. Also, solutions should be left to HR professionals and executives who have the required knowledge and skills, not to the opinion generators.

In the theory and practice of high-performance individuals and organizations, this kind of focus is often referred to as "attending intently." When other conditions that lead to high performance that have been documented in the literature over the past two decades are present, this leads to high-impact results in the arenas of productivity, quality, and service. It is difficult, if not impossible, to jump directly into a laser-like focus. Before that can happen, it is important to know the context or background. Everyone has to be on the same page, even if they get there from different directions.

The section on perspectives offers opinions grounded in context or background. The articles in this section identify a framework for HR that can be useful for practitioners, academics, and consultants. Once this framework is established, it becomes easier to conduct explorations into whatever aspect of HR is on the table. This, in turn, facilitates the development of a laser-like focus that produces a meaningful contribution to the resolution of HR situations.

Reading this section of the *Annual* is great preparation for the HR challenges ahead! This section contains the following articles:

Free Agency: The 21st Century Employment Relationship for Professionals, by Douglas Buck

Story as Organizational Learning: The Role of Story in Expanding Our Capacity to Generate Results, by Elizabeth Doty with Kat Koppett

New Role for HR: Communication Caretaker, by Ronald C. Fetzer

Terrorists Hit HRM, by Jack N. Kondrasuk

Behavior Matters: Building a Legal, Ethical Workplace Culture,
by Stephen M. Paskoff

Doing It Right the First Time: Orientation and Community Building,
by Rick Rocchetti

Developing and Using Behaviorally Based Rating Scales: A Tool for
Appraising Human Resources, by John Sample

Free Agency:
The 21st Century Employment Relationship for Professionals
Douglas Buck

Summary

The world is changing. Today's professional employee who has attained a measure of success through education and work experience is no longer seeking employment that will assure him or her of long-term employment with a single employer as a primary focus in career choices. Today's professionals perhaps have recognized that their parents' conception of employment success as employment stability with one or a few employers is not a reality in contemporary employment relationships. Organizations are expanding globally, "right sizing," contracting out functions, eliminating functions, reengineering functions, and hiring temps to replace full-time employees— all events that have a significant impact on the stability of long-term employment. These are a just a few of the factors that have caused this new employment paradigm that this article will explore. Professional employees who have expended their resources and energies to succeed now are faced with practically applying their knowledge and skills in an employment relationship. Recognizing the tentativeness of the contemporary employment relationship, how should newly emerging professionals proceed? This paper attempts to answer this question.

Free agency typically describes an employment relationship in professional athletics and has been widely "cussed and discussed" by avid sports fans who do not want to see their favorite player leave the local team to possibly go with the "enemy"—one of its significant rivals. In essence, it allows a professional athlete, after expiration of a contract signed with a particular team, to declare free agency and to provide his or her professional services to the highest bidder. This free agency is codified in the league's collective bargaining agreement.

As an example, the National Football League's contract with the Players Union contains this provision:

Section 1. Unrestricted Free Agents

"Subject to the provisions of Article XX (Franchise and Transition Players), any player with five or more Accrued Seasons, or with four or more Accrued Seasons in any Capped Year, shall, at the expiration of his Player Contract, become an Unrestricted Free Agent. Such player shall be completely free to negotiate and sign a Player Contract with any Club, and any Club shall be completely free to negotiate and sign a Player Contract with such player, without penalty or restriction, including, but not limited to, Draft Choice Compensation between Clubs or First Refusal Rights of any kind, subject to the signing period set forth below." (www.nflpa.org/Members/main.asp?subPage=CBA+Complete#art19)

It has been predicted that a recent college graduate can expect to change jobs up to ten times and careers up to four times in his or her working life (Noe, Hollenbeck, Gerhart, & Wright, 2003). Can it be that the free agency metaphor can be applied to the professional employee of the 21st Century? What is causing this phenomenon in employment relationships with many professional employees? Why are many professional employees so quick to change employers and have fewer reservations about it than some of us "traditionalists," who may still long for the "old days" when you earned your employment security by loyally serving your employer? Or is it just a natural progression of our society that has created this paradigm for the future of U.S. professional employment? Could it be that the contemporary American worker is focused more on external interests, less willing to compromise ethics, unable to deal constructively with conflict in an organizational setting, feeling unrewarded as an employee or a manager, confused and concerned with the increasing diversity of the workforce, and more loyal to his or her "profession" than to the organization that employs him or her; or is it a combination of these factors that has caused the "free agency" of individuals? This article explores some of these areas and attempts to answer these questions and explain why the contemporary professional employee may continue the trend of offering his or her expertise to those employers he or she believes will meet his or her wants and needs, regardless of the stability or the length of the employment relationship.

Psychological Contract

The vast majority of professional employees working in the private sector do not have a written employment contract with their employers. This is especially true for companies that have "employment-at-will" policies. In general, employment-at-will permits a manager to terminate an employee for any reason, whether it is a good reason, a bad reason, or even no reason at all (Muir, 2003). Employment-at-will effectively means that either party to the employment relationship may sever that relationship at any time for any reason, as long as the reason does not constitute illegal discrimination. However, in any employment relationship there exists a "psychological contract" between the employer and the employee.

According to Noe, Hollenbeck, Gerhart, & Wright (2003), the psychological contract describes what an employee expects to contribute and what the company will provide to the employee for these contributions. Unlike a sales contract, a psychological contract is not written. Traditionally, companies expected employees to contribute time, effort, skills, abilities, and loyalty. In return, companies would provide job security and opportunities for promotion. However, in the new economy a new type of psychological contract is emerging.

The competitive business environment demands frequent changes in the quality, innovation, creativeness, and timeliness of employee contributions and the skills needed to provide them. This has led to company restructuring, mergers and acquisitions, layoffs, and longer hours for employees. Obviously, this has provided some of the impetus for the more dynamic employment relationships for employees in today's economy.

Rousseau (1999) also states in a study that, as a result of this changing psychological contract, companies are using more alternative work arrangements. These arrangements include independent contractors, on-call workers, temporary workers, and contract company workers. DiNatale (2001) reports that the Bureau of Labor Statistics estimates that there are 12.2 million "nontraditional workers," including 8.2 million independent contractors, two million on-call workers, 1.2 million temporary workers, and approximately 800,000 contract company workers (workers employed by a company that provides them to other companies under a contract). These alternative work arrangements constitute about 10 percent of employees. Again, these "alternative" employees are assuming the work formerly performed by full-time employees, thus contributing further to the new employment dynamic for professionals.

Frase-Blunt (2004) reports that the U.S. Bureau of Labor Statistics says executive and professional temps now account for 11 percent of the temp workforce, up from 7 percent in 1998. Driving much of the growth in the temporary-executive sector is the Sarbanes-Oxley Act of 2002. Many companies have been hiring experienced executives to help them comply with the law's strict corporate accountability requirements. These temp execs are brought in to either replace an individual who has terminated employment after some internal auditing results, or they are joining the organization to assist the senior-level executives to come into compliance with the Act.

Why Do Employees Stay?

Most organizations would like to have a stable workforce and be able to offer their loyal and productive employees a sense of security by continuing their employment as long as they are contributing to the success of the organization. Turnover is costly, with both direct and indirect costs, ranging from recruitment and selection costs to the history lost when the individual leaves, especially the professional employee.

Typically, there are controllable and uncontrollable reasons for turnover, and companies tend to conduct exit interviews of those leaving to detect the controllable reasons. However, according to Hughes (1990), "The traditional approach to measuring and understanding terminations has focused on turnovers. These employees generally represent a small percentage of the total employee population; therefore, placing retention efforts on them exclusively ignores the reasons the majority of the workforce stays with the company. Employers wanting to improve their working environments should stop assuming that exit interviews provide a meaningful picture of why other employees stay" (p. 64).

Perhaps it is more important to investigate the reason that most employees decide to stay in their employment relationship, since this is a much larger population than those who choose to leave or are forced to leave. What are some of the areas of satisfaction or motivation that may enhance a more stable employment relationship that can be utilized by the employer?

Hughes (1990) states, "Employees tend to stay where they are until some force causes them to leave, in other words 'inertia.' As in physics, a body will remain as it is until acted on by an external force. Two factors inside organizations and two outside make people stay. *Job satisfaction* and *satisfaction with the working environment* produce the internal inertia and are directly affected by the positive or negative correlation between the employee's personal value system and that of management. A disparity between personal and organizational values reduces the desire to stay, while compatibility between these two values increases the desire to stay. The external factors that increase inertia include *perceptions of other job opportunities* and *personal and family reasons*" (p. 62). In essence, it is not only external environmental factors that exacerbate the volatility of the employment relationship; the stability of the employment relationship is many times affected by the internal motivations of the individual employee beyond the control of the employer.

The Transition to the Free Agency Paradigm

Now let's look at some of the reasons why the employment paradigm for professionals has been transitioning to a "free agency" paradigm.

Globalization and Relocation of Facilities

Most of the major corporations in the United States have expanded their operations internationally in order to survive competitively. This includes focusing on expanded international markets for their products and services, establishing operating facilities internationally, as well as transferring members of their professional and managerial workforces to foreign locations on temporary or permanent assignments. A number of implications for professional employees often impact the stability of their employment. Dowling, Welch, and Schuler (1999) discuss the reasons for "expatriate failure," defined as the premature return of an expatriate (that is, return home before the period of assignment is completed). This has a significant impact on the company as well as on the individual. It is an immense cost for the company, since it has expended resources to select, train, and transport the employee, as well as family members in many cases, to the foreign location. It also includes the future replacement costs of the returning expatriate. The returning expatriate may also be negatively affected, as the employee's return may be deemed a personal failure from the organization's perspective and cause the individual to sever the employment relationship.

As cited in Dowling, Welch, and Schuler (1999), there has been almost no empirical foundation for the existence of high failure rates in the United States when measured as premature re-entry. However, there have been extensive empirical studies in European multinationals, including U.S. subsidiaries. These studies revealed that, of the firms surveyed, the premature re-entry rate ranged from 5 to 15 percent. They go on to say that, in the absence of more empirical studies, their opinion is that it is to be expected that the U.S. rates would be in the same range. It should be noted that the re-entries included both employees who were directed to return for performance problems as well as those employees who opted to return for personal reasons. There is anecdotal evidence that suggests that a portion of the re-entries result in the individual not having a job in the home organization to go to, since many companies do not offer a return guarantee to expatriates. One more factor has caused professionals to be much more mobile in seeking career opportunities in the marketplace, thus exercising their "free agency" rights.

Increasing Workforce Diversity

According to the U.S. Department of Commerce, both minority populations and purchasing power are going to grow at rates much higher than the population as a whole.

From 2000 to 2045, minorities will account for 86 percent of the total U.S. population growth, increasing from 29 to 46 percent of the total population. The total minority population will surpass the non-minority population sometime between 2055 and 2060 (Carr-Ruffino, 2003).

Carr-Ruffino (2003) states that "People with university degrees and technical expertise come from all types of backgrounds these days. Since the 1960s more and more African Americans, Latino Americans, Asian Americans, Arab Americans, and women have been entering college programs and technical areas that were formerly dominated by Euro-American men. As a result, these 'minorities' have been moving into managerial, executive, technical, and professional careers formerly closed to them" (p. 3). Today's work environment to some extent is beginning to mirror the general population because of affirmative action and diversity programs implemented by many organizations. The "inclusion" of the new diversity initiatives has sometimes met resistance from employees, including professional and managerial, that has created some attrition among these groups.

Perhaps it is relevant to understand some of these adjustment issues by looking at some of the characteristics of employees based on their generational values. Table 1 summarizes research on the ethos of various American generations of this century, based on studies by Gann and Duignan (1986) and S.E. Jackson (1992).

Table 1 provides information that is useful in correlating generations and traits; Table 2 identifies several generations and their cultural ethos. The kinds of experiences, the issues each had to deal with, and the specific cultural beliefs of each generation tend to encourage certain values and can form certain personality traits.

Over one-quarter of the HR professionals recently surveyed by the Society for Human Resources Management (SHRM) said they have seen tensions between workers of different generations increase in the past five years, and about one-third said they expect intergenerational tensions in the workplace to increase in the next five years. One area where employee groups differ slightly according to age is that of work/life balance. The younger the age group, the more it values such balance between work and personal obligations. Among younger workers, it plays a larger role in job satisfaction for women than for men (Schramm, 2004).

The result of integrating a number of individuals with very different values together in a diverse working environment can lead to conflict situations. This is one more reason why we have seen an increased mobility of professionals in the contemporary economy. In the current business environment, an organizational culture that leverages diversity and builds diversity inclusion will create a climate that can facilitate both external business success and internal employee satisfaction, thus assisting in the stability of the employee-employer working relationship.

Those organizations that can introduce an "inclusion breakthrough" may be those that will be able to extend the employment relationship with its professional work-

Table 1. Typical Values and Traits by Generations

Traditionals	Boomers	Generation Xers	Millennials
Loyal	Optimistic	Skeptical	Realistic
Pay dues	Highly competitive	"Show me the money"	Participate in decisions
Show up, on time	Affluence	Latchkey children	Expect diversity
Care about work	TV generation	Computer generation	Internet/cell phone generation
Strong, silent	Express self	Resourceful	Confident
Faith in institutions	Idealistic rights	Distrust institutions	Collaborative
Hierarchy	Question status quo	Independent	"Don't command me"
Chain of command	Change of command	Self-command	

Source: Adapted from N. Carr-Ruffine, *Managing Deversity: People Skills for a Multicultural Workforce,* 2003. Copyright 2003, Pearson Custom Publishing. Reprinted with permission.

Table 2. Generations and Their Cultural Ethos

Birth Years	Era	Key Issues	Cultural Ethos
1930–1945	Traditionals	Survival (Depression, WWII)	Security, savings, defending freedom
1946–1964	Baby Boomers	TV "Me" Generation, self-development	Rebuilding, demanding personal freedom, individuality, seeking personal fulfillment
1965–1975	Generation Xers	Distrust institutions	Spanning the global village, cutting edge, fun, diversity
1976–1985	Millenniums	Safety from violence	Ethnic diversity, global concern, rapidly changing technology

Source: Adapted from N. Carr-Ruffino, *Managing Diversity: People Skills for a Multicultural Workforce,* 2003. Copyright 2003, Pearson Custom Publishing. Reprinted with permission.

force. An inclusion breakthrough is a process to transform the organization from a monocultural organization that values and supports sameness in style and approach to a culture of inclusion that leverages diversity in all its many dimensions. According to Miller and Katz (2002), "An inclusion breakthrough is required—to leverage the diversity of all people and build an inclusive culture—because old assumptions, old styles, old approaches to problem solving and old line-ups are insufficient to help an organization survive and thrive in a turbulent environment" (p. 7). An inclusion breakthrough necessitates a whole new way of life. Many Gen Xers feel that their parents' materialism has led to empty lives. A vital element of an inclusion breakthrough strategy is seizing the opportunity to give talented people reasons to stay, including meeting their need to give something back.

Management Paradigm Shift

Another impact on the mobility of professionals in today's workplace is the paradigm shift of the 21st Century manager. Kreitner and Kinicki (2001) address the issue of the management paradigm shift that is required in order to operate successfully in today's dynamic business environment. Today's workplace is indeed undergoing immense and permanent changes. In the authors' words, "Organizations are being reengineered for greater speed, efficiency, and flexibility. Teams are pushing aside the individual as the primary building block of organizations. Command-and-control management is giving way to participate management and empowerment. Customer-centered leaders are replacing ego-centered leaders. Employees increasingly are being viewed as internal customers" (p. 9). All this creates a mandate for a new kind of manager in the 21st Century. Some of these changes are shown in Table 3.

The future managerial job will require a number of different skill sets, knowledge, abilities, and values to be successful compared with the same attributes for "past" managers. Again, this may cause increased attrition of professional managers who cannot, or who are unwilling to, adapt to these requirements. They may find themselves "in the job market" and will be seeking future positions in an environment and culture more acceptable to them. They will exercise their "free agency" rights to explore other opportunities.

Conclusion

Professional employees and/or managers of the 21st Century can expect to change employers numerous times throughout their working lives. In effect, contemporary professionals are comparable to professional athletes: free agents in the job market, offering their education, skills, and abilities to the organization that can fulfill their wants and needs at any particular time during their working lives. Wants and needs change, and this new paradigm will provide the flexibility for the employee to sever an employment relationship when his or her expectations are not being met. Employment security will consist of, and be dependent on, the individual's inherent confidence in his or her skills and ability to be successful in achieving a variety of professional positions over the span of his or her working life. To some, this may be discomforting; to others it is a challenge

Table 3. Comparison Between Past and Future Managers

	Past Managers	Future Managers
Primary Role	Order-giver, privileged elite, manipulator, controller	Facilitator, team member, teacher, advocate, sponsor, coach
Learning and Knowledge	Periodic learner, narrow specialist	Continuous lifelong learning, generalist with multiple specialties
Compensation Criteria	Time, effort, rank	Skills, results
Cultural Orientation	Mono-cultural, monolingual	Multicultural, multilingual
Primary Source of Influence	Formal authority	Knowledge (technical and interpersonal)
View of People	Potential problem	Primary resource
Primary Communication Pattern	Vertical	Multidirectional
Decision-Making Style	Limited input for individual decisions	Broad-based input for joint decisions
Ethical Considerations	Afterthought	Forethought
Nature of Interpersonal Relationships	Competitive (win-lose)	Cooperative (win-win)
Handling of Power and Key Information	Hoard and restrict access	Share and broaden access
Approach to Change	Resist	Facilitate

Source: Adapted from R. Kreitner and A. Kinicki, *Organizational Behavior.* New York: McGraw-Hill. Reproduced with permission of The McGraw-Hill Companies.

that will be refreshing and stimulating. It "is what it is"—the free agency paradigm for professionals in the 21st Century.

References

Carr-Ruffino, N. (2003). *Managing diversity: People skills for a multicultural workplace* (6th ed.). Boston, MA: Pearson Custom Publishing.

DiNatale, M. (2001, March). Characteristics of and preferences for alternative work arrangements. *Monthly Labor Review,* pp. 28–49.

Dowling, P.J., Welch, D.E., & Schuler, R.S. (1999). *International human resource management: Managing people in a multinational context* (3rd ed.). New York: Southwestern College Publishing.

Frase-Blunt, M. (2004, June). Short-term executives. *HR Magazine, 49*(6).

Gann, L.J., & Duignan, P.J. (1986). *The Hispanics of the United States: A history.* Boulder, CO: Westview Press.

Hughes, D.L. (1990). *Making unions unnecessary.* New York: John Wiley & Sons.

Jackson, S.E. (1992). *Diversity in the workplace.* New York: Guilford Press.

Kreitner, R., & Kinicki, A. (1998). *Organizational behavior* (4th ed.). Boston: Irwin/McGraw-Hill.

Miller, F.A., & Katz, J.H. (2002). *The inclusion breakthrough: Unleashing the real power of diversity.* San Francisco, CA: Berrett-Koehler.

Muir, D. (2003). *A manager's guide to employment law.* San Francisco, CA: Jossey-Bass.

National Football League Players Association. Retrieved September 22, 2004, from www .nflpa.org/Members/main.asp?subPage=CBA+Complete#art19.html

Noe, R.A., Hollenbeck, J.R., Gerhart, B., & Wright, P.M. (2003). *Human resource management: Gaining a competitive advantage* (4th ed.). New York: McGraw Hill.

Rousseau, D.M. (1999). Psychological and implied contracts in organizations. *Employee Rights and Responsibilities Journal, 2,* 121–129.

Schramm, J. (2004, September 9). Age groups mostly in accord. *HR Magazine, 49*(9).

Douglas Buck, *DPA, SPHR, is an adjunct professor at several universities, teaching master's and doctoral courses in human resources, business, alternate dispute resolution, conflict management, and public administration. His education includes a bachelor of science degree in personnel administration, a master of science degree in employee relations, and a doctorate in public administration. He is retired as associate vice president of human resources after thirty-two years in the HR profession. He previously served in executive level HR positions with the Department of Defense, an Ohio public school district, and an Ohio community college. Dr. Buck has a consulting practice in Aiken, South Carolina, where he provides human resource consulting, training, and alternate dispute resolution services to both public and private sector organizations*

Story as Organizational Learning:
The Role of Story in Expanding Our Capacity to Generate Results
Elizabeth Doty with Kat Koppett

Summary

Intuitively, we understand the power of an organization "learning" or "knowing," although most of us find that our organizations' collective intelligence is actually lower than the sum of the individuals that make it up. Therefore, one of the most valuable roles any HR department can play is to support the processes that enable learning at an organizational level. We know story brings individual learning to life. Might we use story to support learning at an organizational level? This article provides a framework, overview, and several sample exercises for using story to support the three core elements of organizational learning: shared vision, a deep understanding of current reality, and the learning processes that improve an organization's capacity to generate the results it truly desires.

When most of us think of learning, we think first of an individual process, the individual acquisition of knowledge or skill. How could we think otherwise, after all those years in school? And now our organizations' strategies depend on our ability to rapidly develop an evolving set of skills in our people. So naturally we focus on how to make these learning and development processes more effective.

Story is one mode that works. Anyone who has spent any time in the classroom knows the power of vivid examples for bringing concepts to life and improving retention; case studies and scenarios for developing critical thinking and judgment; and tapping participants' own past experiences for deepening motivation and improving application. As we continue to explore new ways to apply story effectively, some organizations are experimenting with practices from improv theater, rapid instructional design, and more.

Now, as world-class organizations call on human resource functions to expand their roles, taking a full seat at the table to influence the development of culture and leadership practices in their businesses, we find ourselves facing a new question: *How do organizations learn as a whole?*

Intuitively, we understand the power of an organization "learning" or "knowing." We may have a mental image of our organization adapting and inventing new approaches as the environment and opportunities change, retaining valuable competencies and practices as individuals come and go. But without conscious attention to learning, most of us find our organizations' collective intelligence is actually lower than the sum of the individuals that make it up. (Think "Abilene Paradox" [Harvey, 1988], if you know what I mean.) This is why one of the most valuable roles any HR department can play is to support the processes that enable learning at an organizational level.

Does story have a part in this process? Might we expand and build on the power of story for individual learning to support parallel efforts at an organizational level?

What We Mean by "Story"

Before we explore the relevance of story for organizational learning, we should first ask: What do we mean by "story"? Fundamentally, story is about making meaning. We might define it specifically as *an account of experience so as to give it meaning*—that is, to allow us to draw conclusions about how things work, how to act, or what to care about. That means that "the launch of the NASA Space Program" and "what happened to performance last year" both refer to stories. We might think of myths as stories about ultimate meaning: identity, purpose, the nature of reality.

In a broader sense, we can think of story as *any connection or association that allows us to make meaning.* This conceptualization goes beyond traditional stories to what I call "storylines"—explanations that help us make sense of the world. "People tend to resist change" and "Accelerating economic growth is causing higher turnover" are both storylines in this broader sense, because they represent the meaning we draw from countless bits of data. I mention this now because we will need to include stories in both senses if we are to get at their full power for organizational learning.

Approaches to Organizational Learning

There are two main schools of thought on organizational learning: one centered around Peter Senge and his colleagues at MIT and the Society for Organizational Learning (2004), and the other centered around David Garvin and his work at Harvard.

Peter Senge's work, best represented in the *Fifth Discipline* books, focuses on fundamental questions such as the aim of organizational learning. For him, organizational learning is about "continually expanding our capacity to generate the results we truly desire" (Senge, 1990, p. 1).

This simple description casts learning in a whole new light, broadening our perspective and uniting employees and leaders in addressing whatever prevents them from getting results. It allows us to look beyond individual skills and knowledge to how we function together, what results we truly desire, even how we think together—not for their own sake, nor to counter-balance financial results with the "soft side" of business, but because *these factors are often the most direct means to getting those results.*

For Senge (1995), three barriers tend to limit organizations' capacities to learn:

- Difficulties in seeing and talking about current reality;

- Weaknesses in our ability to engage one another in a shared vision; and

- Limits on our ability to understand and work with complexity.

Therefore, Senge and his colleagues tend to focus on individual and leadership practices for addressing these three barriers. (Please see the References at the end of this article for additional books and resources on organizational learning, including *The Fifth Discipline Fieldbook* [Senge, Kleiner, Roberts, Ross, & Smith, 1994] and *The Dance of Change* [Senge, Kleiner, Roberts, Ross, Roth, & Smith, 1999].) One of the central ideas in *The Fifth Discipline* is the concept of "creative tension": the idea that if we are completely honest about both what we care about creating *and* about current reality, whatever the distance between them, that tension will naturally propel us to seek new capacities that help close the gap (Senge, 1990). (See Figure 1.)

David Garvin's writing focuses on the question of how we close the gap. He proposes specific processes and structures for building learning into an organization's day-to-day functioning, defining a learning organization as "an organization skilled at creating, acquiring, interpreting, retaining, and transferring knowledge and at purposefully modifying its behavior based on new knowledge and insights" (Gary, 1997, p. 5). More than individual practices, Garvin encourages organizations to develop and implement processes to improve learning from experience, experimentation, and intelligence-gathering, and to assess their impact on an ongoing basis (Gary, 1997).

We can integrate these two approaches if we visualize Garvin's focus as learning processes that close the gap between Senge's shared vision and current reality, as is illustrated in Figure 2. According to this perspective, many corporate initiatives can be considered part of the organization's learning processes, including learning and development, Six Sigma and process excellence, action learning, informal communities of practice, and even strategic planning.

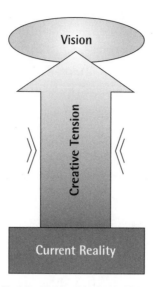

Adapted from *The Fifth Discipline Fieldbook* by Senge, Kleiner, Roberts, Ross, & Smith (1994, pp. 195, 197), describing the work of Robert Fritz.

Figure 1.   Creative Tension Between Vision and Reality

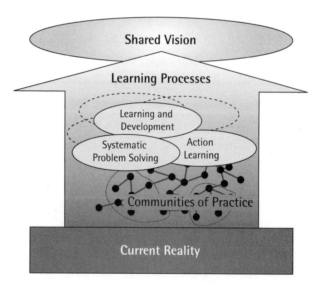

Figure 2.   Integrating Senge and Garvin

What organizations need is an integrating role, one that attends to how shared vision, current reality, and learning processes tie together. Human resource professionals are in a natural position to contribute to this weaving: connecting the processes for cultivating shared vision, understanding current reality, and developing new capabilities into a coherent whole.

Story and Organizational Learning

What is the relevance of story to this process? As I see it, organizational learning is essentially about learning from our collective experience—removing the blinders that prevent us from recognizing and sharing the lessons buried in how things really work and applying them skillfully to new challenges and opportunities. We might visualize this as the process of distilling knowledge out of raw experience (our own or others') through routine processes or intentional experiments and then sharing it. I see this as a modified form of the "ladder of inference" described in the *Fifth Discipline Fieldbook*, as shown in Figure 3.

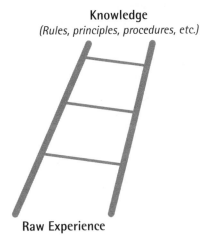

Knowledge
(Rules, principles, procedures, etc.)

Raw Experience

Adapted from *The Fifth Discipline Fieldbook* by Senge, Kleiner, Roberts, Ross, & Smith (1994, pp. 242-243), describing the "ladder of inference," developed by Chris Argyris.

Figure 3.   Ladder of Inference

And what is story but the most ancient human way of conveying experience so we may learn from it? It is innate, perhaps as innate as language for humans, to tell and listen to story. We might see it as a middle step in the process of moving up from raw experience to knowledge, or conversely, going back down as we reexamine old principles that no longer fit. (See Figure 4.) This works not just for knowledge about the world "out there," but also for making sense of our identity and purpose as individuals and organizations.

The problem is that *we do not automatically learn by having gone through an experience.* As a colleague of mine put it rather starkly, "People (in corporations) go through terribly painful experiences and, upon surviving, at best leap to a conclusion about the 'lesson.'" We do all the work of living through challenging experiences but cheat ourselves of the hard-won lessons in the end—the lessons that will actually increase our capacity to generate future results. I believe this is one reason people find their enthusiasm for

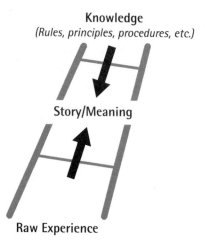

Adapted from *The Fifth Discipline Fieldbook* by Senge, Kleiner, Roberts, Ross, & Smith (1994, 242-243), describing the "ladder of inference," developed by Chris Argyris.

Figure 4. The Middle Step

change flagging over time—they privately sense that there are lessons that have not yet really been learned. As a result, we over-tax our capacities for commitment and ingenuity, depleting our reserves and our ability to commit fully to the next change. After all, we want our hard work and creativity to add something of value—not to serve as a substitute for a real understanding of challenges we have lived through before.

Yet most of the time, we feel we cannot afford to stop long enough to tell the story. We have learned in the professional world to minimize the time we spend recounting experiences and, instead, to "cut to the chase." Our normal ways of communicating in business are like sharing the moral without the story—which, on its own, fails to engage or leaves out critical contextual information in the process.

It is becoming clear that the price of these constraints is too high. For the past ten to fifteen years, leaders in a variety of fields have been challenging old assumptions about the role of story in professional settings—rediscovering its power for engaging imagination, surfacing possibilities, illustrating concepts, and anchoring new behavior and identities. (For a chronology of these efforts, please see the *Chronology of Organizational Storytelling* [Denning & Kahan, 2003] or IBM's Institute for Knowledge Management's exploration of story [*IBM Knowledge Socialization Project*, 2000].)

My sense is that *we are in the midst of relegitimizing the process of sharing experience and meaning in the professional world.* Not all the time, and not every experience. Not to the exclusion of thoughtful analysis and decision making, but as a critical component of a cycle of learning and improving, making inroads and sharing them, and piecing together a shared understanding of the dynamics that generate results. We are beginning to see story's place alongside analysis in the process of working raw sensory data into useful principles and insights.

For example, a new leader recently assumed responsibility for an IT infrastructure organization that had been cobbled together through successive mergers. She found that the most effective way to engage her team and her peers was to craft a storyline that highlighted the implications of the merger history itself: that there was a new need for a horizontal function to consolidate operational excellence across multiple technologies. She then illustrated that storyline with vivid examples from her own team members' experience—early glimpses that point to what is possible on a larger scale in the future.

What I am proposing here is a new perspective—one that I believe will allow HR professionals to make subtle contributions that have tremendous impact. Recognizing the role of story as a meaning-making process opens up a wide range of new "moves." When something is too abstract to seem real, we can ask for a concrete instance. When a situation is turbulent or chaotic, we can guide people in "storying" it to find the patterns. When a serious issue recurs too often, we can invite people to share the experiences behind their assumptions, to reexamine old mental models that no longer serve us. Do you sense the orientation I am offering? This is about facilitating the natural flow up and down the ladder of inference, inviting the story in the middle when the organization goes to either extreme, as shown in Figure 5.

How might this look in relation to the three elements of organizational learning? From our new perspective, there are many possible options. Let's explore how to empower the purposeful sharing of experience for organizational learning at each of the three levels.

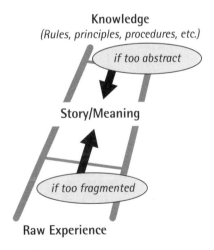

Adapted from The Fifth Discipline Fieldbook by Senge, Kleiner, Roberts, Ross, & Smith (1994, pp. 242-243), describing the "ladder of inference," developed by Chris Argyris.

Figure 5.   Natural Flow Up and Down the Ladder of Inference

Story for Engaging with Shared Vison

Shared vision is at the heart of creative tension, the "inspirational dissonance" (Dosher & Terry, 1997) that generates the energy for learning and change. (See Figure 6.) Too often we compromise, individually and organizationally, on what we really want to create, in order to avoid disappointment. Both employees and leaders tend to need encouragement to share these private hopes.

But when we do invite them, we generally find aspirations that far outstrip conventional plans and strategies. And in the process of exploring, we connect individual passions to corporate imperatives, overcoming the narrow focus that is sometimes a by-product of the emphasis on accountability and measurable performance. As a wise person once said, "True commitment is always voluntary." The degree to which people own a shared vision is the degree to which these voluntary inner resources are turned toward learning.

The qualities of story that most support shared vision are imagination, continuity, and compactness. Stories activate our imaginations, sparking evocative mental images and bringing visions to life with a vividness that is more likely to engage our deepest commitment and impact our actions (Swap, Leonard, Shields, & Abrams, 2001). Because memory and imagination are so closely related, stories provide continuity between past and future, helping us to surface remarkable experiences we want to extend while acknowledging the valued elements of the past we want to preserve. In fact, new thinking shows that the most compelling visions actually emerge out of our past experience, rather than disconnected fantasies about intellectual ideals. Finally, stories carry complex mes-

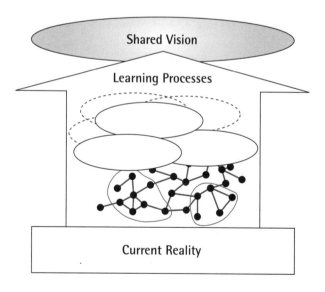

Figure 6.   Moving to a Shared Vision

sages in a highly condensed form, so they can be remembered and shared easily—in a way that re-creates the experience of the vision, rather than just the idea of it (Shaw, Brown, & Bromiley, 1998).

There have been many recent advances in using story to engage people in shared vision. Among the most widely recognized are Stephen Denning's (2001, 2004) work using "springboard stories" to ignite imagination and action and the widespread adoption of Appreciative Inquiry techniques for leading transformation based on what is already working (Appreciative Inquiry Commons, 2004; Cooperrider & Whitney, 2002; Hammond, 1996). I have found that most of the advances in this area support organizational learning by strengthening one of three functions:

- *Enriching Leadership Communication:* Leaders seem to be hungry for coaching on how to use their own stories more effectively—to point to the future, convey their core values, or create storylines that make sense of where we're coming from and how we will move toward the vision. See the work of Stephen Denning (2001, 2004), Noel Tichy (2002), David Armstrong (1992), Annette Simmons (2001), Terri Tate (2004), Evelyn Clark (2004), and the Ariel Group (Halpern & Lubar, 2003) for help on when, how, and what type of story to tell.

- *Hosting Conversations to Surface What Is Working:* As organizations mature and cultivate the ability to share leadership, it becomes possible to co-create shared vision by inviting the whole system into a conversation—using the power of stories and good questions to surface what is working so we can build on and extend it. See the Appreciative Inquiry Commons (2004), Stephanie Nestlerode (2004), and Donna Stoneham (2004), as well as The World Café (2004) and Seth Kahan's (2004) "jumpstart storytelling" to learn more about this growing field.

- *Tapping the Power to Sense What Is Possible:* As we recognize how fundamentally unpredictable our work actually is, more and more leaders are turning to simulations, role plays, improv theater games, and other experiential techniques for sensing what might be ready and waiting to emerge as the natural next step in our organization's evolution. To learn more, see the work of Kat Koppett (2001), Michael Schrage (2000), Peter Senge's latest book on "presence" (Senge, Scharmer, Jaworski, & Flowers, 2004), or upcoming writings on "wisdom labs" by Mitch Saunders and John Ott (Collective Wisdom Initiative, 2004).

(Note that the references listed throughout this article are meant to provide a sampling of thought-provoking ideas and approaches. Unfortunately, this partial list cannot begin to include all of those whose work I admire. If you have a source to recommend, please feel free to forward it to WorkLore's [2004] online bibliography.)

Much of my own work with story has involved helping groups access their own experience as a resource for learning. In the process, I have learned much from my colleagues about incorporating improv theater activities and an appreciative approach to issues or challenges.

Here is an example of simple, practical visioning session that draws from all three of these disciplines. You might try this with a team facing a change of leadership or a significant change in its role.

Story-Visioning Activity

Preparation

a. *Craft your topic and key questions as an Appreciative Inquiry.* Identify a challenge or opportunity worthy of focused attention and invite a small design team to help you craft a topic statement and exploratory questions. Be sure the topic frames the discussion in terms of what you *do* want, rather than what you don't want or don't care much about. For example, rather than talking about "avoiding malpractice suits," a physicians group might focus on "processes that promote excellent care and mutual understanding of risks with patients." Then craft two to four exploratory questions to surface participants' experiences with the topic, including feelings and enabling conditions. For example, our physicians might ask, "Think of a time when you and a patient successfully arrived at a mutual understanding of risk, despite a challenging situation. What happened? What worked? What conditions made it possible? How did it feel?"

b. *Invite participants.* Invite as many perspectives as is practical, knowing that different opinions will add definition to the challenge. Think of yourself and the design team as hosts inviting guests to a gathering.

Session (2 hours total)

a. *Introduce the topic* (5 min.). Explain the topic and the intention to explore what is currently working, based on our experiences. List the topic and exploratory questions on a flip chart.

b. *Tell the stories* (50 min.). Ask everyone to take a few moments to reflect on their experiences with the topic. What images come to mind? Ask each of them to select one and relive it more fully, with all five senses if possible. Finally, ask them to share their experiences, using the exploratory questions as a guide. Allow three to five minutes per person for those who wish to share. (If you have more than 10–15 people, you can do the exercise in pairs and then share the highlights with the group.)

c. *Reflection and brainstorming* (25 min.). Ask participants, "What did you notice? Which examples conjured up the most powerful images or the biggest stretch?" Allow any brief dialogue that comes up naturally; then ask participants, "What do these examples suggest is possible for us?" List answers on a flip chart. Finally ask, "What conditions seem to enable those possibilities?" Create a separate list.

d. *Break* (10 min.)

e. *Warm-up* (5 min.). Ask participants to break into triads to plan a summer outing. Explain that they have two minutes, and the only rule is that before following someone's idea, they should say, "yes, but. . . ." After one minute, have them switch and start saying, "yes, and . . ." between ideas. After another minute, debrief by asking what difference they noticed after the switch. Explain the energy created by building on one anothers' ideas and the creativity unleashed when time pressure prevents us from filtering good ideas.

f. *Provocative propositions* (10 min.). Introduce the idea of provocative propositions and post the definition and an example, such as "Provocative Propositions: Statements that describe an ideal future, one that causes us to stretch, written in the present tense. Example: We have time for our families *and* to show dedication to priorities at work." Explain that they frequently involve combining opposites, as in the example. Then ask participants to work in triads to create one or more provocative propositions based on the possibilities and enabling conditions identified above. Allow them three minutes and ask them to create a single flip chart with their statements. (*Variation:* Instead of using the present tense, have them phrase the propositions as "what if" questions.)

g. *Report out and debrief* (10 min.). Ask them to post and read out their provocative propositions, calling out "yes, and . . ." between groups. Ask, "Do these capture what has passion for us? Is anything missing? Any overlaps?" (If desired, identify a subgroup to wordsmith the final statement offline.)

h. *Close* (5 min.). Ask, "What did we do well in this meeting? What do you wish would happen next?"

Sessions like these create a compelling sense of the desired future while activating the confidence to pursue it, because participants recall the successes they have had in the past. Whichever approach you choose to create and engage your people in a shared vision, you will want to begin a deeper exploration into current reality as well.

Story for Understanding Current Reality

The desire to truly understand current reality is what brings rigor to our learning efforts. It is the reality check that lends meaning and power to the shared vision: If we see how things really are and yet dare to aspire to high ideals, there must be real courage and commitment involved. (See Figure 7.)

Recently, I read an account of the Cultural Revolution in China in which farmers were hard-pressed to increase production, which unfortunately created an environment where everyone had an interest in colluding to report good news. (Not at all familiar, right?) One day a group of farmers brought their weekly production to the warehousing depot, triumphantly announcing they had bred a pig that took up the entire cargo area of the truck. When the government staff went to inspect the pig in the back of the farmers' truck, they discovered that it was made of papier-mache! Rather than force the issue, it became commonplace to hold up these fictitious results as the standards others should meet (Chang, 1991).

Actively seeking to understand current reality allows us to discover these distortions and, in the process, highlights those forces already in motion and those assets and resources already in place to help us get to the results we care about. How much easier is it to make subtle adjustments in a trajectory well underway than to overcome the inertia of a completely new start?

I have found that three qualities of story allow us to overcome the "official story" about reality to get at a truer view: authority, concreteness, and empathy. Because every teller is the ultimate authority on his or her own experience, we tend to hear a broader range of perspectives, particularly from those with lower status, with less triggering of

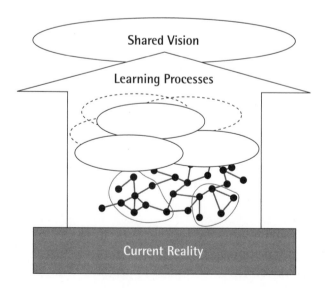

Figure 7.   Checking the Current Reality

judgment and conflict. This ability to take in divergent perceptions is, in turn, the first step toward a deeper understanding of how the system functions as a whole. Secondly, the concreteness of stories allows us to step back down the ladder of inference from abstract terms to what we actually mean in practice, surfacing and clarifying potential misunderstandings. Finally, because we naturally tend to identify with the protagonist of a story, hearing one anothers' stories can help activate empathy and the ability to work with and value diverse perspectives.

You can see, I am sure, that these qualities could lend themselves to a variety of applications. In fact, it is a little artificial to separate out applications for shared vision, current reality, and learning processes. Several of the advances I mention here could just as easily be linked to shared vision or learning processes—and one could argue that Appreciative Inquiry (Appreciative Inquiry Commons, 2004) actually belongs here under "current reality." Yet there is a slight difference of focus when our primary concern is simply to see and understand what is. Recent advances in using story to understand current reality seem to do so in the following areas:

- *Understanding Complexity:* "Mess maps," systems diagrams, and collective storytelling all attempt to uncover patterns inherent in the complexity of organizations. See *The Power of the Tale* (Allan, Fairtlough, & Heinzen, 2001), Bob Horn's (1998, 2004) work with murals and mess-mapping, the systems thinking segment of the *Fifth Discipline Fieldbook* (Senge, Kleiner, Roberts, Ross, & Smith, 1994), and the resources available at Pegasus Communications (2004). Although individual practitioners usually incorporate story, I am eager to see how its use is more fully developed in this field over time.

- *Uncovering Organizational Myths:* Corporate "anthropologists" are skilled at surfacing and capturing the creation and transformation myths that generate and preserve the underlying culture of an organization and its brand commitments. Once we are aware of these "grand narratives," we can work with them to shape the next phase in our evolution and better articulate the value proposition to the customer. See the work of Jonathan Marks (2003), Hanley Brite and Authentic Connections (2004), Rick Stone and the StoryWork Institute (2004), Harrison Owen (1987), Ed Wachtman and Storytellings (2004), and Art Kleiner (2004) for approaches to this area.

- *Surfacing Unmet Needs:* Learner needs analysis, customer observation, exit interviews, and skip-level meetings are designed to uncover the real experiences and needs of those whose voices might be obscured by quantified aggregated data. New approaches are increasingly reliant on "deep dives" into stories, using interviews, role plays, and enactments. See the work of StoryNet (2004) and Storytellings (2004) to learn more.

- *Valuing People:* In venues provided through diversity programs, at retreats, and occasionally as part of change efforts, people are discovering the tremendous satisfaction of simply telling their stories, of being seen and heard. If done respectfully, the process can build relationships, create empathy, and free up inner resilience. See the work of Terri Tate (2004) and her storytelling circles, Nan Crawford and Pacific Playback Theater (2004), Joe Lambert's and Nina Mullens' Center for Digital Storytelling (2004), the StoryWork Institute (2004), and George Simon's Diversophy (2004).

In my experience, the process of exploring stories for one purpose naturally ends up serving another. For example, interviewing employees to understand unmet needs naturally leads to valuing people and begins to surface potential solutions (which we will cover under "Learning Processes" later). Similarly, exploring organizational myths sets the stage for studying complexity or discovering shared vision.

The following activity is designed to help you surface the organizational myths and assumptions that affect progress on strategic priorities or learning efforts. This is especially useful if you are in the process of merging organizations, although you will also find it works with an existing organization where there is a sense of disempowerment or a tendency toward "groupthink."

Organizational History and Myth Session

Preparation

a. *Select a focus.* Consider your strategic priorities and use your judgment to assess whether the cultural norms and assumptions at the level of the team, function/ business unit, or entire organization are having the most impact on progress. Select one of these levels as a focus (but be prepared to change if needed in the session). If you are working through a merger, select those two former organizations as your foci.

Session (1 hour 15 minutes total)

a. *Introduce the focus* (5 min.). Explain the value of understanding the organizational history, myths, and stories that guide decisions and actions and the need to get creative in surfacing them because they are so embedded in our thinking. Introduce the focus organizational level as the team, the function/business unit, or entire organization.

b. *Warm-up* (10 min.). Ask the group to break into pairs. Have one partner give the other three words, chosen at random. The partner's job is to weave the three words into a brief story, using any links he or she can come up with. After three minutes, switch partners. Debrief by asking what that was like and reinforcing that we all naturally know how to tell stories.

c.   *Introduce the "story spine"* (5 min.). Post the story spine (Koppett, 2001) and explain that it is a tool for helping people to craft stories easily. (The story spine: 1. Once upon a time. . . 2. Every day. . . . 3. But one day. . . 4. Because of that. . . 5. Because of that. . . 6. Because of that. . . [repeat as necessary] 7. Until finally. . . 8. Ever since then. . . 9. And the moral is. . . [optional])

d.   *Tell the "history"* (10 min.). Explain that you're going to start with the factual history of the focus organization—what could have been seen or heard by an outside observer and what was "supposed" to have happened in the "official version" of the story. Stand in a circle. Starting with "Once upon a time," have participants tell the story one sentence at a time, using the story spine as a guide. (If you want, record the story on a flip chart. If working with merged organizations, do this with each former organization, having the members of the other organization stand in a larger circle around the tellers, and allow twice as much time.)

e.   *Debrief* (5 min.). Ask participants, "What was that like? Did the structure help? What surprised you in the story we told?"

f.   *Introduce "mythology"/individual reflection* (10 min.). Explain that underneath the factual "history," there is the organizational "mythology" that guides decisions and actions, which is more difficult to uncover but has more impact. Write the following questions on a flip chart and ask each person to reflect and jot down a few notes: "What have been the important challenges, turning points, and transformative decisions since you have joined this organization?" "What stories/events define what this organization is really about?"

g.   *Tell the "mythology"* (15 min.). Explain that you will now use the story spine to tell the organization's mythology—those challenges, turning points, and transformative decisions that have shaped the organization's fundamental character. Identify the person with the longest tenure and explain that he or she will start with "Once upon a time" and complete the first one or two elements of the story spine. Then others will begin to chime in, adding elements to the story spine until they come to a natural ending. Don't worry if events overlap or conflict—this is myth. (If you want, record the story on a flip chart. If working with merged organizations, do this with each former organization, having the members of the other organization stand in a larger circle around the tellers, and allow twice as much time.)

h.   *Dialogue* (15 min.). Ask participants, "How was that different? Do you see connections between the myths and how we function today? What strengths do these shared stories point to? What blind spots?" (If you have more time, feel free to extend this dialogue.)

People are often amazed to see how these myths help make sense of what goes on in the organization day to day. Understanding these organizational myths will allow you to focus your learning processes more effectively, while also crafting storylines that explain what is changing in terms that relate to people's deepest understanding of how things work.

Story for Strengthening Learning Processes

This is where things start to get fun. With a sense of creative tension, especially with a shared vision that builds on and extends the best of current reality, people are naturally drawn to develop and share new capabilities. There is an appetite for new ideas and practices, and the leader's role shifts from mobilizing the organization to guiding, connecting, and reinforcing all the various learning processes underway through programs such as learning and development, benchmarking, Six Sigma and process excellence, intentional experimentation and pilots, communities of practice, or any of the many other ways we improve. Of course, learning processes almost always involve investigations into current reality, but it is generally with an eye to a particular improvement, which is why I have grouped them in this section. (See Figure 8.)

Almost all of these programs involve certain phases focused on invention and discovery, and others are directed more toward diffusion, transfer, and application. As William Gibson reportedly said, "The future is here. It's just not evenly distributed yet"

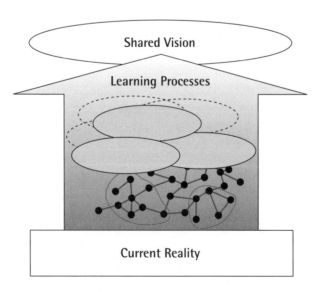

Figure 8.   Mobilizing the Learning Processes

(O'Reilly, 2002). Story can serve as a catalytic ingredient at each of these stages, because it is that "middle step" where we make meaning of new experiences we have and bring to life the insights we want to share.

When the organization has reached the limits of its capacity to absorb change, story can help us activate the "pull" for a new idea. The most familiar way to do this is to use story to make the new idea or practice more vivid, compelling, and concrete, but we can also create "pull" by connecting the idea to current reality, putting it in the context of an overall story about where we have come from and where we are going. Or we can free up time, attention, and energy by clarifying which priorities are receding and providing venues for people to tell their stories so they can let go of old commitments and expectations and move on.

This last use of story points to an even more fundamental aspect of the learning process: people and their communities. When we share experiences, we are doing more than transferring insights or information. We are simultaneously reinforcing the human connections and relationships that foster ongoing learning and the emergence of a shared professional identity. Story turns out to be a critical enabler of the learning communities (or "communities of practice")(Wenger, McDermott, & Snyder, 2002) that many organizations find are the actual stewards of knowledge.

Many practitioners have been contributing specific ways to enable learning processes in these ways, usually by focusing on the following functions:

- *Distilling the Most Valuable Lessons from Experience:* As we explore through experiments, pilot projects, or task forces, we can improve the quality of our results by consciously taking time to reflect on our experiences and what we are learning—surfacing the most valuable insights. Without this time for reflection, we may jump to conclusions and effectively waste our investment in learning. See the section on Reflection, Inquiry, and Mental Models in the *Fifth Discipline Fieldbook* (Senge, Kleiner, Roberts, Ross, & Smith, 1994, pp. 264–275) and the activity below for examples in this area.

- *Reexamining Old Models and Stretching Our Mindsets:* One of the greatest barriers to learning is those things we "know" that "just ain't so." Using scenarios (alternative stories about future events) can help us ease into our mental blind spots and practice dealing with a broader range of eventualities. Dialogue, a complementary approach, helps groups think creatively together, find shared meaning, and reexamine mental models that may no longer be useful. Combined with experience-sharing, dialogue seems to provide even more valuable perspective on our unquestioned assumptions. For scenarios, see the work of Peter Schwartz (1996) and the Global Business Network (2004). For more on dialogue, see Glenna Gerard and Linda Ellinor's book based on David Bohm's ideas (Gerard & Ellinor, 1998) and the Team Learning sections of the *Fifth Discipline Fieldbook* (Senge, Kleiner, Roberts, Ross, & Smith, 1994, pp. 351–441).

- *Narrating Change as It Happens:* As we move toward diffusing a change or improvement across the organization, there is a crucial role for the leader as narrator—articulating where we have come from, where we are going, and where we are now. It is as if the story provides stability as we navigate the unknown. What works here is a slightly more abstract story that describes the pressures, events, and decisions that have led us to the current situation and the actions required to address it. For more information, see the work of Barbara Minto (2003) or my adaptation of her QuestionFirst framework for constructing storylines (WorkLore, 2004).

- *Providing Vehicles for Internalizing the Change:* Because mental models, assumptions, and competencies are so deeply internalized as to become unconscious, we need help drawing them back out and reexamining them in light of new information. Without vehicles for doing this, we have a very difficult time absorbing or making use of new practices, because our minds are already "full." Two ways to foster this approach to freeing up attention and energy include providing rituals and experiences that signal endings and creating venues for people to tell their individual stories so they can recognize and let go of old loyalties and commitments. The works mentioned above for valuing people also help with the internalization of change, including the work of Terri Tate (2004) and her storytelling circles, Nan Crawford and Pacific Playback Theater (2004), Joe Lambert's and Nina Mullen's Center for Digital Storytelling (2004), and the StoryWork Institute (2004).

- *Bringing Individual Learning to Life:* Once we have learned something worth sharing, we tend to build it into our learning and development processes or create learning events as part of rolling out a change. Instructors and change agents have found that story can be used to improve individual learning effectiveness by making ideas more vivid, memorable, and actionable and by connecting ideas to the learner's own experience (Swap, Leonard, Shields, & Abrams, 2001). Self-facilitated action learning groups are the epitome of the learner-centric approach, as individuals use peer support to work through on-the-job professional challenges over time. An important thread in both of these has been the emergence of new ways of interacting with a hypothetical situation, including case studies and simulations that make complex dynamics come to life. See the work of Thiagarajan (2004), Roger Schank (1997), and StoryNet (2004) for more on linking instruction to the learner's experience using story. Liz McGill and Ian Beaty (2001) have a wonderful book on self-facilitated action learning. See the work of Barry Richmond at High Performance Systems (2004) and the "Microworlds" section of *The Fifth Discipline* (Senge, 1990, pp. 313–339) for the use of simulations.

- *Cultivating Communities That Learn:* As mentioned above, when we share experiences we cultivate relationships even as we share information. Because communities form the natural cross-organizational networks that pursue, share, and guide the application of knowledge, many organizations are actively cultivating them. Story can help by deepening and broadening these relationships, while simultaneously helping the members of a community piece together a common mental model of their craft. See the work of Etienne Wenger, Richard McDermott, and Bill Snyder (2002), CPsquare (2004) and experienced members there such as John D. Smith (2004), Seth Kahan (2004) on Jumpstart Storytelling, Arian Ward and Beth Alexander at Community Frontiers (2004), and The World Café (2004).

- *Facilitating the Transfer of Actionable Knowledge:* Apart from formal learning and development events, organizations are seeking conduits for the active transfer of knowledge as it is created or recognized. One of the most effective approaches is to facilitate the creation and sharing of "knowledge stories," which guide the subtleties of when and how much to apply general principles to new situations. The beauty is that the story can then encapsulate the insight *and* its application, allowing us to transfer the "aha" more effectively and bringing others into the experience, rather than just distilling the implications and convincing others to adopt them. Furthermore, as we accumulate "narrative databases," we can analyze patterns in the stories and surface new knowledge about what it is our experts really do. See the work of David Snowden (2002, 2003), Cohen and Prusak (2001), John Seely-Brown and Paul Duguid (2002), and *ASK Magazine* (2004) on project management at NASA.

- *Make Assessment Itself a Learning Process:* The most talented instructional designers I know always emphasize designing tests and other instruments to help consolidate and reinforce the content they test. The same holds true at an organizational level. Rather than focusing on the numbers that tell us whether an investment paid off, telling the story of an experience can point us to the subtler layer of what exactly to build on and share. Besides, in the most leading-edge efforts—such as those pursued by communities of practice—it is the story of the insight that actually helps us come up with the numbers. See the work of Art Kleiner and George Roth (1997) on learning histories and Etienne Wenger, Richard McDermott, and Bill Snyder (2002, pp. 167–178) on "systematic anecdotal evidence."

Since we began this list with gleaning lessons from experience and ended it with comments on assessment, here is an outline for a session to do both. It has the additional benefits of helping a team prepare to share its lessons with others and freeing up energy and attention by providing a sense of completion. This exercise is especially effective at the end of the first phase of a multi-phase project or at the conclusion of a pilot program.

Experience Review Activity

Preparation

a. *Gather background information.* Prepare a list of key dates for your own reference and gather key documents you recall. Prepare a long sheet of butcher paper with an initial sketch of a horizon line, an ascending rollercoaster at the left edge, and the label, "Our Charge" underneath. (See Figure 9.) Gather enough large Post-it Notes® and pens for all participants.

b. *Invite participants.* Invite those who participated and a few people who were affected by the project, as well as any who will join in the next phase.

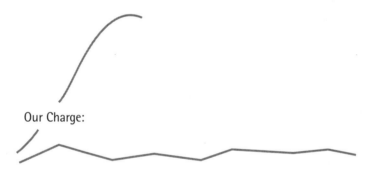

Our Charge:

Figure 9.   Sample Layout

Session (1 hour 30 minutes total)

a. *Introduce the session/individual reflection* (10 min.). Post the butcher paper on the wall. Explain the value of taking time to replay experience so the lessons we take are the most relevant and have the most leverage for future efforts. Ask participants to take a few moments to jot down key events, decisions, and turning points in the history of the project.

b. *Set up the rollercoaster* (10 min.). Introduce the idea that most projects are like rollercoasters, with changes in energy/intensity over time. Ask the group: "Where did we start? What was our original charge?" (It can sometimes take some time to reconstruct the charge, which is actually quite useful. Allow the discussion to progress naturally and record the various aspects of the charge on the butcher paper.)

c. *Construct the rollercoaster* (30 min.). Invite participants to help flesh out the rest of the "rollercoaster." Have them write key events and turning points on Post-its, place them on the butcher paper as "high" or "low" points at the appropriate points on the timeline, and read them out as they do.

d. *Reflection and assessment* (30 min.). Ask the group to step back and look at the result. Is anything out of sequence? Any questions of clarification? When the group feels it is roughly accurate, have someone draw a fat line connecting the Post-its over time. Then ask: "What do you notice about the process? What worked? What tensions were we managing?" Track the key comments on the butcher paper above and below the rollercoaster line. Don't worry about precision; the idea is simply to tie the discussion to actual events rather than overall impressions. Now ask the group to assess the project in terms of process, relationships, and results, on a scale of 1 to 10 (10 being highest). Ask: "What practices or conditions would we keep if we had to do this again? What would we change? If we had to write two or three key principles to help the next group to do such a project, what would they be?" Note the principles mentioned.

e. *Closing* (10 min.). Ask: "Any final appreciations as we end the project? Any personal 'ahas'? With whom should we share this story?"

I have seen teams dramatically improve the lessons they take from a project after reflecting even briefly on what actually happened. And which conclusions are more valid—those gleaned in the last few crunch days of a project or those that take into account the entire process? Exercises like these can also help teams distill insights from intentional experiments or systematic problem-solving processes, because they add rigor and depth to our normal reflection processes, allowing us to translate learning on a small scale into knowledge that serves the organization as a whole.

Recognizing Opportunities in Your Organization

We have completed quite a journey here. Where do you begin in your organization? Of all the options, what would most impact your organization's ability to generate the results it desires?

At the core of these ideas is the proposal to take a new orientation: to help facilitate the natural flow up and down the ladder of inference, inviting the story in the middle that turns experience into meaning and abstract ideas into actionable understanding, as was illustrated earlier in Figure 5. As I see it, you can consider applying this new orientation at the level of the organization, within a specific initiative, and at the level of individual interactions.

Between individuals, we can invite the stories behind people's positions and cherished ideas and create opportunities to tell the stories that make sense of otherwise fragmented experience. We can build in opportunities to hear one another's experiences as we launch communities or transform teams. For specific initiatives, we can ask whether people are taking time to reflect on what is happening and whether they are grounded enough in current reality to recognize resources and trajectories to leverage. We can use a combination of story activities to amplify a new idea, connect to what is already in place, and free up attention and capacity as we begin to share it across the organization.

Ah, and then there is the organization. How might we support its evolution and growth at the most optimal and sustainable pace? Figure 10 shows a "map" of all the terrain we have covered here, including the three levels that affect learning and each of the functions story seems to strengthen.

Which methods would most contribute at this time to your organization's learning?

This is where I would invite you to use your judgment to sense what is happening on a systemic level—to take all the tiny observations, comments, and data points you pick up in everyday interactions and combine them into a hypothesis about what is needed. You might try taking some quiet time on your own to reflect or invite others into a conversation with you.

Then ask yourself: "In thinking about the organization as a whole, what do I (or we) notice? Is it energized, moving, aligned, but perhaps lacking coordination or solutions that last?" Then connecting and integrating learning processes might be the place to start. Are there indications that it is disconnected from aspects of what is really going on, perhaps with frequent crises and surprising new data? Then you might want to start by strengthening the organization's awareness of current reality. And finally, is there a sense of plodding or compliance, that a few at the top have a vision, but few are fully enrolled in following? In this case, the most benefit might come from focusing on creating true engagement with a shared vision.

Your greatest asset in mobilizing energy for these opportunities is your ability to name what is working and what might be possible, and then to invite, propose, and invent new approaches to getting there. Tell the story and connect the challenges faced by the organization to its evolution, its potential.

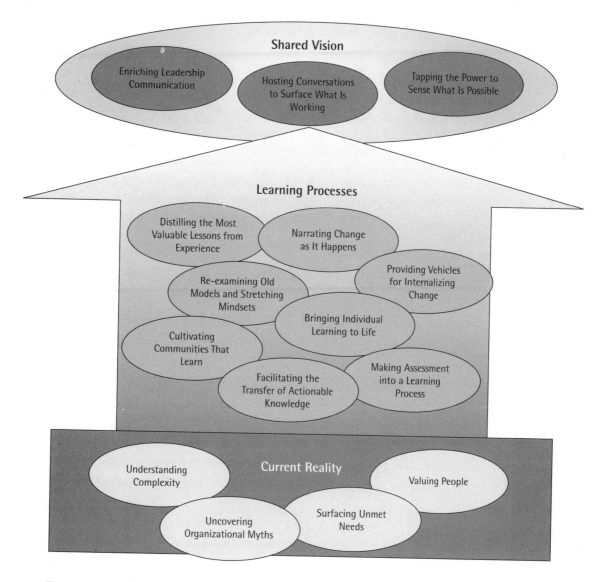

Figure 10. Summary: Applications of Story for Organizational Learning

Where to Go From Here

So how about Monday morning? Why not try reflecting a bit on the opportunities above and then schedule one of the activities suggested here as an experiment? Or you might notice what triggered the most energy for you as you read this article and pick up a book from the References list. Perhaps ask someone else to read this article, too, and then meet for lunch to talk about what might make sense and what questions you still have.

As you proceed, you may notice that something else happens as you relegitimize the processes for sharing experience and meaning, something beyond arriving at a particular insight or lesson. At an individual level, the process of telling our stories reinforces the sense of personal authority, clarity, and confidence that activates inner resources and allows us to contribute to increasingly complex organizational challenges. At an organizational level, this promotes the emergence of shared leadership and the widespread ability to hold creative tension—the creative tension that energizes learning as a systematic process. For many of us, this is an inspiring vision of the future of organizations.

Of course, in the end, story is not the point. Creating the results you care about is. The key is to elevate the quality of thinking, relationships, decisions, and action by more effectively recognizing and integrating the lessons hidden in our collective experience.

References

Allan, J., Fairtlough, G., & Heinzen, B. (2001). *The power of the tale: Using narratives for organisational success.* West Sussex, England: John Wiley & Sons.

Appreciative Inquiry Commons. (2004). [Online]. Available: http://appreciativeinquiry .cwru.edu

Armstrong, D. (1992). *Managing by storying around: A new method of leadership.* New York: Doubleday Currency.

ASK Magazine. (2004). [Online]. Available: www.appl.nasa.gov/ask

Authentic Connections. (2004). [Online]. Available: www.authenticconnections.com

Center for Digital Storytelling. (2004). [Online]. Available: www.storycenter.org

Chang, J. (1991). *Wild swans: Three daughters of China* (pp. 224–225). New York: Anchor Books.

Clark, E. (2004). *Around the corporate campfire: How great leaders use stories to inspire success.* Sevierville, TN: Insight.

Cohen, D., & Prusak, L. (2001). *In good company: How social capital makes organizations work.* Boston, MA: Harvard Business School Press.

Collective Wisdom Initiative. (2004). [Online]. Available: www.collectivewisdominitiative.org

Community Frontiers. (2004). [Online]. Available: www.communityfrontiers.com

Cooperrider, D., & Whitney, D. (2002). http://appreciativeinquiry.cwru.edu/intro/book ReviewDetail.cfm?fcoid=761. Euclid, OH: Lakeshore Publishers.

CPSquare.(2004). [Online]. Available: www.cpsquare.com

Denning, S. (2001). *The springboard: How storytelling ignites action in knowledge-era organizations.* Boston, MA: Butterworth-Heinemann.

Denning, S. (2004, May 1). Telling tales. *Harvard Business Review,* pp. 122–128.

Denning, S., & Kahan, S. (2003). *Chronology of organizational storytelling.* [Online]. Available: www.creatingthe21stcentury.org/Chronology.html

Diversophy. (2004). [Online]. Available: www.diversophy.com

Dosher, A., & Terry, J.P. (1997, Spring). How organizations learn: An intentional evolutionary approach to organizational development and change. *New Designs for Youth Development, 13*(2), 31–37.

Garvin, D.A. (1993, July/August). Building a learning organization. *Harvard Business Review*, pp. 79–91.

Gary, L. (1997). What makes for an authentic learning organization: An interview with David Garvin. *Harvard Management Update*, No. U9706C (pp. 3–5). Boston, MA: Harvard Business School Publishing.

Gerard, G., & Ellinor, L. (1998). *Dialogue: Rediscover the transforming power of conversations.* Hoboken, NJ: John Wiley & Sons.

Global Business Network. (2004). [Online]. Available: www.gbn.com

Halpern, B.L., & Lubar, K. (2003). *Leadership presence: Dramatic techniques to reach out, motivate, and inspire.* New York: Penguin.

Hammond, S.A. (1996). *The thin book of appreciative inquiry.* Plano, TX: CSS Publishing Co.

Harvey, J.B. (1988). *The Abilene paradox and other meditations on management.* Hoboken, NJ: John Wiley & Sons.

High Performance Systems. (2004). [Online]. Available: www.hps-inc.com

Horn, R.E. (1998). *Visual language: Global communication for the 21st century.* Bainbridge Island, WA: MacroVU, Inc.

Horn, R.E. (2004). Bob Horn personal site. [Online]. Available: www.stanford.edu/~rhorn

IBM Knowledge Socialization Project. (2000). [Online]. Available: www.research.ibm.com/knowsoc/index.html

Kahan, S. (2004). *Seth Kahan: Creating communities that generate returns.* [Online]. Available: www.sethkahan.com (Also see website for *Building Beehives: A Handbook for Creating Communities That Generate Returns.*)

Kleiner, A. (2004). Art Kleiner personal site. [Online]. Available: www.artkleiner.com

Kleiner, A., & Roth, G. (1997). *Learning histories: A new tool for turning organization experience into action.* Boston, MA: MIT Sloan School of Management, Center for Coordination Science. (Also available online: http://ccs.mit.edu/lh/21CWP002.html)

Koppett, K. (2001). *Training to imagine: Practical improvisational theatre techniques to enhance creativity, teamwork, leadership, and learning.* Sterling, VA: Stylus Publishing.

Marks, J. (2003). *Many voices, one story.* Presented at New Vistas: Story Work in Organizations Pre-Conference. Chicago, July 8–9, 2003.

McGill, I., & Beaty, L. (2001). *Action learning: A guide for professional, management, and educational development.* London, UK: Kogan Page.

Minto, B. (2003). *The Minto pyramid principle: Logic in writing, thinking and problem solving.* London, England: Minto International, Inc.

Nestlerode, S. (2004). *Omega point: Choosing to shape the future.* [Online]. Available: www.omegapoint.net.

O'Reilly, T. (2002, April 9). *Inventing the future.* In O'Reilly Network. [Online]. Available: www.oreillynet.com/lpt/a/1697

Owen, H. (1987). *Spirit: Transformation and development in organizations* (pp. 12–41, 143–146). Potomac, MD: Abbott Publishing.

Pacific Playback Theater. (2004). [Online]. Available: www.pacificplayback.com

Pegasus Communications. (2004). [Online]. Available: www.pegasuscom.com

Schank, R. (1997). *Virtual learning: A revolutionary approach to building a highly skilled workforce.* New York: McGraw-Hill.

Schrage, M. (2000). *Serious play: How the world's best companies simulate to innovate.* Boston, MA: Harvard Business School Press.

Schwartz, P. (1996). *The art of the long view: Planning for the future in an uncertain world.* New York: Doubleday Currency.

Seely Brown, J., & Duguid, P. (2002). *The social life of information* (pp. 91–117). Boston, MA: Harvard Business School Press.

Senge, P.M. (1990). *The fifth discipline: The art and practice of the learning organization.* New York: Doubleday Currency.

Senge, P.M., Kleiner, A., Roberts, C., Ross, R., Roth, G., & Smith, B. (1999). *The dance of change: The challenges to sustaining momentum in learning organizations.* New York: Doubleday Currency.

Senge, P.M., Kleiner, A., Roberts, C., Ross, R., & Smith, B. (1994). *The fifth discipline fieldbook: Strategies and tools for building a learning organization.* New York: Doubleday Currency.

Senge, P.M., Scharmer, C.O., Jaworski, J., & Flowers, B.S. (2004). *Presence: Human purpose and the field of the future.* Cambridge, MA: The Society for Organizational Learning.

Senge, P.M., with Simon, F. (1995). *Building a learning organization: Insights on theory and implementation.* Presented by San Jose State University. San Francisco, November 10, 1995.

Shaw, G., Brown, R., & Bromiley, P. (1998, May/June). Strategic stories: How 3M is rewriting business planning. *Harvard Business Review.*

Simmons, A. (2001). *The story factor: Inspiration, influence and persuasion through the art of storytelling.* Cambridge, MA: Perseus Books Group.

Smith, J.D. (2004). *Learning alliances.* [Online]. Available: www.learningalliances.net

Snowden, D.J. (2002). *Narrative patterns: Uses of story in the third age knowledge management.* Presented at Action Enabled Learning: The Power of Narrative Conference, New York, April 24–25, 2002.

Snowden, D.J. (2003). Complex acts of knowing: Paradox and descriptive self-awareness. *Bulletin of the American Society for Information Science and Technology, 29*(4).

Society for Organizational Learning. (2004). [Online]. Available: www.solonline.org

Stoneham, D. (2004). *Positive impact coaching and consulting.* [Online]. Available: www.positiveimpactllc.com.

StoryNet. (2004). [Online]. Available: www.thestorynet.com

Storytellings. (2004). [Online]. Available: www.storytellings.com

StoryWork Institute. (2004). [Online]. Available: www.storywork.com

Swap, W., Leonard, D., Shields, M., & Abrams, L. (2001, Summer). Using mentoring and storytelling to transfer knowledge in the workplace. *Journal of Management Information Systems,* pp. 95–114.

Tate, T. (2004). *Terri Tate, inspirational humorist and story coach.* [Online]. Available: www .territate.com

Thiagarajan, S.T. (2004). The Thiagi group. [Online]. Available: www.thiagi.com

Tichy, N.M. (2002). *The leadership engine: How winning companies build leaders at every level.* New York: HarperCollins.

Wenger, E., McDermott, R., & Snyder, W. (2002). *Cultivating communities of practice: A guide to managing knowledge.* Boston, MA: Harvard Business School Press.

WorkLore. (2004). [Online]. Available: www.WorkLore.com

The World Café. (2004). [Online]. Available: www.theworldcafe.com

Elizabeth Doty *is the founder of WorkLore (www.WorkLore.com), a consulting firm that helps individuals and organizations uncover the insights hidden in their experience, often through the use of story, learning communities, and systemic thinking. She received her master's in business administration from Harvard Business School and, prior to founding WorkLore, served as senior associate of Symmetrix, Inc., a change-management consulting firm based in Boston. Recent clients include Hewlett-Packard, Intuit, Archstone-Smith, and CTB/ McGraw-Hill.*

Kat Koppett *is the co-founder of StoryNet, LLC (www.thestorynet.com), a consulting and training company devoted to using the power of theatre and storytelling techniques in organizations. The author of* Training to Imagine: Practical Improvisational Theatre Techniques to Enhance Communication, Teamwork, Leadership and Learning, *Ms. Koppett holds a B.F.A. in drama from New York University and an M.A. in organizational psychology from Columbia University.*

New Role for HR:
Communication Caretaker
Ronald C. Fetzer

Summary

Human resource professionals, because of the variety of services they provide and the support they offer for their organizations, do experience first-hand employee reactions to communication processes, strategy implementation, and communication technology integration within the unique context of the organization. By aligning the basic communication process with a specific proposed competency, HR professionals as communication caretakers for all organizational communication efforts have an opportunity to build trust, a critical component, and create specific programs, services, and resources that improve the organization's ability to use communication more effectively. After an analysis of communication within organizations, which reflects the critical role that trust plays within the dynamics of this process, some communication caretaker strategies and activities are proposed and supported with operational guidelines in an effort to demonstrate the benefits of such efforts by HR professionals within their respective organizations.

Anne Seibold, author of *The Trusted Leader: Bringing Out the Best in Your People and Your Company*, suggests there are two levels of trust. She believes at one level HR managers want to be trusted as individuals by their staffs. But more broadly, on a second level, HR professionals are concerned about their level of trust across the total organization (McGrath, 2004). Gaining trust takes time and a carefully constructed strategy, especially on the part of the HR department, given its charge to take care of employees' personal needs at work. HR professionals have learned from experience that employee trust has positively influenced the success of HR recruitment, selection, performance outcomes, job satisfaction, loyalty, performance management, and retention services.

The intent for most employees when using organizational communication in the workplace is deliberate and purposeful. Many organizations address the importance of communication, even mentioning it in the company vision or mission statements. And most strategic plans include specific communication strategies to implement their business plans. However, it is challenging at best to create communication processes that are deliberate and purposeful, yet effective and efficient when striving for beneficial results. In this age of electronic communication, it is so easy to access, archive, and obtain information on demand. Still, employees hold some concerns about the "openness" and "truthfulness" of organizational communications. Without an understanding of some basic communication competence and a support system to communicate effectively and efficiently, employees will frequently feel overwhelmed trying to communicate within the organization. Often it is not the job responsibilities that tire and frustrate employees, but the day-to-day communication on the job.

Two important questions are worth serious consideration by HR professionals. First, how do employees achieve effective communication in today's organizations? And second, where do they get help and support when struggling with organizational communication processes? This article proposes that such support should come from human resource (HR) professionals, who historically have been seen as experts at helping employees with processes. Furthermore, they access and have opportunity to observe organizational communication everywhere in the organization.

This article addresses these questions and propositions by first offering some basic definitions. It examines the opportunities and challenges for HR professionals to be part of the solution. A description of the proposed role of communication caretaker serves to identify why HR practitioners are suited for the challenge to monitor and support communication. Specific HR caretaker strategies are offered, as well as some guidelines for maintaining a continuous improvement approach concerning organizational communication.

Working Definitions

Charles Conrad and Marshall Poole (2005) define *organizational communication* as strategic discourse from two unique perspectives. The first perspective is the emergence of the organization, which is influenced by the strategic choices for designing its structure and creating operational processes. These initiatives are established by developing a vision, mission, and goals that are defined using a variety of complex communication processes. This phase of organizational communication calls for leadership initiatives to oversee and maintain the support needed for organizations to routinely communicate. Since it is the responsibility of the HR function to identify and match open job positions with employees who have the requisite skills, which include effective communication, it stands to reason that HR professionals would be good resources when one is looking for caretakers to lead these organizational communication initiatives.

The second phase of the Conrad and Poole definition describes how the initial strategic choices made by the organization's leadership directly create situations that require employees to make strategic choices in order to control their own workplace situations. This is accomplished through the use of various organizational communication processes that are customized by these employees as they react to their choices within their workspace. In short, "organizational communication is any type of communication activity occurring within the organization where people, acting alone or in groups, create, sustain, and manage meaning and personal perceptions using verbal, nonverbal, and written communication to achieve specific goals that are intended to support the overall goals of the organization" (Conrad & Poole, 2005, p. 4).

According to Shockley-Zalabak (2002) the primary objective of organizational communication is to achieve a shared reality among all of an organization's employees by using appropriate verbal and written communication skills. It requires specialized strategy, multiple communication tools, resources, and processes. It requires various types and levels of information technology and communication to support employee work efforts. In many situations it will require that technical training and continuous development activities be made available to all employees if they are to achieve the basic purpose of effective organizational communication, namely a shared reality. In summary, it appears to be a major HRD initiative for HR professionals to monitor and guide.

Communication is so entwined within an organization that some scholars say that communication *is* the organization. Most organizational communication scholars examine communication from one of four perspectives. They see it as (1) information transfer, (2) a transactional human process, (3) a strategic organizational control technique, or possibly (4) a continuous balancing effort between struggling to be creative, but also being constrained in order to complete specific outcomes (Eisenberg & Goodall, 2004).

The term "communication caretaker" is proposed as a new role for the HR professional. By definition, a caretaker is someone who gives physical and emotional support to others.

Support for an organization is much like the support of a caretaker for one individual. Schein (1987) views the organization as a collective of individuals coping with problems of adaptation and integration who consider what works well and is valid, worthy enough to be maintained and taught to new members entering into the organization as the correct way to perform. Schein's thinking has a unique similarity to many HR strategic documents, as well as to the wording found in employee job descriptions.

Consider that for the past twenty-two years in the Annual Industry Report published by *Training* magazine, "new hire orientation" has made the top ten list as one of the most frequently delivered training programs by 96 percent of the organizations that routinely participate in this annual research (Galvin, 2003)! The employee handbook, a major responsibility for HR departments, provides the organization's core messages and is the organization's primary communication channel to ensure that employees know how to act as engaged, productive employees.

With these working definitions established for organizational communication and communication caretaker, it is now possible to understand why HR professionals should consider the role of organizational communication caretaker as their functional responsibility.

Communication Caretaker: A New Role for HR Professionals

From an organizational perspective, it is important for HR professionals to recognize how they can serve to monitor, support, implement, and guide this complex communication process. For starters, any complex process used in organizations needs to reflect consistency and reliability. It should be efficient, user friendly, and transparent so that employees can use it on demand. Such requirements can only be met when tools and resources are available to support such a process. There has to be training, performance management, and evaluation of the process to keep it continuous yet supportive of the organization's changing needs.

Since HR supports and maintains many employee-related processes, it has the staff with the knowledge, expertise, and operational experience to work closely with the organizational communication process. Within the context of an organization, who is more prepared than HR professionals to provide employee support to the organizational communication process? So what is really "new" about this proposed HR role of communication caretaker? Rather than new as in revolutionary, possibly it is more *evolutionary*, given some of the evolving issues and changes appearing in today's workplace.

Given the large number of changes, some new trends are emerging that will affect all organizations and their employees. HR must now address many issues such as *employment security*, which is based on competencies and knowledge, as opposed to the traditional notion of *job security*, which was viewed as a guarantee of permanent employment. The makeup of the workforce is becoming more diverse as more minorities enter. For example, white, non-Hispanic employees will decrease from 73 percent in 2000 to nearer 53 percent by 2050. Simultaneously, Hispanics will double from 11 percent to 24 percent. Afro-Americans will increase from 12 percent to 14 percent, and Asians will increase from 5 percent to 11 percent (Toossi, 2002). And the pace of technology will steadily rise as well. Job-related stress will have to be constantly monitored.

Insecurity and distrust will remain, and possibly grow, as organizations continue to streamline in order to compete, leaving downsized employees feeling violated.

Organizations need guidance, leadership, and expert individuals who can serve as experienced caretakers. The question is, are HR professionals prepared to take on this new role that needs to address the emerging trends challenging organizations and their employees?

Strategy Planning: The First step for Communication Caretakers

HR has been responsible for supporting the beliefs, values, and norms of the organization for a number of years since business strategy has gained prominence as a necessary organizational function. HR departments have been holding strategy-planning meetings for years to develop HR initiatives that directly align with an organization's vision, mission, and strategic business plan. This is certainly a major communication effort for every organization and its HR staff. So one may question who is taking care of the complex communication process that supports and drives these strategic initiatives. Is it the CEO, senior management team, middle management (for the few still around), first-line supervisors (whose ranks are also quickly thinning), or the HR department?

Certainly HR is expected to have the capability, commitment, and conscience to contribute to organizational strategy planning. Additionally, HR is expected to collaborate, communicate, and maintain the continuity to support followthrough with strategy implementation. This amounts to a great deal of caretaking (physical and emotional) on the part of HR. Presently, the first and most obvious output is a product, the employee handbook, which for many organizations today is not really a book but rather an online electronic information system. The second obvious output is a service, new employee orientation, which is a requirement and ritual for every new employee entering the organization.

The concern for the hows and whys of HR strategy planning has and continues to be of great interest to HR practitioners, researchers, and business students thinking about a career in HR. The Society for Human Resources Management (SHRM) offers its members a wide variety of resources dedicated to HR strategy planning, design, implementation, and evaluation. SHRM has a published code of ethics for guiding its membership that directly addresses strategy as a core responsibility for HR professionals to provide to their respective organizations (SHRM, 2004).

For some time HR professionals have been addressing the challenge of HR strategic planning and the mandate to align with the strategic business plan of the organization.

This traditionally expected alignment requires the HR professional to have an expert working knowledge of HR services and programs, a real understanding of organizational processes and work flow, an accurate assessment of workforce capability, and the know-how to support a wide variety of organizational communication processes.

The "5P" Strategic Planning Model developed by R.S. Schuler (1992) suggests that the HR professional must be attentive to five essential components of strategic planning. His strategy model defines what HR departments must attend to, namely HR philosophy, policy, programs, practices, and processes. Schuler warns that this strategy planning model is only activated after the organization's business strategy is created and defined by top management based on its analysis of the organization's needs.

Bamberger and Meshoulan (2000) more recently advocate two distinct theoretical perspectives. The first aligns with the traditional thinking of Schuler that HR strategic planning follows after the organization's strategic planning by its senior management, in order to achieve alignment. However, a second perspective is an incremental HR planning approach that is greatly influenced by internal forces and resources, which are driven by technical and efficiency criteria. Obviously, this latter approach can be greatly supported by the various organizational communication procedures, practices, and tools used to design, implement, and evaluate strategic planning. If HR departments subscribe to this second approach, incremental strategic planning, then they take responsibility to provide the technical expertise, the tools and resources, and the emotional support, which is, in effect, the role of communication caretaker.

Similar to the rational planning perspective of Schuler, the incremental planning approach of Bamberger and Meshoulan also requires a clear understanding of the strategic planning process. However, this incremental approach, which is more open to influence by political interests, examines the corporate-level mission. HR examines the strategy plan for the clarity of mission-based objectives. It then determines how HR services will support any broadly defined programs recommended to maintain the strategy plan. And last, HR will examine and align its efforts with policies put forth that are created to facilitate the organization's reaching its defined objectives (Bamberger & Meshoulam, 2000). As communication caretakers, HR professionals must use complex organizational communication skills to support the strategic process.

Given the complex process of organizational communication and strategic planning as proposed by Schuler or Bamberger and Meshoulan, HR professionals can, and should, consider the value of serving as communication caretakers to the organization. Additionally, serving in this caretaker role may offer creative opportunities for improving and streamlining other HR services and programs already in use.

Organizational Communication: A Contextual Perspective

The standard classic model for visualizing the communication process is deceivingly simple. The elementary explanation of the human communication process in Figure 1 is familiar to most HR practitioners.

Unfortunately, the same is not quite so true when examining the larger and more complex domain of organizational communication. The uniqueness of organizational communication is clearly pointed out by Virginia Richmond (2005) when she cautions that it is a process whereby individuals stimulate meaning in the minds of other individuals by way of verbal and nonverbal messages within the context of a formal organization. The challenge is the term "context" when analyzing organizational communication. Not all communicators are good at communicating all of the time. For example, a CEO presenting an annual report to a room full of employees and shareholders may find it more difficult on his flight going home to talk for an hour one-on-one with the individual seated next to him on the plane.

The communication process can take many turns and meet blockages when two employees attempt to communicate via this classic process model. Without framing the communication process, too many variables may be unaccounted for, only to surface after the communication effort has been disappointing, at best. The idea of a shared reality between two people may not appear to be too challenging unless it happens during the annual performance review for one of them.

The communication situation between a CEO and the entire membership of her organization is quite another matter. Her dynamic presence speaking to all 1,200 employees in the company auditorium can get dramatic support with sound, lighting, and the shared energy of a capacity audience. On the other hand, her presentation may have less than desirable results, even with technical support services, when done as a simultaneous broadcast throughout the company's intranet directly to every office cubicle for the 6,000 employees who could not make it to the corporate auditorium. This CEO's presentation may neither seem "real" nor "shared" by the 7,200 employees!

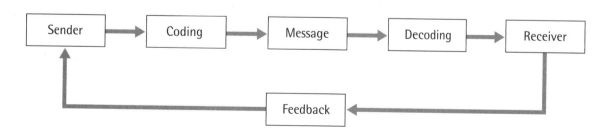

Figure 1.   Classic Communication Process Model

One of the emerging perspectives regarding organizational communication comes from the research and writing of Dr. Stanley Deetz. He believes organizational communication is a process of developing meaning and social production of perception, common identities, social structures, and affective responses (Deetz, 1994). In short, he suggests that organizations experiment with communication strategy as they develop. The groups and social structures in organizations continuously change as multiculturalism increases. Furthermore, mediated experiences (electronic) are increasingly exceeding direct sensory experience (face-to-face), so the social and political policies related to organizational communication must focus on the process of constructing meaning rather than focus simply on its transmission. So communication skill needs within organizations are also changing as the structure and operations of organizations are changing.

It makes sense that many organizational communication researchers and scholars are now turning to metaphor analysis when studying organizations. By using this metaphoric analysis, scholars can more easily focus on process rather than structure. Cheney (2004) describes several of the more popular metaphoric analyses, as listed in Table 1.

Much of organizational communication research is based on relational interaction. Cheney and others (2004) view organizational communication as more than merely a set of specialized skills designed to operate in a defined structure. They discuss communication competencies as a complex series of skill sets that are interconnected with interpersonal relationship experiences over time to permit individuals within organizations to learn from one another about what constitutes successful communication.

Table 1.   Metaphors for Communication in Organizations

Metaphor	Descriptive Imagery
Conduit	Transmission line, channel, pipe line for flow or protection
Lens	Eye, scanning device, filtering process, single source for viewing
Linkage	Relationships, connections, networks, patterns, cliques, isolates that have associations and commonness
Performance	Episodes, rituals, role plays, actor/audience-based activities
Symbol	Representations, artifacts, narratives, shared meanings with cultural alignments
Voice	Chorus, presentational expression, group participation and control
Discourse	Verbal or print language, public dialogues, multimedia conversation with defined publics, contrived and narrowly defined messages for targeted groups

Source: Based on G. Cheney, L. Christensen, T. Zorn, & S. Ganesh (2004).

Table 2. Organizational Communication Context in Relation to the Classic Communication Flow Model

Organizational Communication Context				
Sender(S)	Encoding	Message/Channel	Decoding	Receiver(R)
Interaction Management	Experientially Based	Message Design	Experientially Based	Interaction Management
Skills/Attitudes	Preference Styles	Channel Formats	Preference Styles	Skills/Attitudes

According to these researchers, there are three specific competency categories most frequently used within the context of organizational communication. These are (1) interaction management skills and attitudes, (2) experientially based perceptions and preferences, and (3) message designs and channel formats. Table 2 reflects these skills, style preferences, and technologies in alignment with the traditional classical communication process model.

Interaction management skills and attitudes have direct bearing on both the sender (S) and the receiver (R). These are the skills and attitudes most frequently studied by organizational communication experts to measure influence in the unique context of organizational communication for both the S and R. These include the trust level, open communication, subject-matter expertise, view of content and timing, and the reporting relationship of the S and R.

The second category, style preferences, is experientially based on personal choice and aligns with the encoding and decoding stages of the traditional communication process model. These include how S and R use communication, and nonverbal and social style preferences as the S encodes and the R decodes during the communication process.

The third category includes technology supporting message designs and channel formats, which is in direct alignment with message creation and delivery used for transmission. Table 3 displays the total alignment between the skills, personal preferences, and technology with the basic traditional communication process model.

Interaction Management Skills/Attitudes: Sender Perspective

Trust is an attitude of assured reliance on the character, ability, strength, or truthful communication of another individual or the representative leadership of an organization. Trust, as a contextual factor in organizational communication, may appear more difficult to identify within an organization, but far easier to identify within individuals. Trust

Table 3.   Context of Organizational Communication

Organizational Communication Context				
Sender(S)	Encoding	Message/Channel	Decoding	Receiver(R)
Interaction Management	Experientially Based	Message Design	Experientially Based	Interaction Management
Skills/Attitudes	Preference Styles	Channel Formats	Preference Styles	Skills/Attitudes
S/R trust level	Communication style	Information/ communication technology	Communication style	R/S trust level
Subject-matter expertise	Nonverbal style	Email	Nonverbal style	Subject-matter expertise
Pos/neg view of content	Social style	Inter- organizational linkages	Social style	Pos/neg view of content
Pos/neg view of timing		Response time		Pos/neg view of timing
Reporting relationship		Surveillance/control		Reporting relationship
		Formal/informal language use		
		Voice/print interchangeability		
		Portability		
		Live/delayed transmission		

building occurs over time before two individuals consider one another trustworthy. Johnson and Johnson (2003) advocate that individual trust between two people may take a long period of time to develop over a series of multiple interactions, but can be destroyed quickly with a single situation.

Experts have much to say about building trust within an organization. David Johnson and Frank Johnson are experts on the role and development of trust in groups. They note in their book, as brothers in a large family, that their experimentation with trust started very early in their lives. In their recent edition of *Joining Together: Group Theory and Group Skills,* the authors propose that establishing and building trust begins with openness. The openness of sharing information, ideas, thoughts, feelings, and reactions is the essence of trust. These factors are all embedded within the human communication process. In effect, open communication is inherent to creating and building trust.

Bennis and Nanus (1985) describe trust as the "glue" that maintains organizational integrity. The managers in their study were not necessarily liked, but because these managers were constant, predictable, and reliable in their interactions over time with their employees, they were perceived as trustworthy. By exhibiting personal stability, even when involved with extensive organizational change and innovation, managers can position themselves to be worthy of trust. Trust building as a part of the communication process works much the same way. If a manager, when talking with her employees, is truthful and forthright with her messages, even though employees may not always like her messages, they will come to recognize this manager over time as reliable, predictable, and consistent.

Therefore, the ability to gain a high trust level when communicating is a top priority for both S's and R's. When communicating in the workplace, most individuals believe they are trustworthy; however, they are not always as certain about the other person(s) with whom they are interacting.

Shockley-Zalabak, Ellis, and Cesaria (2000) have researched factors that support trust building within organizations and have identified three significant factors. These factors are accuracy of information shared with employees, clarity of explanations given for managerial decisions, and the frequent use of open dialogue.

This third skill, the frequent use of open dialogue, is a serious consideration for both S's and R's. Open dialogue is normally thought of as freely sharing information, ideas, thoughts, feelings, and reactions to issues held in common by individuals involved in one-on-one or in small-group situations within the context of an organization. However, the more recent concern of disclosing too much information or sharing information too freely with the "wrong" individual(s) is becoming a concern for S's more so than R's.

In short, researchers over the years have come to identify four central components of effective communication within organizational settings that have been historically viewed more as management's responsibility. The four most noted organizational communication behaviors in the literature clearly support the idea that effective supervisors should:

1. Emphasize the importance of communication in the relationships;

2. Be empathic listeners who respond positively to employee questions, listen to suggestions and complaints, and display a willingness to take fair and appropriate action when needed;

3. Ask or persuade rather than tell or demand;

4. Freely share information, such as giving advance notice of changes and offering some explanation as to why any specific change is being made (Eisenberg & Goodall, 2004).

Subject-matter or content expertise can have significant influence within organizational communication for both the S and the R. Beyond ethnocentric bias about the contextual importance of the actual content to either the S or R, there are also issues of personal power when controlling information, such as determining the amount of information to be shared, when to share it, and with whom to share or not share the content. However, Eisenberg and Witten (1987) caution that openness of communication is not without problems. In their research, they advocate that ethics and confidentiality should not be compromised for the sake of full and honest disclosure without sensitivity to the communicative context of a situation.

The positive or negative view of the content is related to subject-matter expertise held by the S or R. This reflects the S's or the R's personal opinion concerning the subject of the message content. Obviously, when the S viewpoint is opposite that of the R, the communication situation can be greatly affected. Conversely, when the views of the S and R are nearly the same, either positive or negative, this is one less filter or barrier to impede communication effectiveness. The same can be said of the perceived appropriateness of the timing of the communication encounter as viewed by the S or R. Often, the timing for sharing specific information is important. It has been said that "timing is everything." The organizational communication context concerning the timing, when or when not to share information, is heavily influenced by organizational politics. In such a situation, when the S and R hold opposing views concerning this issue of timing, communication effectiveness can be greatly reduced.

The reporting relationship between S and R, like the variable of timing, is another organizational communication factor that can influence the communication process. Eisenberg and Goodall (2004) report about organizational communication behaviors managers need when talking with their employees. In the past, the relationship between manager and employee was viewed mostly from the perspective of the supervisor. Recently, the notion of "managing the boss" has become a popular theme in the career development literature.

Encoding

Encoding is the process of formulating messages and choosing content and symbols to convey meaning in order to meet the goal of a shared reality between S and R. Interestingly, encoding by the S and decoding by the R are inherently critical steps in the communication process, and this is particularly true given the context of all organizational communication. Both of these phases are process-based yet require different skills for the S and R. Both processes are highly influenced by the individual preferences of both the S and R in terms of communication style, nonverbal style, and social style.

When the S is encoding the choice and structure of language, this person is also conveying feeling as well as ideas. The clarity of ideas when being composed or verbally expressed is heavily influenced by both verbal and nonverbal delivery. The socialization preference of the S encoding, which includes the assertiveness to initiate the communication, greatly influences the exchange as well as how the message is encoded. This same situation is true with the R, who is simultaneously decoding and also has a preference for being assertive when communicating. Therefore, socialization preference can make for a rather complex and interesting exchange between the S and R at work.

Within the context of organizational communication, a wide variety of emotions are displayed during dialogue. For these reasons, factors such as the empathy display and level of eye listening used by both the S and the R will contribute to their exchange. It is not surprising that the concept of achieving a shared reality between S and R is such an arduous task within the context of organizational communication. For example, the many nuances of encoding and decoding between S and R in a performance review often display the dynamics of the communication exchange more than the factual content of the messages during this exchange.

Communication style can, as viewed on an assertiveness continuum and cross-correlated on a continuum of responsiveness, suggest that individuals prefer one of four common communication styles. Figure 2 displays how assertiveness and responsiveness can generate four distinct communication styles. For example, an emotive S and an equally emotive R would have a really challenging time in the context of a performance review, since both would be asserting to speak rather than making a responsive effort to listen to the other. If the S and R are more attuned to communication style, they not only know what their own preferred styles are, each can become savvy at identifying the communication style of the other person. This knowledge will empower one of them to switch to a more complementary style. In the case of the S being highly emotive (high assertive and high responsive), the R can recognize this and adjust to the more complementary style of reflective (low assertive and low responsive) (Fetzer, 1990).

Nonverbal communication style very closely relates to communication style. The critical nonverbal elements most frequently used by S and R while coding and decoding are displayed in Table 4. Often nonverbal style is not given much deliberate thought by the S or R. Usually it is thought of as spontaneous, but as with any communication behavior within the context of a specific situation, the behavior reflects a style preference, meaning there is opportunity to choose. Repeatedly choosing the same style behaviors reflects a personal preference. Over time, personal preferences evolve into personal communication habits that are comfortable for the S, and can

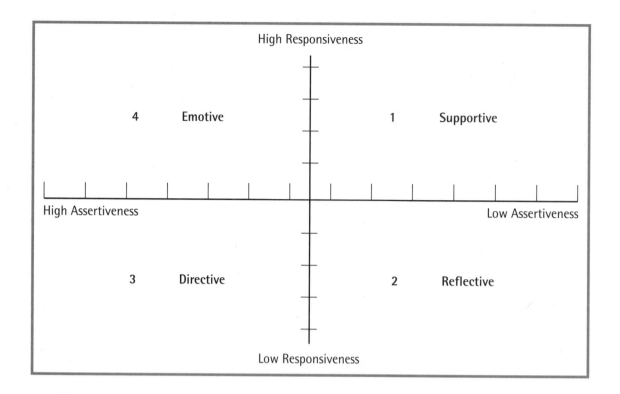

Figure 2.   Communication Style Grid

be predicted by the R when communication is frequent in the workplace. Or possibly with all of S and R attention focused on work responsibilities, many preferred or habitual communication behaviors go unnoticed by both.

In communication situations when the R knows the S well, such as in a boss-employee relationship, the R watches for nonverbal behaviors to decode the message. Bosses and employees become acutely aware of the role nonverbal behaviors play during encoding and decoding phases. If the dialogue is face-to-face versus speaking on the telephone, the nonverbal cues support a shared reality. However, if the dialogue is on the phone, many nonverbal cues are not available to S and R.

HR professionals in global organizations are often faced with situations in which employees are located at remote work sites, and they are forced to communicate about very personal situations such as a negative performance review, a family illness, or even something as difficult as talking about the death of a family member, and possibly finding it necessary to do so over the phone without benefit of a face-to-face exchange. Their communication styles must be flexible due to the broad scope of the communication situations.

Social style preference came to prominence with the work of Merrill and Reid (1981). Similar to communication style, social style uses a continuum of nonassertive to assertive. correlated to a continuum of responsive (emote) to nonresponsive (control).

Table 4.   Nonverbal Factors in Communication Coding and Decoding

Nonverbal Factor	Description	Example
Sign and Symbols	Specific word choices, figures of speech	In-house, contextual work-related terms; visual aids encoded into messages
Proxemics	Use of intimate, personal, casual, public space	Distance between S and R during exchange when standing, sitting, interacting in workplace
Kinesics	Gestures, body posture, facial expression, seat positioning	Use of hands, greeting, leave-taking; choosing where to sit at a table; leaning in or out
Chronemics	Perception and use of time	Appointment timeliness; body clock time vs. actual clock time; respecting time of others
Haptics	Use or avoidance of touching when talking	Recent workplace harassment has biased, yet touching is a powerful expression of empathy
Dress/Appearance	Clothing worn and personal hygiene	Work uniforms, dress codes, health laws have wide interpretation; dress is self-expressive
Olfactics	Sense of smell and sensory awareness of scent	Cologne/perfume can pose problems in the workplace, especially in open office systems
Oculesics	Use of eyes to communicate, listen, gain attention	Eye listening for feedback while simultaneously speaking to others; checking others' reactions
Paralanguage	Voice, pitch, accent, volume, non-word noises while speaking	Vocal segregates, "ah," "um," "uh-huh"; filler words to avoid silence or "thinking aloud"
Silence	Non-response, non-reaction, stillness	Conveys apathy, confusion, shock, hostility, contemplation, sadness, respect, and many other human feeling that reflect style and emotions

Merrill and Reid identify four distinct social styles: Driver (controlling, nonresponsive, high-assertive); Expressive (high assertive, emotive-responsive); Amiable (non-assertive, emotive-responsive); and Analytical (non-assertive and controlling, non-responsive).

Social style, like communication style, is a preference that, over time, also becomes a matter of personal choice and habit. Both the S when encoding and the R when decoding either can choose their style preferences deliberately or use them without awareness. However, this does not mean that either communicates exclusively in a single style. Each can, with practice, alternate social style preference, and they often do so in workplace communication based on the context. In the context of a boss and a direct-report employee discussing a work-related matter, recognizing and adapting to one another's social style is not nearly as challenging as when several employees meet with their boss in a group staff meeting. It takes deliberate effort, some training, and some practical experience to adapt one's personal style to productively participate in group meetings where multiple preferred social styles are influencing the communication exchanges. For this reason, it is not uncommon for a group of employees to come out of a staff meeting, each having quite different perceptions of what was discussed and what were the specific meeting outcomes. Communication style preferences are ethnocentric-based, meaning most individuals believe their own style is superior and more effective than others. This explains why the diverse individual perceptions of a shared reality often exist.

In organizational environments, small group and large group meetings usually require a higher level of encoding and decoding, so more controls need to be in place to support a shared reality. There is more pre-work to do, planning of details, agenda setting and revision, and greater need to use handouts, record minutes, use some form of parliamentary procedure, set time limits for discussion of controversial topics, and possibly assign specific attendees responsibility for individual agenda items to balance the participation and clarity of dialogue exchange. All of these control techniques support the encoding and decoding occurring within a group meeting. It is not surprising that when people sit in a series of meetings all day at work, they leave work exhausted and feeling as if they have performed hard physical labor.

When examining communication, nonverbal, and social style preferences, it becomes apparent that encoding is a very individual process. Given the amount of communication education and accumulative experiences with it in classrooms prior to entering the organizational workplace, most people assume the encoding phase should be a simple and natural process for routine use on the job. However, this does not appear to be the case. In the workplace, individuality is important to employees, and this is especially true in an environment that routinely promotes and rewards individual accomplishment as opposed to group work. The possible combination of various style preferences does keep organizational communication creative, exciting, and full of surprises. Very possibly the same can be said of message design and channel formats, the next factor to examine in the communication process.

Message Design and Channel Formats

The message design and the channel formats are at the center of the communication process and are reflected as such in the traditional communication model. Separating the message from the messenger is not easy. In fact, some communication researchers clearly believe the message is not a separate component in the communication process, but rather is an extension of the S and the R. Shockley-Zalabak (2002) suggests, "Sources of messages intend meaning, but messages, in and of themselves, do not carry meaning. Meaning, or interpretation of messages, is assigned when the receiver decodes the message" (p. 22).

Conrad and Poole (2005) suggest that availability of information and communication technologies (ICT) is having a significant effect on organizational communication. The use of ICTs has changed organizational communication and significantly increased its accessibility to all people inside and many more outside of the organization. The communication networking possibilities appear endless. Process is clearly the intent of some organizations to such a degree that they are viewed literally as virtual organizations. Brick and mortar is certainly not a prerequisite to be considered an organization, which now gives a whole new meaning to "corporate headquarters."

The use of email is making access to information easy. It's also easy to control when and how much attention and time to give to such communication exchanges between employees and their supervisors. The use of ICT in the workplace is significantly compressing communication time, allowing employees to do more in less time. The employee's work and workplace have become portable. The laptop computer permits the workplace to move with the employee, which is convenient. Such ICTs allow employees more options for when, where, and how they choose to work. Employees communicate more freely with no concern for distance or time, which has promoted spatial dispersion for the organization. For example, HR departments can continually keep in touch with all employees in an organization regardless of office locations and service facilities, which can exist literally anywhere in the world, operating continuously regardless of time zone. Benefits, internal job postings, online training, compensation schedules, retirement planning, and much more can all be available 24/7 to all employees. The introduction of ICT into the HR function has dramatically altered how HR services and programs are delivered to employees.

One must consider how this is affecting organizational communication in the workplace. Are there any negative effects to introducing so much ICT so rapidly into the organization? Shockley-Zalabak (2002) warns that the time to plan for a response (decoding) is shortened. For example, a threaded series of email or chat room interactions allows less time to give a thoughtful, well-planned response. Many employees have experienced the pain of not thinking through an email response immediately after hitting the "send" button. Shockley-Zalabak also suggests that the use of ICT channels for exchanging messages has greatly reduced face-to-face communication, making the exchange (delivery) much less interpersonal.

This is an area of concern for HR, having less opportunity for interpersonal face-to-face communication exchanges given the programs and services it must support for employees. It is a challenge to find creative ways to keep the interpersonal context in ICT applications. One of the most visible HR services is the increased delivery of online training courses rather than using the traditional classroom with all employees facing the trainer and one another.

Conrad and Poole (2005) discuss another change, one with much fear and anger associated with it: the issue of surveillance and control with the use of ICT. Personal privacy is greatly affected by ICT. Conrad and Poole suggest that this lack of privacy often goes undetected by employees, as with the common use of surveillance cameras in the workplace. Surveillance is even less detectable with personal and mainframe computers where time usage, information requested, information sent, and specific persons contacted can all be tracked. The use of "cookies," a technique to identify people contacting an information site, creates many privacy issues in the workplace. Currently privacy is a very important communication issue HR departments are addressing because of the need to create and implement organizational policies and guidelines.

The Society for Human Resource Management has completed a major study on security versus privacy since the 9/11 events (Segal, 2002). After much discussion with its membership, its published policy report to members concludes that employers should reserve the right to search as broadly as possible, noting that while reserving the right is one thing, implementing it is quite another. Ironically, the solution suggested is for HR practitioners to integrate an interpersonal approach by creating, communicating, and introducing "people friendly" surveillance and privacy into their organizations. SHRM has created an online privacy policy for the organization and its members, which serves as an example for HR professionals who need to create written policies for their own organizations.

ICT devices now have available various types of keyboards, large and small; punch pads; and electronic writing tablets, which use pens that use neither lead or ink, but rather a stylus and tapping system that only a few years ago most people thought would no longer be needed with the demise of the telegraph. Such toys and gadgets, to the consternation of many older generation employees, when used correctly do support organizational communication. HR needs to address how these technology-driven messages can accommodate the lack of communication richness, which does exist in traditional face-to-face dialogue.

Group meeting technology, by combining phones, computers, satellites, and video technology, allows meetings to take place at any time and anywhere, defying geography and time zones. Groups meeting can use many channel formats such as teleconferencing, audioconferencing, and computer conferencing. There are software products to help employee groups with decision making, and these can be integrated with a variety of information management systems. The day of the face-to-face meeting with all members actually sitting around the same table in the same room may soon become a thing of the past. Encoding and decoding are dramatically changing as message designs and channel format options increase. Group meetings can take less time and more business can be conducted, while also more easily accommodating work and personal schedules. The HR professional can promote and support technical training and workplace job aids to provide group-meeting resources that support such group-based organizational communication. As a communication caretaker, HR can provide employee support for using ICTs that build and promote group trust, manage group conflict, and encourage group creativity. With such care taking, employees can feel a sense of accomplishment and pride in their group communication, and they can possibly experience some interpersonal communication enrichment when participating in their meetings.

The impact of live versus delayed message decoding greatly influences how organizational communication functions. Group communication, when carried out online, also has synchronous (live) or asynchronous (delayed) options. This empowers employees to choose when to participate, giving them more personal control over their workflow. HR professionals have online training that can operate continuously 24/7 for employees located anywhere in the world, regardless of time zone, to provide technical training on demand. Not only has ICT created a whole new dimension for training and development delivery, but it also provides additional options for message design and channel formats when encoding and decoding within the communication process.

The message design and channel format options have increased dramatically due to technology advancements. Due to their rapid introduction into the workplace, many employees have not completely realized the impact of ICTs on this phase of the communication process. What is frequently heard from employees is the amount of frustration felt concerning the speed of technology, the constant state of flux, and their influence on both one's work and personal life. This is most obvious in the portability of work, namely taking it home to continue working with it on personal time. Ironically, this frustration is a benefit for others who feel they have more control and choice over how, when, and where they work and can manage their own personal lives. From an HR perspective, many of these message design and channel format factors do pose concerns around HR issues of privacy, performance management, advancement opportunity, personal expression, and use of empowerment in the workplace. Given what has been shared about message design and channel formats, it is appropriate to examine decoding from the perspective of the R.

Decoding

Decoding, as reflected earlier in Table 3, is an interpretation process R's perform upon receiving messages via specific channels, which allows them to process what is seen, heard, felt, and sensed. The intent of decoding is to assign meaning to a message generated by the S. In short, the R uses communication, nonverbals, and social style preferences to decode. The purpose is to achieve this shared reality, which originated in the mind of the S. The R, when using communication, nonverbals, and social styles, has the same preference options that are available to the S. It would appear that the two processes are not all that different. However, considering the many combinations of style preference options, Ss and Rs can literally be at opposite ends of a complex communication continuum when encoding and decoding.

As with the encoding process for Ss, interaction management skills and attitudes are equally important for Rs as they decode in this communication process.

Interaction Management Skills/Attitudes: Receiver Perspective

The interaction management skills factors are the same ones available to the R, as displayed in Table 3. The factors of trust level, the subject-matter expertise, the positive and negative views on content and time, and the reporting relation between the S and R are very influential within this organizational communication process.

Level of trust and the importance of trust building are of equal concern for the R. It can take some time over a series of exchanges for the R to feel trustful of the S; furthermore, trust can be shattered very quickly within a single exchange.

Within the organizational communication context, R's may pose mental questions that are of little concern to S's, such as, "Why is the boss talking to me?" or "Wow, what did I do wrong now?" Such mental questions by the R are not so much issues of trust, but rather another factor, communication climate. Shockley-Zalabak (2002) defines communication climate as the reaction to organizational culture. Conrad and Poole (2005) define it as the collective beliefs, expectations, and values regarding organizational communication within each organization. The communication climate is an important factor to watch. Many HR departments routinely do communication and satisfaction audits with their employees, asking questions about the status of organizational climate. Just as the word climate implies, communication climate is something that can change quickly and frequently.

Communication climate should also be of concern for the S. However, unlike the R, the S considers climate when preparing messages, thinking proactively about how to maintain a positive communication climate while encoding message design.

Richmond, McCroskey, and McCroskey (2005) discuss communication climate, proposing that bosses can affect climate using their power, such as ordering free lunch for staff or giving employees a longer lunch break to celebrate a success. These kinds of periodic actions can contribute to the organizational climate, but not maintain a supportive climate to ensure effective communication exchanges in the workplace. This type of communication climate is based on routine use of an organizational communication process in such a way that is predictable, reliable, and operates effectively over time. For example, communication climate can change quickly if the computer system shuts down, phones stop working, or bosses and employees stop trusting and supporting one another. HR caretakers can help to ensure these problems are quickly attended to, monitored, and even anticipated, by providing training and alternative organizational communication processes when such situations arise.

Positive communication climate building and maintenance is everyone's responsibility. It really comes down to a simple question: "Is it more enjoyable to work in a positive or negative communication climate?" Most individuals want the positive climate. So supporting a positive communication climate is everyone's responsibility, and HR professionals as communication caretakers need to get this message out to all employees.

Regarding the status of communication climate, when all is said and done, HR professionals as communication caretakers have the greatest opportunity to generate the most positive influence over communication climate. With their access to and responsibility for job descriptions, communication protocols, communication training programs, performance management systems, and strategic planning support, they are responsible for the organizational processes that influence and monitor communication climate. Instituting some policies and guidelines for the organization will have a positive influence on communication climate and an even greater overall influence on the total organizational communication process.

The organizational communication context has been examined from a traditional communication model as depicted within the competency categories of Cheney and others (2004), namely interaction management skills and attitudes, experientially based perceptions and preferences, and message design and channel formats. Table 3, Context of Organizational Communication, describes these contextual factors and reflects their relationships to the human communication process. This leads to the important question: How does the HR professional use this organizational communication model as a guide to assume this role of communication caretaker?

HR Communication Caretaker Activities

HR professionals, as noted earlier, as communication caretakers have the resources and experience to work from a well-established HR support service base to link and realign organizational communication and ICT initiatives to processes and services already operating within their organizations. It begins with strategic planning for organizational communication processes and ICT integration throughout the organization.

Table 5 displays eight essential strategies for communication caretakers.

The first strategy is to determine the organizational communication status quo within the organization so the caretaker will have an accurate assessment of employee feelings, communication climate, communication resources, and current support operations and an accurate picture of ICT resource utilization. This can be done with surveys, inventories, focus groups, and the use of outside consultants if necessary.

Table 5.   Organizational Communication/ICT Caretaker Strategy

Organizational Communication Strategy	Caretaker Action	Intended Outcome
1. Determine organizational communication status quo	a. Design/conduct organizational communication survey b. Conduct ICT equipment inventory c. Conduct organizational communication support needs requests	a. Identify employee feeling/climate b. Identify resources/operational status/availability/convenience c. Identify who needs what to determine resource utilization
2. Verify knowledge, skills, abilities of the current workforce	Conduct organizational communication/ICT needs analysis survey/focus groups	Use data results for designing organizational communication/ICT training curriculum
3. Determine organizational communication/ICT policy for the entire organization	Use representative focus groups/content experts to create policy guidelines	Print and electronic document to include strategy, operational guidelines, privacy/surveillance protocols
4. Integrate organizational communication/ICT strategy into organizational strategy	Use representative group to align/integrate incremental organizational communication and ICT strategy into organizational strategic plan	Establish a coordinated resource utilization plan for all organizational communication and ICT programs, services
5. Create in-house organizational communication/ICT training program	Design a series of courses to meet all needs identified in previously conducted NA	Operational organizational communication/ICT curriculum for use throughout the organization
6. Produce an on-demand training operation to support organizational strategy	Design online/land-based training program delivery system to service all organizational members worldwide	Keep all employees trained in all organizational communication/ICT technology needs and changes as adapted into organizational operations
7. Maintain an organizational communication/ICT continuous feedback system	Create a continuous integrated organizational communication/ICT feedback response system	Continuous caretaker capability to track all organizational communication/ICT technology problems/issues and resolve them at the point of need for maximum people/technology integration efficiency
8. Create organizational communication/ICT board of overseers	Utilize the board of overseers to support the communication caretaker	Board assists caretaker in supporting/maintaining the organizational communication/ICT system

The second strategy is to assess the capabilities and the needs of all employees concerning their knowledge, skills, and abilities in order to determine the overall competency levels of the organization's workforce. This action is one of the most important steps because it needs to align directly with the organization's business plan in order for the organization to sustain a competitive market advantage.

The third strategy is to determine an organizational communication/ICT set of policies and guidelines for the organization. This strategy needs to use a team-based approach that fully represents all units of the organization. Since this action, in addition to creating guidelines, also includes the sensitive areas of privacy and surveillance, it is important to get as much feedback as possible from all employees throughout the organization. It takes time to implement this action strategy, but it is vital because of the far-reaching effects on the organization's ability to recruit quality talent, to manage performance effectively, and certainly to retain its top talent.

The fourth strategy is to align organizational communication and ICT policies with the organization's strategic plan. It would do well for the communication caretaker to use an incremental HR planning approach as proposed by Bamberger and Meshoulan (2000), given the fast pace of new technology development taking place in most organizations. A traditional strategic planning approach will not serve efficiently and can easily slow down the integration process.

The fifth strategy is to create an organizational communication/ICT curriculum that serves the needs of the total organization. Depending on the other training programs in use and the expertise of the training and development staff to design and implement their own programs, this action and intended outcome could be executed quickly with minimal cost or could be very costly if using external consultants who would need to be brought up-to-speed on the total initiative before they could generate any curriculum specifically customized to the requirements of an organization.

The sixth strategy is to provide on-demand training delivery that supports the total organization. The organization's delivery needs are dependent on facility locations, number of employees needing training, and certainly the resources that can be allocated for the total system. Ideally, if all programs could be land-based and online with synchronous and asynchronous capability, the organization would get much more flexibility from its curriculum in terms of offering it on-demand and at the point of need.

The seventh strategy is to maintain and support a continuous feedback system in all organizational communication and ICT initiatives, operations, and resource utilization efforts. The ideal situation is to design a feedback system that is continuous and transparent. When the system is designed to track and collect feedback at the source of the problem, this allows for a much better integration of the organizational communication and ICT technologies for employee use. The more seamless this integration between people and technology becomes, the greater will be the performance of the employees.

With improved performance, the ability to meet organizational strategic objectives is better for all involved. The efficiency will not only benefit the total organization, but will allow employees to feel good about their work contributions and that they are being supported by management.

In a recent research study, Joseph Heinzman (2004) clearly demonstrates a direct and significant relationship between job satisfaction and job commitment. When asked, employees clearly indicated the importance of speaking out to their boss, receiving feedback, sharing information at work, and being involved in decision making on the job.

If HR professionals in their role as communication caretakers can create a continuous feedback system, provide training in open communication, and define how to contribute to a positive communication climate, the benefits of it can be far-reaching for all of the employees as well as for the organization as a whole.

The eighth strategy is to create an organizational communication/ICT board of overseers. Any smart caretaker knows that taking care of oneself is paramount to taking care of others. A board of overseers can be extremely supportive to the caretaker. If this board is created internally, then it offers fair representation to all employees and work units in the organization as well as promoting credibility in such a communication climate. If this board is not merely a group of "worker bees," but is truly empowered to oversee, it will contribute rich momentum and energy toward the total strategic initiative.

And last, a smart caretaker, in his or her role as leader, recognizes the need to prepare for his or her replacement so the process continues without disruption.

Once an organizational communication/ICT strategic plan is designed, then the communication caretaker begins the implementation journey. Since the main purpose of this initiative is to improve communication through the entire organization, it might do well to consider some basic guidelines proposed by numerous experts such as Gibson, Ivancevich, Donnelly, and Konopaske (2003). The many guidelines, suggestions, and best practices synthesize into a short list. HR caretakers should:

1.   Follow up on all verbal and written communication as a courtesy as well as a method to validate success and failures;

2.   Provide communication software and online technical support so that users can maintain the necessary flow of information at the point of need so that all employees access, store, and retrieve data as it is needed;

3.   Make it a practice to collect and use feedback routinely;

4.   Use empathy in all communications by placing oneself in the other person's role, keeping everyone sensitive to the needs and feelings of others;

5. Always encourage mutual trust because it is the foundation of effective organizational communication and a positive communication climate;

6. Be sensitive to the use of other people's time, role modeling this sensitivity to encourage others to do likewise;

7. Simplify language to keep drudgery and confusion out of the essential information that needs to be shared among employees; and

8. Use active listening (focused attention) and reflective listening (routinely provide feedback response) to maintain successful interactive communication exchanges whether they are face-to-face or ICT-based.

These guidelines will empower communication caretakers to carry out their primary role, which is to give technical and emotional support to their fellow employees.

In Conclusion

This article proposes a new role for HR professionals. This role of communication caretaker is defined as a newly proposed HR role to support the overall internal communication processes of an organization. Based on an expansion of the classical communication model, the initial phase; interaction management skills and attitudes, which include trust level, content expertise, and timing of the message; and the relationship between the sender and receiver, are critical for any organizational communication to get off to a positive start. When communicators recognize and understand their communication, nonverbal, and social interaction styles, it becomes much easier to construct messages and choose the most efficient and effective channel format to deliver any message.

As HR professionals take on this new role of communication caretaker, an eight-step strategic process has been proposed to integrate that role within existing HR services and activities. And finally, this strategic process is supported with a few continuous improvement recommendations for practicing effective organizational communication. By choosing this incremental approach as a strategic process for creating support services and activities for their employees, HR professionals can use the Context Organizational Communication Flow Model presented here to integrate effective communication practices that will support and ensure positive organizational communication by all employees regardless of the organization's mission, goals, structure, size, or number of locations throughout the world. This proposed role of communication caretaker has much to offer any organization and its employees as they face the many dynamic changes and challenges of this new century.

References

Bamberger, P., & Meshoulam, I. (2000). *Human resource strategy: Formulation, implementation, and impact.* Thousand Oaks, CA: Sage.

Bennis, W., & Nanus, B. (1985). *Leaders: The strategy for taking charge.* New York: Harper and Row.

Brown, J., & Isaacs, D. (1994). *Merging the best of two worlds: The core process of organizations as communities.* In P. Senge (Ed.), *The fifth discipline fieldbook.* New York: Currency/Doubleday.

Cheney, G., Christensen, L., Zorn, T., & Ganesh, S. (2004). *Organizational communication in an age of globalization: Issues, reflection, practices.* Long Grove, IL: Waveland Press.

Conrad, C., & Poole, M.S. (2005). *Strategic organizational communication in a global economy* (6th ed.). Belmont, CA: Thompson Wadsworth.

Davis, B., Skube, C., Hellervik, L., Gebelein, S., & Sheard, J. (1995). *Successful manager's handbook: Development suggestions for today's managers.* Minneapolis, MN: Personnel Decisions, Inc.

Deetz, S. (1994) *Transforming communication, transforming business: Building responsive and responsible workplaces.* Cresskill, NJ: Hampton Press.

Drapeau, A. (2004). *Interview on organizational trust.* In D. McGrath (Ed.), *Thoughts from the top: A collection of interviews with business gurus.* Aurora, Ontario: HR.Com Publishing.

Eisenberg, E., & Goodall, H.L. (2004). *Organizational communication: Balancing creativity and constraint.* New York: Bedford/St. Martin.

Eisenberg, E., & Witten, M. (1987). Reconsidering openness in organizational communication. *Academy of Management Review, 12,* 418–426.

Fetzer, R. (1990). Communication style inventory. From *Communication training for managers.* Yellow Springs, OH: Fetzer Enterprises.

Galvin, T. (Ed.). (2003, October). The 22nd Annual Industry Report. *Training.*

Gibson, J., Ivancevich, J., Donnelly, J., & Konopaske, R. (2003). *Organizations: Behavior, structure, processes* (11th ed.). Boston, MA: Irwin/McGraw-Hill.

Heinzman, J. (2004). *The relationship of age, tenure and job satisfaction to organizational commitment: A study of two mid-western firms.* Dissertation. Nova Southeastern University, Ft. Lauderdale, Florida.

Jablin, F. (1979). Organizational entry, assimilation, and exit. In F. Jablin, L. Putnam, K. Roberts, & L. Porter (Eds.), *Handbook of organizational communication.* Thousand Oaks, CA: Sage.

Johnson, D., & Johnson, F. (2003). *Joining together: Group theory and group skills* (8th ed.). Boston, MA: Allyn and Bacon/Pearson Education.

Kipnis, D., Schmidt, S., & Braxton-Brown, G. (1990). The hidden cost of persistence. In M. Cody and M. McLaughlin (Eds.), *The psychology of tactical communication.* Philadelphia, PA: Multilingual Matters.

McGrath, D. (Ed.). (2004). *Thoughts from the top: A collection of interviews with business gurus.* Aurora, Ontario: HR.Com Publishing.

Merrill, D., & Reid, R. (1981). *Personal style and effective performance.* Radnor, PA: Chilton.

Redding, C. (1972). *Communication within the organization.* New York: Industrial Communications Council.

Richmond, V., McCroskey, J., & McCroskey, L. (2005). *Organizational communication for survival: Making work* (3rd ed.). New York: Pearson Education.

Schein, E. (1987). *Organizational culture and leadership.* San Francisco, CA: Jossey-Bass.

Schuler, R. (1992). Strategic human resource management: Linking the people with the strategic needs of the business. *Organizational Dynamics, 21,* 18–31.

Segal, J. (2002). Security versus privacy. *HRMagazine, 47(2).*

Senge, P. (1991). *The fifth discipline: The art and practice of the learning organization.* New York: Doubleday/Currency.

Shockley-Zalabak, P. (2002). *Fundamentals of organizational communication: Knowledge, sensitivity, skills, values* (5th ed.). Boston, MA: Allyn & Bacon.

Shockley-Zalabak, P., Ellis, K., & Cesaria, [[init]]. (2000). Measuring Organizational Trust. Paper delivered at International Association of Business Communicators, San Francisco.

SHRM. (2004). *Code of ethical and professional standard in human resource management.* Alexandria, VA: Author.

Tjosvold, D. (1984). Effects of leader warmth and directiveness on subordinate performance on a subsequent task. *Journal of Applied Psychology, 69,* 422–427.

Toossi, M. (2002, May). A century of change: The U.S. labor force, 1950–2050. *Monthly Labor Review,* pp. 15–28.

Ronald Fetzer, *Ph.D., is retired emeritus faculty in the communication department at Wright State University, in Dayton, Ohio. He is currently a visiting professor, department of communication, at Miami University, in Oxford, Ohio, and is serving on the HRM graduate faculty in The Huizenga School of Business at Nova Southeastern University in Ft. Lauderdale, Florida. He has operated an HRD consulting practice for over twenty-five years, working with clients throughout the United States and internationally.*

Terrorists Hit HRM

Jack N. Kondrasuk*

Summary

The United States, as many other countries of the world, has been significantly affected by the events and aftermath of terrorist attacks. Those events produced significant changes in human resource management, businesses, the U.S. government and society, and the world in general. The travel and insurance industries were badly damaged, the nation pulled together, and HRM practices changed to include emphasizing stricter employment screening and security measures. However, many of the initial changes diminished over time. The most likely terrorist events in the future are probably biological, chemical, and radiological attacks against targets where many die and the economy is hurt. HRM can do things to prevent and respond to deleterious effects of those attacks. Developing a crisis management plan is a good first step.

In this paper we look at the effects of terrorist attacks (on society, employers, and specifically on human resource management), how to prevent negative effects of the attacks, and how to respond to those effects that we cannot prevent. Our main focus is on how terrorism relates to human resource management (HRM). There have been many articles in the popular press that express their authors' opinions about terrorism and its effects. However, there are few empirical, objective research articles—especially about the effects on HRM. This paper is an attempt to bridge that gap.

*The author wishes to thank the following University of Portland students, who assisted in providing information for this project: Brent Haverkamp, Krys Moen, Brendan Hochstein, Amy Holloway, Matt Grosshans, Brian Regaldo, and Elizabeth Gomes.

Background

Defining Terrorism

"Terrorism" is a term used in government communications and by the mass media. However, those in the group being assailed and their supporters may view themselves as "freedom fighters" or by some other less pejorative terms. There is no one universally accepted definition of terrorism. However, for use in this paper, "terrorism," as defined by the U.S. Federal Bureau of Investigation (FBI), is the unlawful use of force or violence against persons or property to force the terrorists' political or social views onto a government or its citizens to influence them to change in some way (Terrorism Research Center, 2002). Our definition focuses on foreign-based terrorist groups and excludes groups emanating from within the United States.

Effects of the 9/11 Attacks

Many international, political, societal, and economic effects have been related to the terrorist attacks on the United States on September 11, 2001. Many of those effects have been well-documented—the "war on terrorism," the creation of the Office of Homeland Security, and the governmental inquiry into the events leading up to the attacks. In this section, we focus on those societal and economic effects most likely to impact HRM practitioners.

As for societal effects, the initial response of the U.S. populace was shock, sorrow, and outrage after 9/11. Views of people changed. There were both hatred and acts of discrimination against Muslims and Arabs (Quinn, 2003), as well as a new national inquisitiveness to learn more about Islam (Ghio, 2001). Employees became more concerned about spending time with loved ones and balancing work and home time as well as extending more effort to help others in need. People in the United States became more concerned about the needs of others. The citizens of the United States were drawn closer together into a more cohesive populace (Cohen, 2002).

Many economic effects came from 9/11. Security costs jumped significantly (Cohen, 2002). Large increases in security provisions have occurred at airports in the United States and around the world, as well as at large public gatherings. The insurance and travel industries were expected to post tremendous losses as a result of 9/11. The insurance industry set records in losses in 2001 (Brown, Krozner, & Jenn, 2002; Oster, 2002). The travel industry found many trips cancelled immediately after 9/11, with the airlines, hotels, and travel agencies especially hard hit (Hotel Online, 2001). The DOT's Bureau of Transportation Statistics showed that the airline industry declined significantly after 9/11 (Smallen, 2002). There were adverse effects on U.S. metropolitan economies (Bolger, 2002; DeVol, Bedrousian, Fogelbach, Gonzalez, & Wong, 2002). Cooper and James (2002) said that consumers kept spending, but that businesses cut back greatly after 9/11.

Many changes directly affected employers immediately after 9/11. Crisis management teams and plans took on increased emphasis. Disaster plans were either taken out of mothballs and updated or new ones were created by employers previously without them. Business travel and meetings away were drastically curtailed. Companies designed high-security, armored meeting rooms for their executives and boards of directors (Maher, 2002). Increased security procedures led to slower and more costly movement of goods, services, and people; Bernasek (2002) estimated that it would cost the United States an extra $151 billion a year because of the 9/11 terrorist attacks. Employers gave many more leaves of absence and time off to employees troubled by the events of 9/11. Job applicants and present employees shunned work in high-rise buildings and mail rooms (Cohen, 2002).

However, with the passage of time, the initial effects of 9/11 tended to fade and much of life returned to pre-9/11 behaviors. National surveys have shown little lasting change on the U. S. population and businesses since 9/11 (American Society of Association Executives, 2002; Conway, 2001). Bolger (2002) states that the insurance industry has already recovered from the tremendous losses initially estimated as a result of 9/11. An article in an employment law newsletter states that a recent survey found that 80 percent of the responding employees said they were at least as productive as before 9/11 (Keith & Symes, 2002). Many of the economic changes that occurred after 9/11 were considered by some to be from the economic conditions existing in the United States before 9/11 and were not the result of the 9/11 attacks (Cooper & James, 2002). Although U.S. citizens are more cautious now about being in large public gatherings, shopping malls, high-rise buildings, and on airplanes, people have returned to pre-9/11 behaviors in these venues (Cauldron, 2002). Stress levels have fallen, but U.S. citizens expect, and are willing to tolerate, greater security costs—especially for airline travel.

Future Terrorist Targets and Weapons

Terrorists have a myriad of potential targets in the world. They are thought to be more likely to attack high-profile landmarks, military and civilian government facilities, large public gatherings, water and food supplies, communications systems, transportation systems, utilities, corporate headquarters, and crowded public places with low security (NBC News, 2002). It is believed that Al Qaeda's criteria for targets in the United States are attacks that cause severe damage to the economy, kill many people, destroy areas of high symbolic value, and/or cause maximum psychological trauma (FBI, 2003). These criteria put any organization at increased risk if its location houses many people or if damage to the organization would cause a decline in the economy. It even means that any people or organizations near such locations could suffer collateral damage, even though they, themselves, do not meet the above criteria.

Terrorist weapons include biological, chemical, nuclear, radiological, and cyber warfare. Terrorists know economies could be decimated and/or thousands could die, of course, but their fundamental motive would be to strike fear and panic in tens of millions more (Fox News Online, 2003). Biological weapons are referred to as the poor man's nuclear weapon. The toxins include anthrax, smallpox, plaque, botulinum toxin, ricin, and viral hemmorrhagic fevers. Dispersal ranges from putting germs and toxins in food to spraying contagious viruses over a city. They often start with flu-like symptoms and produce mortality rates of up to 90 percent (Fox News Online, 2003). Chemical weapons generally attack the nervous system. They include mustard gas, sarin, soman, tabun, and the extremely deadly VX, which can kill in a few minutes. Nuclear weapons produce the most devastating effects on humans and animals due to their powerful explosions and subsequent deadly radioactive fallout. However, they are the most difficult weapons to obtain because their components are rare and very expensive. Although atomic bombs and hydrogen bombs (a thousand times more destructive) are extremely deadly, "dirty bombs" (regular explosives attached to radioactive material) are considered a prime choice for terrorists because of ease of procurement (Fox News Online, 2003). Using computers as weapons is relatively new. Whether hacking into a military or business computer system to extract proprietary information or causing disruption in the organization's functioning, it definitely can harm the country's defenses and economy. Transmitting destructive computer viruses can do similar damage.

The Response from HRM

Given the possibility of terrorists attacking targets in the United States with any of the weapons listed above, what effects will it have on HRM (defined as activities done by both line managers and the HR department)? What can an employer do to prevent deleterious effects of terrorist attacks? For those situations where negative effects cannot really be prevented, how is the employer to best respond when they do occur?

A week after the 9/11 attacks, the main professional association in the human resource management field, the Society for Human Resource Management (SHRM), surveyed its members about the effects of the attacks. Responses indicated that 76 percent of companies allowed employees to cancel or delay business travel, 62 percent allowed employees time off if needed as a result of 9/11, 45 percent cancelled meetings and events, 56 percent anticipated tightening security, many employees were concerned about possible layoffs, and HR departments were more concerned with crisis management plans (SHRM, 2001). A month or two later, other surveys found increased stress, employees seeking a better balance between their work and off-work lives, more fear of flying in airplanes, and more layoffs (Poe, 2001). These same reactions could be expected after any significant terrorist attacks in the future.

By a year after 9/11, many of the preceding effects diminished. SHRM did additional surveys of its members in August of 2002 (Cohen, 2002) and found that over half of the respondents stated that the 9/11 attacks made no difference to them, time off for emotional needs related to the effects of 9/11 dwindled from 62 percent to 35 percent, and cancelled meetings and events dropped from 45 percent to 25 percent. On the other hand, some activities and actions did not change much over time. Blood drives and money donations, expectations of tighter security measures, and having a crisis management plan changed very little over the year since the 9/11 attacks. Moreover, some changes increased. Productivity, contrary to expectations, actually improved over this time period. Another set of surveys showed similar declines in effects of the 9/11 attacks over time. The Jackson Lewis survey of HR professionals in November of 2001 showed that the terrorist threat was the number-one HRM issue (Bryant, 2003). However, in mid-2003, the general public viewed terrorism as far less important; a Kaiser Family Foundation survey found that the general public placed health care concerns, inflation, and housing costs as greater concerns than terrorist attacks (Up Front, 2003). Let's look now at specific areas of HRM.

Employment

The main concern after an attack is to make sure that the business continues to function. In case the place of business or headquarters is damaged or destroyed, it's a good idea to have a plan stating who (employees) does what (jobs) with what (resources, equipment) (Tynan, 2003).

If employees are injured in the attack, employee replacement could be key to helping the business continue to function. This can be helped by continually training employees to do a variety of different jobs. This way, if an employee in your business has to take an extended leave of absence, or even if an employee is killed in an attack, someone else in the company can continue to do the job. Other than training employees, it is also helpful to accurately document the job descriptions for each job within your company, to ensure that someone could perform the job if an employee is incapacitated (Tynan, 2003). Other options for continuing to function after an attack are outsourcing jobs or using temps; these approaches can be helpful, at least in the short run.

The hijacking of planes on 9/11 and subsequent failed attempts to blow up bridges and buildings forced organizations to look much more closely at who they were hiring (as pilots, truck drivers of hazardous cargo, and security personnel) (Overman, 2001). In the SHRM (2001) survey, it was found that 23 percent expected greater screening of applicants to eliminate terrorists. There may have been fewer job opportunities for those perceived as Middle Eastern and/or Muslim. The Equal Employment Opportunity Commission, churches, and leaders in the U.S. government came out strongly against possible unfair racial discrimination in such treatment. The attacks, producing significant emotional trauma for their direct and indirect victims, raised questions about the rights of traumatized employees under the Americans with Disabilities Act. Are those traumatized employees considered disabled? Also, do their emotional or, in some cases, physical wounds qualify them for state workers' compensation benefits? (Heidrich, 2002).

There are fewer top job applicants in the recruiting pool as a result of the 9/11 attacks. Immigration and security procedures have tightened up on foreign nationals entering the United States. Previously there were 583,000 foreign nationals coming in to study at U.S. universities; they made up about 33 percent of all the science and engineering doctoral degrees and 40 percent of all Ph.D.s in computer science. That number is dwindling now (Arnst, 2003). It is also likely that expatriate employees are more difficult to obtain. Managers seem more resistant to going overseas to work due to security fears.

Training and Development

It would seem that much more training would occur regarding terrorism. In the initial SHRM (2001) survey, 35 percent of the respondents expected increases in training for crisis management and disaster recovery. However, a year after 9/11, there had been little evidence of an increase in training for detecting or responding to terrorism; the latest SHRM survey states that only 19 percent of the respondents expected greater training in this area (Cohen, 2002). A survey with different results was conducted by the American Society for Training and Development (ASTD) after 9/11. The study showed a distinct shift to distance learning (by intra- and Internet and videoconferencing); training was much more likely to be conducted on the employer's premises and not require travel by airplane to a distant city. In the ASTD survey, training actually increased in diversity, security, stress management, and change management after 9/11 (Cauldron, 2002).

It could be expected that more training would now be done to help employees gain skills in recognizing, preventing, and responding to threats of terrorism. Specific training topics could include mail handling and bomb threats, signs and symptoms of various chemical and biological toxins, and how to handle emotional stress in these dangerous times. Employees must be trained in how to distinguish between alarms to leave the building (for example, fire) and those indicating employees should stay in the building and seal it (for example, nuclear fallout). Due to the quickly changing terrain of terrorism, continual retraining would be highly advised.

Compensation and Benefits

The changes expected here would probably involve employee benefits (although one could imagine that certain jobs might now receive additional "hazardous duty" pay for greater threats of terrorism). There was an increase in the percentage of employers offering EAPs; according to the SHRM surveys, it went from 49 percent to 54 percent over eleven months after 9/11 (Cohen, 2002). There was more long-term therapy for traumatized and stressed employees (Leonard, 2002). Questions arise regarding health care benefits being related to terrorist attacks. Will employers or employees pay the costs for hospitalization and medical care after a terrorist attack? Who will fund the cost for vaccines and drugs to prevent bio-terrorism (for example, smallpox or anthrax outbreaks)? Will there be more employee travel/accident insurance?

Employee Leave Policies

Creating an employee leave policy that applies to an event like a terrorist attack is difficult because there is no way of predicting what specific type of attack will take place or how it will affect the employer and employees. Some of the things that may arise after a terrorist attack include mental health issues, physical injuries, and family issues. Mental health issues can include depression and post-traumatic stress disorder. Part of the employee leave policy should include time allowed for employees to see a counselor during the work day or to take longer periods of time off work, such as a week or more to seek therapy for the condition. However, it is important to realize that not every employee will react the same way, so any policy in place should be somewhat flexible. The most important thing about creating such a policy is to let employees know they are supported and that they can have the time they need to get appropriate help.

Military Leave Policies

Under the Uniform Services Employment and Re-Employment Rights Act (USERRA), employers must grant military leave to reservists and National Guard troops (whether the military service was a call-up of reservists/guards or a new enlistment). The rules for USERRA are extensive, with many exceptions. In general, unless it would be an undue hardship for the employer, leave must be granted to all regular employees (both full-time and part-time), but not to temporary employees. The employer may need to provide benefits and seniority continuation. In general, employers must consider employees who are absent due to military service to be on "unpaid leave" while they are gone. Accordingly, the employer must provide such absent employees with the same rights and benefits (unless they are determined by seniority) that are generally provided to other employees on unpaid leaves. For example, if the employer allowed other employees on unpaid leave to use accrued paid vacation or other types of paid leave during such an absence, then employees on military leave also must be entitled to use such paid leave benefits. Employees on unpaid leave also are entitled to buy continued health insurance coverage under COBRA. Defined contribution plans must permit returning veterans to make plan contributions that they may have missed while absent for military service (USERRA, 2003).

Employees returning from military leave who have met the proper USERRA notice requirements must be reinstated to the same or better positions regarding seniority, status, and pay as long as the employees are still able to perform the applicable job duties (Segal, 2003). If the employee returning from military leave suffers from a disability caused or aggravated by military service and cannot perform job duties performed before taking the military leave, the employer may still be obligated to provide a position that is the nearest approximation of the former job. Returning employees also are entitled to reinstatement of seniority and benefits in the same manner as if they had remained employed for the entire period of service. Employers who violate the USERRA are liable for reinstatement of the employee, payment of back pay, along with compensatory damages (doubled for employers' willful violations), and attorney fees (USERRA, 2003).

Occupational Health, Safety, and Security

This is the area expected to be most affected by possible future terrorist attacks. An employer's first responsibility in case of a terrorist attack is the health and safety of its employees. Employers are legally responsible for the health and safety of their employees under OSHA rules (Conlin, 2001). Without employees, an employer's business cannot function, which is why taking care of employees should be a top priority. Many executives in HR departments were at the forefront of helping their employees on 9/11. Poe (2001) and Leonard (2001) profiled HR professionals who helped their employees to safety, helped account for those missing, set up communications links for those missing, and brought in EAP counselors for onsite help to those with stress problems.

In the future, HR departments will probably be more involved in trying to minimize the loss of employees from a terrorist attack—especially the loss of key personnel such as executives, members of the board of directors, and scientists and others with irreplaceable skills. HR planning could include spreading out the workforce into different locations to preclude having all key employees being killed in one terrorist attack. Management and production staffs could be relocated to more secure areas. Travel, especially by airplane, could be reduced by using videoconferencing and virtual reality meetings and avoiding the need for travel by better long-range planning. Companies could provide bodyguards and vary travel routes taken by executives and key personnel for traveling to/from work or as a part of work. Concrete bunkers could be provided for executives and board members to gather in to continue to run the company in case of an attack.

Related to safety is the issue of security; a BNA Bulletin to Management (2002) indicated that in over half of the organizations, HR departments were responsible for security in their companies. The security unit would be expected to increase security in the wake of 9/11 and other recent terrorist attacks in the world. Conlin (2001) suggests that increased attention be paid to security outside the company, like the commute to work, adjoining neighborhoods, parking lots, proper outside lighting, emergency call boxes, and security cameras. Entry to and exit from the premises should gain attention. Overman (2001) stated that employee ingress/egress must be further constricted and separate from that used by non-employees, such as visitors, customers, and suppliers (who should be watched more closely). Detectors for explosives and weapons and ID badges should be improved. Inspections should be made of suspicious substances such as liquids. Stairwells should be designed to accommodate police and firefighter entry against simultaneous exiting of building occupants. Mail and the mail room will probably need more security procedures to minimize hazards such as letter bombs and anthrax letters.

While concern over security has increased, surprisingly, security departments do not seem to have grown much since 9/11. Of the growth that did occur, much was window dressing, with some of the quick-fix programs already dropped. For instance, immediately after the 9/11 attacks, 34 percent of the employers established employee committees on safety and security, but only 14 percent had them about a year later (Cohen, 2002).

Crisis Management Plan

Perhaps the main anti-terrorism contribution that can be made in the HRM area is to develop and implement a crisis management plan. Crisis management plans are assumed to be very useful for minimizing negative effects from a terrorist attack. Estimates of their use vary. Tynan (2003) estimates that only 10 percent of small- to medium-sized businesses have such plans in action. In contrast, the SHRM surveys found that about half the respondents in the initial SHRM survey stated they had a crisis management plan; nearly 90 percent had one about a year later (Cohen, 2002; SHRM, 2001). Another survey found that 25 percent of those who said they did have a "current" crisis management plan had not practiced it in the last five years (Armstrong, 2003). Lack of use should not detract from the importance of developing and implementing a crisis management plan, though.

The typical process to develop a crisis management plan consists of getting the appropriate support, creating a team, obtaining resources, doing a risk assessment, developing a detailed plan, communicating the plan, preventing harmful effects, and responding to those negative effects that are not preventable. The first step must be for senior management to believe in and sell the vision of a crisis management plan (Conlin, 2001). But it is not only top management that must buy into the plan. According to Suttrell (2002), a disaster plan will only be successful if it has a complete buy-in from all users. This may include the highest levels, such as the CEO of the corporation, other employees, customers, and other tenants in the building.

A crisis management team needs to be selected, organized, and funded. To perform this task, a staff skills inventory should be completed and there should be designated staff assignments for terrorist attacks (Conlin, 2001).

The crisis management team needs to perform a risk assessment (Conlin, 2001). This not only includes an inspection and analysis of the physical facility but also a survey of employee safety concerns. It is important that management understand the concerns of fellow employees so that training needs can be assessed and relevant training provided. The crisis management team should assess the circumstances and determine an appropriate risk category. The risk categories could be (1) no risk, (2) low risk, (3) medium risk, (4) high risk, and (5) imminent danger (Davis, 2001). Some things to ask are: What are the employer's main areas of vulnerability? Who are the tenants in my building and the buildings around me? Are the organizations foreign owned, controversial, or likely targets in any way (Suttrell, 2002)? Notice that it is also important to assess your neighbors. Even though assessing an employer's security risks seems to be an essential task in the present environment of possible terrorist attacks, through April of 2003, only 20 percent of businesses in one survey had done a risk assessment since 9/11 (Armstrong, 2003).

Once a company has determined what types of attack it may encounter, it is important to determine what responses are necessary to those attacks. Biological and chemical attacks need a much different set of responses than incendiary bombs. With an explosion causing a fire, employees need to evacuate the building as quickly as possible. In the case of an external chemical attack, employees should stay in the building. It is important to turn off all ventilation in order to prevent the spread of the chemical toxins. It is vital that all employees take cover in interior rooms, preferably without windows, and seal the rooms off with duct tape and plastic sheeting. They should make sure that the shelter is properly stocked with appropriate supplies—especially devices to communicate with authorities to determine when it is safe to leave the building.

Should a crisis incident occur, the crisis management team should be ready to follow and complete specific action guides, written step-by-step checklists of actions and decisions that have been specially designed and practiced for certain types of critical incidents such as bomb threats, anthrax exposure, armed intruders, radioactive materials exposure, hostage situations, and utilities disruption. It is recommended that these action guides be kept in a central location and also provided on specially designed databases compatible with the various handheld or pocket personal computer devices so that crisis management team members have ready access to them (Loescher, 2003).

An important part of developing a crisis management plan is the communication of the plan to the entire organization. It is helpful for all individuals in the organization to have their own copies of the plan for reference. Seminars and periodic drills can be effective in practicing and applying the principles of the plan. It is helpful to form teams for each floor of the building and decide who will be in charge of leading the employees at the time of crisis. These teams should be trained in CPR, first aid, basic firefighting, and all of the evacuation procedures.

There are numerous steps one can take to prevent some of the harmful effects of a terrorist attack. Such steps include better parking security, installing shatterproof glass, moving air intakes to avoid tampering or external entry, creating a remote mailroom, limiting access to the building, better screening and control of non-employees entering the buildings (for example, scheduled deliveries only), using physical barriers, asking employees to police their workspaces, cooperating with local government officials, obtaining counter-terrorism advice from outside consultants, and posting/practicing evacuation routes throughout the building (Suttrell, 2002; What to do. . ., 2003). One of the best ways to develop a good evacuation strategy would be to invite the local fire and police departments to the facility for an inspection. With this inspection, the fire and police departments can determine the fastest evacuation route out of the building as well as any safety precautions the company can take to make the facility better equipped for an emergency. Subsequently, in the chaotic event of a terrorist attack, any previous knowledge that the police and fire departments had of the facility would expedite a quicker response from them in the emergency.

The crisis management team must be ready to respond to a terrorist attack. Members should arrange for a command center and for a crisis kit. This kit should be secured in the designated command post location for use by the crisis management team during a critical incident. The kit should include a responsibilities checklist to identify who does what, a staff roster with emergency phone numbers and identification of those with special skills, keys/entry codes to building doors and locks, crisis response equipment such as two-way radios and cellular phones, blueprints of the buildings, maps of evacuation routes, and the relocation sites for each section of the facility if needed (Conlin, 2001).

The crisis management team should be prepared to communicate with various groups after an attack. It must have ways of communicating with emergency officials such as police and firefighters. The team should also be prepared to communicate with management, employees, and the media (Downer, 2003). Finally, thought and training should be put into post-crisis review so that the organization can learn from the situation and improve planning for future events.

Employer Terrorist Insurance

When the organization has done as much as it can to prevent and respond to the problems of a possible terrorist attack, it can still add an element of protection by purchasing terrorism insurance. The popularity of such insurance has grown considerably since 9/11. However, since there was such a costly charge to the insurance companies for 9/11, they became hesitant to provide coverage for terrorist attacks. Addressing this problem, the U.S. Congress subsequently passed legislation that encourages terrorist insurance to be sold. With HR 3210, insurance companies are able to sell up to $100 billion worth of insurance, yet only be accountable for a fraction of the claims. The U.S. government pays 90 percent of all claims arising from terrorist attacks after an insurance company settles its first $10 billion worth of claims. This legislation both reduces the insurance industry's hesitance to sell such insurance and helps companies protect their assets, operations, and employees. At present, costs for terrorist insurance vary greatly from $30 per $100,000 coverage in New York, Chicago, Washington, and San Francisco to $18/$100,000 in Seattle, Los Angeles, Philadelphia, and Boston to $1/100,000 in the rest of the United States (Brady, 2003).

Conclusion

The United States suffered unprecedented devastation from terrorist attacks on 9/11. Those attacks produced significant changes in the United States and, indeed, in the world. Although many of those initial changes have not endured, the U.S. government and employers will never again be the same. Al Qaeda and other terrorist organizations are still seen as having the potential to inflict significant damage to the United States and its citizens—especially with biological/chemical weapons and dirty bombs. To reduce the negative effects of any future terrorist attacks from an HRM perspective, more attention could be given to screening job applicants, developing employee replacement plans, training employees regarding dealing with terrorism, developing employee benefit programs to deal with terrorism, increasing security, and developing crisis management plans. Although we may not be able to entirely stop terrorists who are willing to sacrifice their lives for their causes, we can be better prepared to prevent and respond to such attacks, and minimize their damage.

References

American Society of Association Executives. (2002, February). Survey data: Impact of September 11 on the American workforce. *Association Management, 54*(2), 22.

Armstrong, C.M. (2003, May 19). Corporate homeland security. *Business Week*, p. 67.

Arnst, C. (2003, May 19). How the war on terror is damaging the brain pool. *Business Week*, pp. 72–73.

Bernasek, A. (2002). The friction economy. *Fortune, 145*(4), 104–112.

BNA Bulletin to Management (2002). *SHRM-BNA survey #66: Human resource activities, budgets & staffs, 2000–2001,* 1–3.

Bolger, A. (2002, May 24). Industry recovers from September's terrorist shock. *Financial Times,* p. 10.

Brady, D. (2003, April 14). Terrorism: Put the money where the danger is. *Business Week,* p. 40.

Brown, J.R., Krozner, R.S., & Jenn, B.H. (2002, October). Federal terrorism risk insurance. NBER working paper #9271.

Bryant, M. (2003, May 29). 2001 Jackson Lewis workplace survey. [Online]. Available: bryantm@jacksonlewis.com.

Cauldron, S. (2002). Training in the post-terrorism era. *Training & Development, 56*(2), 24–30.

Cohen, D.J. (2002). *HR implications of the attack on America: One year later.* Alexandria, VA: SHRM/eePulse.

Conlin, M. (2001, November 19). When the office is the war zone. *BusinessWeek,* p. 38.

Conway, J. (2001, December 12). Towers Perrin survey finds leaner merit increases and other cost-cutting measures expected for 2002, employers say. *Business Wire, Inc.* [Online]. Available: Conwayj@towers.com.

Cooper, M., & James, K. (2002, September 16). Consumers have done their part. Now, businesses will have to pitch in. *Business Week,* p. 19.

Davis, C.K. (2001). Planning for the unthinkable: IT contingencies. *National Forum, 81*(1), 4.

DeVol, R.C., Bedrousian, A, Fogelbach, N.G., Gonzalez, R., & Wong, P. (2002). *The impact of September 11 on U.S. metropolitan economies.* Santa Monica, CA: Miliken Institute.

Downer, D.F. (2003, April 1). A new world presents new challenges for HR staffs. *Washington Business Journal.* [Online]. Available: www.washington.bizjournals.com/washington/stories/2001/11/19/focus5.html.

FBI. (2003). Testimony of Robert S. Mueller, III, Director, FBI: Before the Select Committee on Intelligence of the United States Senate: February 11, 2003. [Online]. Available: www.fbi.gov///congress/congress03/mueller021103.htm.

Ghio, R.S. (2001, September 10). *National outrage and its impact on the workplace.* [Online]. Available: www.shrm.org.

Heidrich, G. (2002, April 8). The illusion of protection: Terrorism, war and workers' compensation. *Insurance Advocate,* pp. 22–23, 48.

Hotel Online. (2001, October 11). Tourism exposure across the U. S., Pacific, and South Atlantic states at greatest risk. [Online]. Available: www.hotel-online.com/News/PR2002_4th/Oct02_USTourism.html.

Keith, C.L., & Symes, D.P.R. (2002, January). HR trends. *Oregon Employment Law Letter, 8*(5), 4.

Leonard, B. (2001). A job well done. *HRMagazine, 46*(12), 34–38.

Leonard, B. (2002). After September 11, a changed workforce. *HRNews, 21*(9), 1, 7.

Loescher, G. (2003, February). Be prepared. *World Today,* p. 7.

Maher, K. (2002, May 23). Playing it safe. *Wall Street Journal,* p. B1.

NBC News. (2002, May 28). *Are we prepared? NBC Nightly News.* [Online]. Available: www
.msnbc.msn.com/id/3053419/

Oster, C. (2002, April 8). Can the risk of terrorism be calculated by insurers? "Game theory"
might do it. *The Wall Street Journal,* pp. C1, C8.

Overman, S. (2001). Companies go back to work. *HRNews, 20*(11), 1, 8.

Poe, A.C. (2001, December). After shocks of the 11th. *HR Magazine, 46*(12), 46–51.

Porteus, L. (2003, July 8). Weapons of mass destruction handbook. *Fox News Online.* [On-
line]. Available: www.foxnews.com/story/0,2933,76887,00.html.

Quinn, B. (2003, February 9). Racism rekindled in Southern Oregon. *The Oregonian,* pp.
A12, A19.

Segal, J.A. (2003). Military leave minefields. *HRMagazine, 48*(4), 60–64.

SHRM. (2001). More caring, security predicted following attacks, poll shows. *HRNews,
20*(11), 14, 17.

Smallen, D. (2002, January 9). BTS indicators report shows impact of September 11 on
airlines. U.S. Department of Transportation, Bureau of Transportation Statistics. [On-
line]. Available: www.dot.gov/affairs/bts0102

Suttrell, R. (2002). Strategic security. *Buildings, 96*(8), 38.

10 steps to take when terror alert rises. (2003, December 23). *Security Magazine.* [Online].
Available: www.securitymagazine.com/security/cda/articleinformation/coverstory/bnp
coverstoryitem/0,,115542,00+en-uss_01dbc.html.

Terrorism Research Center (2003). Terrorism defined. [Online]. Available: www.terror-
ism.com.

Tynan, D. (2003, April). In case of emergency. *Entrepreneur Magazine,* pp. 59–61.

Up front/The big picture/An anxious lot. (2003, June 2). *Business Week,* p. 8.

USERRA. (2003, February 20). The Uniformed Services Employment and Reemployment
Rights Act. USERRA, 38 USC Sec. 4301. [Online]. Available: www.osc.gov/userra.htm.

Jack Kondrasuk, *Ph.D., SPHR, is an associate professor at the Dr. Robert B. Pamplin, Jr., School of Business Administration at the University of Portland in Oregon. He has worked in HR departments in large corporations,
worked as a management and HR consultant, taught HRM in universities, served in national leadership positions in HR professional associations, and conducted research in HRM during the last thirty-six years—specializing in research on terrorism since 9/11.*

Behavior Matters:
Building a Legal, Ethical Workplace Culture
Stephen M. Paskoff

Summary

When it comes to building a legal, ethical workplace culture, recent scandals and lawsuits prove that distributing a code of conduct and sending people through rote training on the various laws is not enough. Human resource professionals have an increasing role in helping shape organizational strategies to build a foundation for integrity, respect, and accountability in the workplace. By focusing on three areas of responsibility—prevention, detection, and correction of inappropriate behavior—HR professionals can provide the bridge between strategic concepts and everyday on-the-job conduct.

Sexual harassment. Racial discrimination. Fraud. Class action suits. Record-breaking jury awards. For many of us, simply reading those words brings to mind certain organizations that, whether they were well-known before or not, will now be forever associated with high-profile, well-publicized scandals. And whether the cases involved financial or human resource violations, the overwhelming costs to the leadership, the organizations, their ability to compete, and the bottom line were just as devastating.

Acutely aware of these examples, most leaders will tell you they're making sure the same won't happen in their own organizations. They're sending out carefully crafted values statements to everyone. All employees are required to sign a notice saying they've received the "code of conduct" and other policies. Companies may even be sending people through some online training on the various legal requirements. And yet, most of the organizations involved in these high-profile scandals had codes of conduct. Many implemented online training programs. And nearly every major U.S. company has a lofty mission and values statement. In light of all this, human resource professionals need to take a hard look at their culture and environment and ask themselves, "What makes us different? What are we really doing to make sure it doesn't happen here?"

Building a legal, ethical workplace culture is a process, one that demands a strategic approach. As with any strategic initiative, it's important to keep the overarching objectives in sight. Is your objective simply to conduct training? Or do you want to build a culture where individuals treat one another professionally and in line with your standards? Is your goal merely to comply with a specific legal requirement? Or do you want to create an environment in which employees are comfortable raising concerns so you can address issues before they escalate into potentially catastrophic problems?

All too often I've seen organizational leaders define their mandates and the successful execution of their duties by only the narrowest criteria. Simply put, their definition of success is more about meeting short-term financial objectives and focusing on tactical steps (we issued a policy and posted our values statement.), rather than examining what really needs to be accomplished to meet their overarching goals (have we built the foundation for ethical, legal, and diverse operations that foster excellence and bottom-line results?). There's more to building a proper workplace culture than sending out policies or doing just enough to prove compliance with a particular legal regulation.

In this article, I discuss the growing strategic responsibilities of human resource professionals and the role they play in developing a foundation for integrity, respect, and accountability in the workplace. In particular, I address three key areas of HR involvement: prevention, detection, and correction of inappropriate workplace behavior.

Prevention

Aligning Behaviors and Values

The way people conduct themselves at work is a good indicator of the organization's culture. Employees generally model their behavior on the examples they see around them—particularly the behavior of their managers. These are the organization's unwritten rules, the ones that reflect "the way we do things here." So while it's nearly impossible to prevent every potential problem from occurring, by aligning employee behavior with company values and policies, companies will go a long way toward building a proper culture. The challenge comes in making it happen.

Values statements are a start. Their intent is to provide a high-level view of the kind of organization the leaders want to create. Unfortunately, values statements generally contain broad phrases such as:

- We will treat people with respect.

- We value diversity.

- We will conduct our business with complete integrity.

- We recognize that employees are our most valuable asset.

When employees are asked to explain what those values mean in terms of their daily business conduct, each person may have a different and sometimes conflicting interpretation. Human resource professionals need to provide the bridge between strategic concepts and everyday, on-the-job conduct. They must encourage leaders to use clear, candid language tied to real performance expectations, translating the mission and values into day-to-day behaviors. They should remind leaders that, from a business standpoint, when it comes to maintaining ethical and legal operations, it's the behaviors that matter. As so many recent examples in the corporate world have shown, simply having a well-publicized values statement or code of conduct is not enough.

Using the behavioral approach, leaders can ensure that the unwritten rules—which form the model for how everyone behaves—complement the written rules. Effective leaders speak passionately and, in their own words, about what the values mean to them. They speak just as convincingly about human resource issues as they do about sales issues or performance issues. And they back up their words by expecting concrete results, just as they would with any other important business issue. I've heard CEOs give powerful effect to statements as simple as, "There is certain conduct I won't tolerate, and I don't want you to either." They derive credibility from the way they communicate key messages, the context in which they communicate them, and the actions they display to reinforce them as integral to achieving the organization's mission.

Because most employees follow the behavioral examples of managers and others who have been successful in the organization, effective HR professionals know it's not about quoting policies or legal regulations; it's about incorporating the values, standards, and behaviors into their everyday activities and decision making. If any member of management is allowed to undermine the organization's objectives by ignoring them, failing to learn them, or acting contrary to them, it can have a domino effect that extends far beyond just an individual, department, or team.

For example, when employees are required to attend training on compliance and ethical issues, but leaders don't attend themselves because they're "too busy," the leaders are sending a message to the staff that the training isn't really that important. If they attend the training but joke about the content or belittle the subject matter, it is unlikely that employees will take the training seriously either. And if they contradict the organization's standards by telling inappropriate jokes or making inappropriate comments or failing to deal with others who do so, they're sending a subtle message that the organization isn't really serious about those rules. Again, it's the unwritten rules that prevail.

Putting Behavioral Standards to Work

Once behavioral ground rules are established, HR must equip its managers and employees with skills and tools to actualize the concepts.

Managers and employees need a few key skills to support honest and lawful operations. They don't need to be experts on the law, and they don't need to change their long-held beliefs. They simply need to know how they're expected to behave at work and what they should do when faced with various work environment issues and decisions.

Specifically, managers must be agents of the organization. This means they need to monitor not only their own conduct but also the behavior of others who interact in the workplace, including other managers, employees, customers, and vendors.

As the direct lines to employees as well as the public, managers have special responsibilities for building and maintaining the workplace. In a variety of areas, the courts have emphasized the importance of the manager's position. They have said, in essence, that when a manager is made aware of inappropriate behavior, the company is aware of it. Therefore, if managers become aware of any behavior that violates policy, safety, or the law, they have to be prepared to effectively document the situation and know how to support any type of investigation the organization may need to conduct. When difficult issues arise, though, they should recognize that the organization has experts—including HR and legal professionals—who are best equipped to handle them, and they should be encouraged to seek out those experts for assistance.

Managers can also prevent disruptions and minimize the potential for litigation by behaving in a consistent and professional manner with all employees, regardless of the situation or an individual's race, sex, ethnicity, or other personal characteristics. Learning how to consistently apply policies and make appropriate business decisions should be required elements of a manager's development plan.

Employees also have a responsibility to monitor their behavior and treat one anther professionally and with respect. Monitoring their own behavior ensures that everyone can focus on the job at hand without unnecessary distractions. To foster more productive working relationships and a spirit of teamwork, they must be able to interact respectfully with all their fellow employees, regardless of differences in background, beliefs, or personalities.

Just as importantly, employees must recognize that the company needs them to speak up if they become aware of policy, law, or safety violations. Employees are often the first to be aware of such issues; by speaking up, they can help management stop problems before they escalate. By the same token, employees also have a responsibility to support these efforts by recognizing that when a colleague raises a concern, it is in the interest of protecting the work environment.

Education and Training

To ensure that proper responsibilities and skills are developed, it's vital that HR take a lead role in identifying and implementing an outcome-focused, comprehensive learning solution. In fact, a number of recent cases have shown that failing to provide training on key discrimination and harassment issues may either lead to liability or increase the risk of higher damage awards. In *Hoffman-La Roche, Inc. v. Zeltwanger* (2002 Tex. App.), a Texas state court upheld a jury verdict awarding a former employee nearly $10 million in a sexual harassment suit based partially on the fact that the firm failed to provide training to employees on harassment and the use of complaint procedures and that it only provided copies of the manual containing its anti-harassment policies to managers and supervisors. In *Breda v. Wolf Camera & Video* (2000 WL 114138, 11th Cir. Aug. 14, 2000), an employee complained to her store manager of repeated sexual harassment by a co-worker, but no action was taken on the complaint, and she eventually resigned as a result. The U.S. Eleventh Circuit reversed a summary judgment in favor of the company, saying that the store manager's failure to act opened the door for liability. Had the manager received adequate training about supervisory responsibilities, the potential for liability could have been eliminated.

Federal sentencing guidelines also underscore the importance of effective training as a tool for building honest and ethical operations. Ironically, though, the legal institutions have begun to recognize the importance of training before many organizations have. What the courts are saying is that you can't just issue policies and value statements and assume that's enough. You need training and educational tools to give them life.

Even when they recognize the need for training, however, many organizations make the mistake of deciding that they will meet that need by just delivering something—anything. The problem is that they may end up implementing a program that doesn't engage and reach its audience, isn't comprehensive enough, doesn't meet the needs of the workplace climate, or in some other way fails to deliver the results. Organizations have to use the right training tool for the job. If you need to tighten a bolt, you consider the available tools, what each was designed to do, and which would be most effective in getting the job done. You wouldn't choose a hammer to tighten the bolt, just as organizations shouldn't choose a training tool that won't be effective in meeting their objectives.

In essence, though, many organizations "choose the hammer" without even considering what they're trying to accomplish. Many employers say their mission is to provide an inclusive workplace that welcomes diversity, is characterized by professional standards of behavior, and does not tolerate discriminatory and harassing conduct. Of course, by realizing these objectives, they will also increase the legality of their operations and reduce the risk of litigation and penalties. Very few leaders say their mission is to guard against and prevent lawsuits. And yet many choose learning programs that focus on legal obligations, the requirements of the law, and the avoidance of claims.

Providing information on legal issues is important, but it is not the same as providing specific skills and tools that can guide daily on-the-job behavior. The common mistake many organizations make is that they use training as a strategic part of their plan when, in fact, training is a tactic. The organization's vision is the strategy; training should be a tactical component of that overall strategy.

For that very reason, it is vital that participants view the training as one element of an overarching initiative. For it to be truly effective and credible, training cannot be delivered in a vacuum with no connection to the broader goals of the organization.

Furthermore, while many companies say that training on workplace standards is vital and just as important to the business as achieving sales goals and producing flawless products, the way they choose training solutions contradicts that message. Instead of focusing on what will work the best and deliver their desired results, they try to find the cheapest solution or the one that involves the least time away from work. If these are the goals, it is almost pointless to do anything. Companies would be better served designing something quickly and inexpensively and then simply communicating the message by email alone. This would certainly minimize training costs and reduce time away from the job.

e-Learning implementations sometimes result from this flawed decision-making process. I've spoken to HR executives who say they've chosen e-learning because (1) it seems cheaper than classroom training (a questionable premise when all setup, administration, and equipment costs are considered); (2) it can reach people at their desktops; and (3) participants can use it anytime they want without the confines of traditional classroom scheduling. All of these rationales may be correct; however, what should be the most important consideration—whether the training will generate the outcomes that meet your objectives—is frequently forgotten in the haste to embrace the logistical attractions of e-learning.

e-Learning as an element of an overall training implementation can have many tactical advantages and practicalities, but it is not a training strategy in and of itself. Choosing e-learning or any other learning tool for its logistical benefits without considering the quality of the learning experience and whether it can help lead to the real outcomes of the initiative is missing the point. Even beyond the fact that it may do little to build an ethical, collegial workforce, it may not even be enough to prove effective compliance.

To avoid falling into this trap, HR professionals should ask these simple questions before they decide on any learning content and delivery system:

- What are the reasons we are delivering this instruction? What do we hope to accomplish when we have completed the delivery?

- Are the content and delivery methods we are choosing going to serve the objectives we have defined as the rationale for the training?

Detection: Creating a Welcoming Environment for Concerns

As we've discussed, managers and HR professionals need to monitor the workplace to ensure that everyone's behavior aligns with organizational values and policy. As a part of this responsibility, they also need to recognize the importance of employee involvement. True leaders expect their team members to let them know when potentially troublesome issues arise. Creating a culture where employees are encouraged to raise their concerns and are protected from retaliation when they do so is vital to the strength of the organization. Unfortunately, many companies do just the opposite by allowing employees who speak up to be bullied, harassed, or ostracized, thus discouraging others from coming forward.

This is not only bad business practice, but it's illegal. A federal jury awarded a former Motel 6 desk clerk $2 million after he was fired for complaining that the hotel discriminated against black patrons (*Petaccia v. Motel 6, G.P. Inc.*, No. 96–115-CIV-FTM-17D M.D. Fla., June 18, 1998). In another case, a federal jury awarded a terminated TV anchor $8.3 million for sex and age discrimination, stating that she had been retaliated against for complaining about sex discrimination at the station (*Peckinpaugh v. Post-Newsweek Stations Connecticut, Inc.*, No. 396-CV 02475, D. Conn. Jan. 28, 1999). Beyond the legal ramifications, however, creating a culture that promotes speaking up is essential because it helps the organization as a whole operate more fairly and effectively. HR professionals, along with their managers, must send and support the message that the company rewards honesty rather than penalizes it.

Specifically, HR needs to make sure its managers have the skills to foster an environment in which employees are empowered to speak up, whether the concerns are related to safety, policy, ethics, or legal issues. Managers help create a welcoming environment by communicating openly with employees and responding appropriately to their concerns. The tone, manner, and content of their communications are all factors that can either inhibit or encourage speaking up by employees. HR professionals need to realize that many managers don't come into their jobs with these skills; they need specific, practical instruction that relates to their everyday realities and that they can easily apply.

Correction: Taking Action When Problems Arise

The ultimate goal, of course, is to prevent as many problems as possible. But as we know, you can't prevent everything. There will always be some people who try to circumvent the rules. For this reason, it is essential that an organization's leadership, managers, and HR team be prepared to act to correct problems.

The courts are generally unsympathetic toward an organization with management that doesn't act promptly and effectively. In 2000, the North Carolina Supreme Court upheld a half-million-dollar punitive damage award based on a 1992 claim that a university failed to stop sexual harassment from occurring. The former employee alleged she complained about a co-worker's sexual harassment to her supervisor, another manager, and an employee relations representative, and none of them took action to address her complaints (*Watson v. Dixon*, No. 103A99, N.C. July 13, 2000).

In another case, four employees will recover $2.3 million in an EEOC settlement based on a claim that the organization failed to take steps to address allegations of sexual harassment against an affiliated firm's former president, even after it received complaints about his behavior (*EEOC v. Simat, Hellieson & Eichner, Inc.*, No. 97 Civ. 7168, S.D. N.Y. February 14, 2003).

Costly lawsuits are only one of the risks of failing to correct inappropriate behavior. All too often when behavior that could have been addressed early on is allowed to continue, it permeates into the core of the workplace culture. This type of conduct becomes a part of those unwritten rules of behavior, breeding more of the same. Had the manager recognized his or her duty and known how to respond, damage to the workplace environment could have been avoided. In light of these risks, HR must ensure that all managers understand when and how to take action and where to go for help if they're not sure what to do. Taking action to correct policy, safety, or legal violations needs to be a measure of effective management performance.

Accountability Counts

A few years ago, I received an urgent call from a client's HR executive. He was concerned about one of his managers who just didn't seem to "get it." When I asked what he meant, he told me that the manager had been through training, but was still behaving inappropriately—telling sexual jokes, making stereotypical comments, and the like. The client wanted me to come back and conduct another training session. Maybe that would make the manager "get it."

When I hear these kinds of statements, I wonder: What is it that a highly paid, intelligent member of management doesn't "get"? I seriously doubt that he doesn't understand the concept that he is expected to refrain from telling sexual jokes at work. More likely, the person believes he or she can get away with the behavior because, for one reason or another, he or she thinks the rules don't apply. And until that perception changes, no amount of training will make the person "get it."

Holding people—everyone—accountable to consistent standards and expectations is key to changing that perception. Behavior must be tied to performance, and a failure to follow the organization's behavioral standards and values should be treated just like any other performance deficiency. Without accountability, none of the other efforts can succeed fully.

Just as crucial, organizations must put a system in place at the outset of the initiative to measure the program's success and be prepared to make course corrections as necessary. As with other business goals, such as safety and customer service, being able to track behavioral changes in line with expected standards of conduct is vital. HR should establish up-front what factors it will track to indicate success of the project, for example:

- A diminution of external charges of discrimination;

- An increase in use of internal systems for registering complaints about inappropriate workplace conduct;

- An increase in the number of issues that are resolved internally; and

- Changes in employee perceptions regarding the organization's culture (as revealed through surveys, etc.).

Because these factors must be tied to the overall strategic objectives, measurement provides HR professionals with real data to communicate business-linked results and support resource allocation for future initiatives.

Partnering for Success

HR is in a unique position, with opportunities for building partnerships throughout the organization. By developing managers and employees to understand and fulfill their responsibilities, HR can create a workforce that works collaboratively to meet the values and expectations set out by the leadership. Additionally, HR should seek out allies in the leadership ranks—credible, respected leaders who can play a part in laying the foundation for success. Specifically, these leaders will have several characteristics in common:

- They are able to express their commitment to workplace initiatives in simple, understandable language and as forcefully as they do with any other serious business initiative;

- They do so in a variety of company communications, including annual reports, periodic memos, postings, emails, and public meetings;

- They clearly outline specific standards and expectations, the responsibilities of all members of the organization to meet those standards, and that the ability to meet those standards will be a factor of individual performance; and

- They secure and allocate resources to communicate their messages throughout the organization.

Several years ago I worked with a power company that was trying to encourage its employees to be more willing to file complaints within the organization rather than outside of it. The steps this organization followed can be an example to many other organizations striving to improve communication and employee ownership in the task of building a proper workplace. The company made a commitment to welcome all complaints and it communicated this commitment to everyone. HR provided clear instruction about how to raise complaints to every manager and employee within the company. Everyone was told what the standards were, employees were involved in changing the culture, and they were trained on the company message, why it was important, and how they were expected to support it. As a result, both managers and employees understood their roles and responsibilities, and, over time, complaints that would previously have been filed with outside agencies were brought up within the organization. The company also correctly recognized the necessity of training employees as well as management about the specific, individual responsibilities everyone had as corporate citizens.

Contrast the above example with the case of a large national retailer that chose to have a company attorney deliver training only to senior executives, based on an assumption that this would be sufficient to satisfy legal compliance and minimize risk. In essence, a decision was made to protect a small group of executives from potential liability rather than communicate a standard of behavior or corporate citizenship throughout the organization. Not surprisingly, the retailer has had a number of highly publicized issues arise involving practices at the field level where the bulk of daily decisions are made. Insulating a small group of executives was not effective in keeping them out of the news and protecting the workplace environment.

The Long-Range View

Firms successful in building longlasting values are consistently reevaluating their efforts and looking for new and different ways to achieve their goals. One company, recently named the top learning organization in the country for its commitment to employee development, is continually thinking ahead to the "next phase." Its leaders recognize that a one-shot training event or series of activities is not sufficient to meet their vision and business mission. They have implemented long-term, integrated learning solutions that reinforce key concepts and keep a consistent theme and message in front of their employees. Additionally, every few years they have set aside a day to shut down facilities and focus everyone on workplace environment issues. To their employees, the leadership has a clear vision and an obvious commitment to addressing these issues.

When I encounter organizations that have experienced problems with litigation, damage to reputation, high turnover rates, and other human resource concerns, they usually have a lot in common. They all have policies and lofty mission and values statements incorporated into annual reports and other public documents. But many have failed to back up their visions with action. They've trained selectively and focused on minimizing legal risk rather than on their objective to change behaviors. Their leaders have failed to make human resource issues part of their business agenda and scorecards.

Building a proper work environment is a process, and an ongoing one at that. But it doesn't require exploring emotional issues or changing employees' lifelong attitudes and beliefs. It requires a commitment to changing behavior at work. Organizations that have put this commitment into practice have recognized the business outcomes it brings. With the right approach, right tools, right partners, and right actions, HR professionals can make great strides toward building a civil, legal, and productive workplace that fosters excellence, diversity, and bottom-line results.

Stephen M. Paskoff, *Esq., is founder and president of ELI, a leading provider of integrated learning solutions that assist organizations in changing workplace behaviors, communicating standards of conduct, and building legal, ethical cultures. Prior to establishing ELI, Paskoff was a partner in a management law firm and an EEOC trial attorney. A graduate of Hamilton University and the University of Pittsburgh School of Law, he is a member of the Georgia and Pennsylvania bars.*

Doing It Right the First Time:
Orientation and Community Building

Rick Rocchetti

Summary

Individual hiring managers, new employees, and the unit benefit from being intentional about the orientation process and having a systematic way of going about the process. This article outlines the process of orientation, notes some of the benefits of having an intentional process, and applies the model to a recent hiring situation. The author integrates several models and many ideas that have resulted in making the joining up process faster and more effective.

I'm in a battle. I'm out to change the way organizations orient new employees. I have a belief (and some experience) that demonstrates that we in organizations do not do beginnings well and that it is hurting our overall effectiveness and performance. A way we might change this outcome is to be more intentional about employee orientation and have a way of thinking about the process that works for the new hire, manager, HR, and the organization.

By not being intentional about the joining up process, we:

- *Create needless inefficiency.* A new employee is in a new land. He or she needs to be oriented so that he or she can find his or her way in the organization/community. If someone does not know the vision, expectations, and so forth, it causes needless chaos, conflict, and confusion when what is needed is clarity, alignment, and focused energy.

- *Create disillusionment unnecessarily.* Lack of attention to the process tells the new hire how he or she will be treated throughout his or her career. It creates a demotivating environment very early in employment and one that is difficult from which to recover. It is a short-term response to a long-term question. The question is around survivability and sustainability. How are they attained and maintained?

- *Create rework.* When confronted with a lack of information and support, people fill in the gap with their own information, make assumptions, and commit behaviors that may cause problems with the new hire or the system.

- *Provide inadequate stewardship.* As a business owner and as a mid-level manager (3,800 employees) in an organization with extremely limited resources, I understand the impact of lack of intentionality and not having something under process. Not dealing with this issue costs money—directly and indirectly.

- *Create a recipe for failure.* It is potentially a recipe for creating a credibility issue for you, the new hire, and/or your unit. Low or no credibility will most probably lead to performance problems and separation.

I want to share how I think about orientation. I want to share what models, theories, and experience inform my thinking. I also want to share what an orientation process might look like in your unit by sharing what it looks like in the unit I lead. Before I move in that direction, here are a few of my assumptions:

- I think of organizations as communities. I have rights, duties, and obligations to fulfill within the context of the community.

- Different parts of the orientation process require different emphases, depending on the situation.

- The orientation process needs to have some boundaries, such as goals, outcomes, objectives, and a timeframe, so that it will be efficient, effective, and timely. Intentionality is a key part of the process. So is choice—mine, the new employee's, and the team's unit.

- The process needs to take into consideration the whole system at various levels.

- I want to co-create this process with the new hire and the unit.

- While I present the orientation process as having discrete steps (which it does), there is much overlap.

- The orientation process is a process, not a one-time event. Conversations will need to be held more than once in order to fully complete the process.

Desired Outcomes

When I think about bringing someone in, the first question I ask is: What is the outcome I am looking for in the orientation process? It has to meet my needs, the new hire's needs, and the needs of the unit/organization. Specifically, those needs are

- Know and understand why he or she is there, that is, purpose;

- Have a sense of group identity/a sense of belonging;

- Have trust in his or her competence and the competence of group members;

- Feel safe enough to make a contribution;

- Have a clear sense of the mission, goals, objectives, and expectations;

- Understand the community's culture and its way of being in the world (how we make our contribution);

- Understand his or her role and the way his or her contribution is to be made; and

- Have some clarity about the vision that the unit is pursuing and its priorities.

By achieving these outcomes, the new hire has a better opportunity to be successful. For the unit/organization, it sets the stage for the long-term success of the enterprise. It is about setting the proper infrastructure in place now so that the long-term issues of survivability and sustainability are better enabled at the individual, group, and organizational levels. It is about shortening the distance between low productivity and satisfaction and higher levels of productivity and satisfaction. It is an example of what Charlotte Roberts (Senge, Kleiner, Roberts, Ross, Roth, & Smith, 1999) calls "conscious oversight." Conscious oversight is a discipline of organizational stewardship that examines how to create communities of "care and nurturing for people and systems with an eye toward generational impact" (Senge, Kleiner, Roberts, Ross, Roth, & Smith, 1999, p. 545). The orientation process is part of this community-creating process and, for me, sets the context for entering into an organization and being prepared to contribute.

The Process

A helpful way to think about the orientation is thinking about group formation or team building. One team-building model I find helpful is the Team Performance Model by Allan Drexler, David Sibbet, and Russ Forrester (Reddy & Jamison, 1988). The model addresses the concerns/goals of the process of integrating into a community or team. We'll explore the first four stages of the model—orientation, trust building, goal clarification, and commitment—as a way to think about the orientation process. The model identifies major issues that need resolution at each stage of team development. If those issues are resolved, the person is ready to move to the next stage. If they are not resolved, or not resolved well, the person/team is essentially stuck and must get some sort of response to the issues of the stage to be or remain effective.

Orientation

In the *orientation* stage, the employee must deal with the questions around purpose, identity, group membership, and acceptance. This stage essentially deals with the question of why. Why is the department here? Why is the unit or team here? Why am I here? And what is expected? What are we to contribute, and can I? Do I even really want to contribute? Is this really worth my time, effort, and commitment? The anxiety present must be dealt with if the employee is to be effective. The question for the hiring manager is how to set the stage for these conversations to take place, with depth, early in the career of a new employee.

When a new hire is made, new possibility is introduced into the organization. What is the possibility that this person demonstrates, even if only vaguely to him- or herself and the organization? What is the difference that this person will make? What is the significance of this person in this team/unit? Part of the role of the hiring manager in this phase is to create the space for the seeds of that possibility to be sown.

Trust Building

In the *trust building* stage, the initial concerns of orientation give way to other people the new hire interacts with. Questions here involve issues of trust in competence and connection. This, according to the Team Performance Model, is a function of inter-dependencies. How much does the new hire have to work with this person or group? How competent is he or she in relating to the task? Does he or she have the knowledge, skills, and abilities for the work and is he or she committed? It is my responsibility to set the stage and create the space for the appropriate people to have a chance to get to know one another and share their competence with one another.

There is a dual purpose for this. First, I want to establish for the new employee that he or she is working with competent people (and vice-versa) and, secondly, I want to create the space for the entire group to display its true character to one another, so that trust can be built on the level of competence that "I trust you are competent to do what you say you can do" and then to build on the level of trust as "connection." Other words for this aspect of trust are affection/openness (Will Schutz, 1958). My role here is to create a place where people can share and disclose with one another in order to build the relationships that they need in order to do their own work and the work of the organization. This involves making the space safe enough for people to take risks. It also means helping the new hire understand when this may not be possible.

Related to this stage is Peter Koestenbaum's (2002) Leadership Diamond-*Reality*. In Koestenbaum's model, at a pragmatic level, reality means paying attention to detail. I want to ensure that the new hire is grounded in the realities of the job, the team, the unit, the department, and so forth. This would include a basic view of the culture, of "how we do things around here."

Another aspect of the Leadership Diamond—*Ethics*—comes into play. To Koestenbaum, ethics means service: "It's an attitude of love and compassion, of caring, of including people, of valuing them, of hearing them, of suffering when they suffer, and of being proud when they succeed" (2002, p. 107). Again, at a pragmatic level, this means that I want to see how much of a team player this person will be, how he or she views group membership, and how this person interacts with key people that he or she will depend on in the future.

Goal Clarification

In the *goal clarification* phase, my role as a hiring manager is to help the new employee understand the vision of the unit and the specific goals for the year. This phase really helps to underscore and clarify the real work of the work group. It's here that the employee decides whether or not to commit his or her full energy to the task/work of the group. Is this compelling enough/challenging enough? Is he or she able and willing to commit to this work? It is also at this stage that assumptions can be surfaced about the vision, goals, methods, and so forth so that the employee can more fully contribute to the work of the group. This phase is related to the Leadership Diamond's area of *Vision* or big picture thinking (Koestenbaum, 2002).

Commitment

The last part of joining up, the *commitment* phase, is where the "rubber meets the sky" (Block, 2002). This is where all of the other phases come together or not. It is a difficult phase because choices have to be made about how the work will be done, how resources will be allocated, what work will get done, and in what order. Just as important, this phase is about the work that will not be done. Difficult choices have to be made. If the work of the previous phases has been done well, a new employee will want to get on with the work and be able to do so. This will be possible because he or she has clarity about the vision, mission, goals, and objectives as well as clarity about his or her role in the process. If the work of the previous phases has not been done well, dependence and resistance will result and the work of the previous phases will need to be revisited. Additionally, from the Leadership Diamond perspective, *courage,* or sustained initiative, will be more difficult (Koestenbaum, 2002).

Application

We had a recent experience applying the model at work. I provide some examples of what we did at each stage, where we are now, and how well we did.

The context for this example is that another manager and I were hiring an external applicant for a position that had a dual reporting relationship. After the offer had been accepted, here is what we did.

Pre-Hire Date Meetings

We (both mangers) met several times to review and agree on what we wanted individually and collectively from each other and from the new employee. The title for this position was "Employee Relations Training Specialist" for a municipal government. This position was above entry level and at a professional level. We agreed on what the organization needed from this position and what we each needed from this position. We discussed potential areas of conflict and how we would resolve them. We discussed and agreed on the process of joining up that we were going to use. We agreed on roles and separated duties.

Orientation Phase

We set up weekly meetings that extended over an eight-week period. We also had several unscheduled "meetings" where we would check in and see how the new employee was doing. After a couple of months, we moved to a more informal meeting schedule. Specific activities included:

- Setting ground rules for how we were to interact with one another;

- Review of why this job was necessary and what we were trying to create;

- Role of local government in general and this one specifically;

- Review of recent organizational needs assessment;

- Review of mutual expectations;

- Review of how these three divisions worked together;

- Going to lunch together;

- Initial assessment of skills and abilities and initial development planning;

- Discussion of potential challenges;

- Asking questions;

- Review of organizational, departmental, and unit philosophies; and

- Presenting employee with organization gear to wear—with logo.

Trust Building

We had established some initial levels of safety by our use of ground rules and by being very intentional about introducing the new employee to others within the organization. The employee relations manager and I met periodically to discuss how we thought we were doing and to make adjustments accordingly. During this stage, we spent time establishing our new hire with the key people she would be interacting with initially. Key activities included:

- Initial briefings about the culture, the history of the organization, etc.;

- Initial briefings about overall mission/vision/goals of the department;

- Initial conversations about specific challenges the new hire would face and how they might be resolved;

- Structured introductions to key people that included sharing backgrounds, values, experiences, and goals;

- Providing time for the new hire to establish relationships with key people;

- Providing low-risk opportunities for the new hire to get out in front of people and interact through facilitating activities in a training session; and

- Asking questions—providing a forum for dialogue.

Goal Clarification

In this stage, we became more formal in our discussions of the missions, visions, and goals of each unit. In the Training Division, we had just created a variation of the Corporate University that included a developmental curriculum. We spent a lot of time identifying assumptions and clarifying specific meanings. On the employee relations side, we made clarifications around the goals of investigations, and so forth. Specific activities included:

- Sharing visions and goals for the year for each unit;

- Discussing progress of new hire in the orientation process;

- Providing opportunities for our new hire to see both managers in action;

- Continued opportunities to apply skills to tasks;

- In-depth analysis of skills needed versus skills demonstrated—development planning;

- Continued role clarification and assigning of more specific duties;

- Providing feedback and adjusting duties accordingly; and

- Asking questions—providing a forum for dialogue.

Commitment

In this stage, we talked about how the new hire would play an active role in achieving the goals for the existing year. Specific activities included:

- Identifying specific projects for which our new hire would be responsible;

- Discussing relative priorities;

- Discussing budget implications and priorities;

- Discussions with increasing depth on divisional strategy;

- Dialogue on how individual values and goals aligned and contributed to organizational values and goals; and

- Discussing limits of decision making.

What Have We Learned from This Process?

We have learned the following:

- The process works.

- Being intentional and having a process helps to get to interdependence quicker.

- Having a certain level of control ensures a higher-quality experience and, ultimately, a more satisfied and productive employee.

- It doesn't happen overnight, but it does happen.

- It's like an investment. The more you invest early, the earlier compounding starts!

- Based on feedback from our new hire and others, the process has been beneficial for us as managers, our new hire, and the organization as a whole.

- It is a continual and ever-deepening process.

References

Block, P. (2002, October 23). Presentation at The Learning Consortium Leadership Conference, Durham, North Carolina.

Koestenbaum, P. (2002). *The philosophic consultant* (pp. 107–328). San Francisco, CA: Pfeiffer.

Reddy, W.B., & Jamison, K. (Eds.). (1988). *Team building: Blueprints for productivity and satisfaction.* Alexandria, VA: NTL Institute/San Francisco, CA: Pfeiffer.

Schutz, W. (1958). *FIRO: A three dimensional theory of interpersonal behavior.* New York: Rinehart.

Senge, P., Kleiner, A., Roberts, C., Ross, R., Roth, G., & Smith, B. (1999). *Dance of change.* New York: Currency Doubleday.

Rick Rocchetti *has consulted to all types of organizations for over twenty years. His expertise is in leadership, systems, strategy, and culture. He has advanced degrees from Fordham University and The American University. He currently directs both the organization development and training and development functions for the City of Raleigh, North Carolina. He also has a consulting/training practice.*

Developing and Using Behaviorally Based Rating Scales:
A Tool for Appraising Human Resources
John Sample

Summary

This article traces the developmental history and utility of an important innovation in assessing employee behavior. Behavioral expectation and observation scales as conceived by Smith and Kendall (1963) and others are discussed in terms of scale development processes, alternative uses in organizations, advantages and limitations of different types of scales, and the problems associated with training raters to use the scales effectively. The review ends with a discussion of frame of reference (FOR) training, a process used to increase accuracy of evaluations.

Effective assessment of performance is necessary to meet Equal Employment Opportunity Commission (EEOC) requirements, which now cover any measurement tool or procedure that impacts any significant personnel decision. Such assessments are viewed as "tests," and they must be job related and valid (Cascio & Aquinis, 2004). However, most appraisal forms and procedures are subjective judgments of various traits that are thought to be important on the job. In *Wade v. Mississippi Cooperative Extension Service* (1976), a U.S. District Court held that such trait-rating systems are often biased and not job related and that there must be (1) a relationship between the appraisal instrument and job/task analysis and (2) evidence that the appraisal instrument is a valid predictor of job performance.

A typical appraisal intervention is some form of goal or objective setting. Goal-oriented approaches have several advantages, one of which is to separate organizational means (resources and activities) from intended ends (outcomes and results). However, such approaches may measure only selective aspects of an individual's total contribution to the organization (Goodale, 1977). A suggested alternative is the collaborative development and routine use of behaviorally based methods that assess job dimensions of competencies not measurable by goal or trait approaches.

This article focuses on one such approach to assessing performance. Behaviorally based rating scales were introduced in the 1960s by Smith and Kendall (1963). According to Katzell and Austin (1992), the outgrowth of the original work by Smith and Kendall (1963) is considered one of the exemplary innovations in industrial-organizational psychology that emerged during the mid-1960s through the mid-1980s. A search of the Social Science Citation Index for the years 1963 through 2004 identified no less than 345 instances in which the Smith and Kendall (1963) article was cited by authors in their publications and research.

Examples of the use of behaviorally based scales in various contexts include the following partial listing: aviation, higher education, child welfare workers and rehabilitation counselors, health care and nursing, local government, hotels, sales personnel, police officers, and the insurance industry.

Specific Applications for Behaviorally Based Assessment Tools

The original focus for behaviorally based scale development was in the employee appraisal arena. It has been almost forty-five years since Douglas McGregor (1957) described his uneasy feeling about performance appraisal. McGregor's concern was that traditional performance-appraisal systems suffer from a lack of behavioral specificity, making it difficult to give meaningful feedback to organizational personnel. Although good performance might lead to promotion, poor performance now might lead to transfer, so that employees' skills are more congruent with their jobs. The use of behaviorally based scales in assessment centers is described by Goodstone and Lopez (2001) and Engelbrecht and Fisher (1995).

Recruitment, Selection, and Supervision

A legally defensible job can be based in part on behaviorally based scales (Cascio & Bernardin, 1981). Such scales aid in the recruitment (Naffziger, 1985), selection, and placement (Maurer, 2002) of human resources. Job descriptions and specifications frequently do not include behavioral expectations. Behavioral specificity enables the manager to more effectively fit the person to the job. Once a person is on the job, socialization (that is, the process of learning the organization's norms and values) can be enhanced with behaviorally based scales. Supervisors can use these types of scales to not only assess employee performance but also as a coaching benchmark to improve performance (Maiorca, 1997). Kearney and Whitaker (1988) advocate the development and use of behaviorally anchored disciplinary scales (BADS) as a tool for managers in the public sector, and the motivational context of jobs has been described using retranslation of anchored scales by Kent and Davis (2002).

Evaluation

Program evaluators can use behavioral-expectation and observation data in their summative and formative reports. Personnel can be evaluated using behaviorally based methods. The behavioral responses of clients and customers to sales and marketing people can be evaluated using behaviorally based scales. Blood (1974) suggests that such scales can be useful in assessing agreement on organizational policy and communication patterns.

Training and Development

Blood (1974) cites a compelling need for the use of BES in the development of training programs in which "the skills to be trained for are specified in term of actual job behaviors rather than simply the name of the skill domain. . . . Trainees in a program based on these materials would learn expected behaviors, and they would learn how their performance is to be evaluated" (p. 514). The American Society for Training and Development competency study by McLagan (1983) provides behavioral anchors for each competency. Dunn (1992) provides case examples from a psychiatric hospital in which assessment and training using BARS were utilized. Michell (1987) describes a process in which managers were involved in training to promote creativity. BARS were used as pre- and post-test measures of creativity enhancement. Leat and Lovell (1997) describe an organizational model and process for needs assessment using behaviorally based scales.

Validation Studies

Data from behaviorally based scales are useful for determining the validity of a number of human resource management functions. These scales can serve as criteria against which to evaluate predictors for selection and promotion decisions (Campbell, Dunnette, Arvey, & Hellervik, 1973). Predictor scores from employee and managerial selection processes can be correlated with job performance criterion based on these types of scales. The scales themselves can be used as predictors of performance improvement in training programs.

Developing BES, BARS, and BOS

The effectiveness of a human resource management and development program can be measured by functional relationships between predictor variables (for example, employment tests, job interviews) and criteria variables (for example, performance ratings, time to reach required performance). In this context, Toops (1944) states that in "making predictions, generally there must be . . . a unitary, general success score, or criterion score for each person" (p. 271). However, not all management decisions involve *prediction.* A manager may wish to *evaluate* the consequences of a particular personnel action or program. According to Cascio and Aquinis (2004), the distinction between predictors and criteria is based on the time the measure is used. If measures such as written or performance tests are administered *prior to* making a decision (that is, to hire, to promote), then the standards are predictors. If measures are administered subsequent to a personnel decision (that is, to evaluate performance effectiveness), then the standards are criteria. Without relevant predictors and criteria, a manager may not be able to generate performance measures that have utility throughout the human resource management cycle (Smith, 1976).

Behavioral expectation scales (BES) and behaviorally anchored rating scales (BARS) differ from behavioral observation scales (BOS) in one major respect: BES and BARS are based on inferred (but not necessarily observed) performance (Smith & Kendall, 1963); BOS are based on actual, observed performance (Latham & Wexley, 1977).

In their original research, Smith and Kendall (1963) bemoaned the existing technology for developing effective performance-rating scales. One of their major concerns was with the proclivity of scale developers, especially psychologists, to impose their own values in scales. A second concern was with the unjustified assumption that scale developers would agree on important characteristics of employees. A third concern was that scales need to have at least face validity for the respondent. Smith and Kendall concluded that:

> "Better ratings can be obtained, in our opinion, not by trying to trick the rater (as in forced-choice scales) but by helping him to rate. We should ask him questions which he can honestly answer about the behaviors which he can observe. We should reassure him that his answers will not by misinterpreted, and we should provide a basis by which he and others can check his answers." (p. 151)

Developing Behavioral Expectation Scales (BES)

The development of behavioral expectation scales (BES) is a sequence of five phases.

Phase I: Development of Performance Dimension

People who are knowledgeable about a specific position (job incumbents, their supervisors, customers or clients, etc.) help to develop performance dimensions for the position. These dimensions define the critical parts of the job. There usually are between five and ten dimensions (Schwab, Hennemann, & DeCotiis, 1975). The development may include an analysis of available job descriptions, a published job/task analysis, and so forth. Performance dimensions usually are generated as a group activity.

Phase II: Development of Critical Incidents

A group of job-knowledgeable persons generates specific examples of job behaviors (effective, average, and ineffective performance). This phase utilizes the critical-incident method developed by Flannagan (1954).

Phase III: Retranslation

A different group of job-knowledgeable people allocates a randomly ordered list of behavioral incidents to the performance dimensions identified in Phase I. This ensures that behavioral incidents are matched correctly to performance dimensions. A behavioral incident is eliminated from further consideration if the raters are not in agreement about which performance dimension it relates to. This process reduces the percentage of acceptable behaviors. The literature suggests from 50 to 80 percent for agreement (Cascio & Aquinis, 2004; Schwab, Hennemann, & Decotiis, 1975; Smith & Kendall, 1963).

Phase IV: Scale Development

Once the critical incidents are assigned to appropriate performance dimensions, a five- or seven-point scale is used to indicate the extent to which each incident represents a specific level of performance (highly effective, moderately effective, or very ineffective). Means and standard deviations are computed for each behavioral item, and items with standard deviations exceeding an arbitrary standard (for example, 1.5 or 1.75) are eliminated from further consideration (Campbell, Dunnette, Arvey, & Hellervik, 1973).

Phase V: Final Scale Development

Smith and Kendall (1963) advocated the construction of a vertical, graphic scale for each performance dimension. Typically, each dimension is supported with six to nine behavioral incidents. Exhibit 1 is an example of a performance dimension with behavioral anchors, using a seven-point scale. The behavioral incidents are concise statements of observable behavior. Smith and Kendall (1963) advocate the editing of all behavioral incidents so that they represent "not actual behavior but inferences or predictions from observations" (p. 150).

The training and development competency study by the American Society for Training and Development (McLagan, 1983) adapted Smith and Kendall's approach for developing behavioral anchors. Thirty-one competencies were identified in the knowledge and skill areas of the training and development field. As least two behavioral anchors were developed for each competency. Table 1 provides examples of basic, intermediate, and advanced behavioral anchors for the competency "adult-learning understanding."

Exhibit 1.   Example of a Behaviorally Anchored Rating Scale for a College Professor

---

7   When a class doesn't understand a certain concept or feels "lost," this professor could be expected to sense it and act to correct the situation.

6   This professor could be expected to answer the students' questions about learning and conditioning without making students feel stupid and without making the students feel that they are "bothering" the professor.

5   When confronted with questions after class, this statistics professor could be expected to stay and talk to the students until the next class must begin.

4   This professor, when a student comes to his office for help, could be expected to go through one explanation of the material and tell the student to read certain chapters of the text and to come back if he still has troubles understanding the material.

3   During lectures, this professor could often be expected to tell students with questions to see him during his office hours.

2   If a student asks this statistics professor to help him with "t-tables" a few days before the final exam, this professor could be expected to say that he has no time because he is very busy composing the exam and to tell the student to ask a TA.

1   This professor could be expected to not see students individually, except during his regularly scheduled office hours.

Based on Harari & Zedick, 1973.

Table 1.   Examples of Behavioral Anchors for a Training Competency

	Sample Behaviors Illustrating Levels of Expertise		
Competency	Basic	Intermediate	Advanced
1. Adult-Learning Understanding Knowing how adults acquire and use knowledge, skills, and attitudes. Understanding individual differences in learning.	When preparing visuals for a presentation, the T&D specialist assures that there are *no more then five to seven* points on each slide. Knowing that support and review are *important after a learning experience*, the T&D specialist implements a series of *follow-up brochures that review key points and application ideas* from a course.	In order to assure that the managers participating in a management development program get the most out of their learning, the T&D specialist develops a half-day module *on how to self-manage the learning process*. The module is designed to be *highly participative* and present the latest findings about *how adults learn*. When asked to develop a career development program, the T&D specialist develops a program that *uses participative methods, learning contracts,* and *continuing learning plans*. A writer preparing a self-study manual for experienced nurses that includes action-planning modules at the end of each section to e*nsure that the nurses have a formal opportunity to relate the theories to their own practices*.	Microcomputer customers complain that the written instructions and information provided by local representatives is too confusing. The learning specialist reviews the manuals, interviews customers, and observes local representatives. He or she then *develops a workshop entitled "How to teach adults about microcomputers,"* complete with a set of job aids for interpreting the manuals. The course is presented to all company representatives. A T&D specialist, interested in exploring the applications of a broad range of learning theories to the training and development field, invites *ten leading learning theorists* to be featured at a one-day colloquium. The T&D specialist *identifies the issues to be addressed and moderates and provides commentary on discussions during the meeting*.

Source: McLagan, 1983, p. 5.

Table 2.   Example of Behavioral Observation Scale

Behavioral Items	Never (0–19%)	Seldom (20–39%)	Sometimes (40–59%)	Generally (60–79%)	Always (80–100%)
Dimension: Planning, Organizing, and Scheduling Program Activities					
1. Develops a comprehensive program plan and documents it well.	1	2	3	4	5
2. Obtains required approval and distributes plan to all concerned.	1	2	3	4	5
3. Regularly assesses performance of staff in relation to work plans.	1	2	3	4	5

Developing Behavioral Observation Scales (BOS)

The procedures for developing behavioral observation scales (BOS) are similar to those for developing BES. The researcher meets with persons who are knowledgeable about the job position. Flannagan's (1954) critical-incident method is used to generate behavioral examples of work performance. Care is taken by the researcher to help participants avoid describing traits or attributes. Dunnette (1976) reports that fourteen or fifteen participants can produce between two hundred and three hundred behavioral differences during several sessions. In successive sessions, the behavioral incidents are edited and classified into performance dimensions, and incidents that describe essentially the same dimension are grouped into one performance dimension (Latham & Wexley, 1977). A five-point Likert scale is developed for each behavioral item, and the rater records the frequency with which the employee was observed demonstrating the indicated behavior. Several performance dimensions and their accompanying behavioral items compose a behavioral observation scale (BOS) (see the example in Table 2). Individual scores are determined by summing the raters' responses to all the behavioral items.

BES, BARS, and BOS: Advantages and Disadvantages

It has been over forty years since Smith and Kendall (1963) first described the developmental procedures for behavioral expectation scales (BES), and the literature from organizational and industrial psychology still reports the attractiveness of BES and BOS formats. The apparent advantages of BES and BOS are significant and are as follows:

- The developmental procedures directly involve those who are most affected by a performance-measured system—those being rated and those who perform as raters. According to Campbell, Dunnette, Arvey, & Hellervik (1973), the development of BES for store managers was a valuable learning experience because they "seldom, if ever, give careful attention to what they really mean by effective performance" (p. 22). Studies by Burgar (1978), Friedman and Cornelius (1976), and Warmke and Billings (1979) strongly support participation in as many phases of scale development as possible.

- Behavioral scales provide the rater with performance dimensions and behavioral items that are specific and nonambiguous (Fogli, Hulin, & Blood, 1971). Because the behavioral items are written in the language of the user, they are less subject to misinterpretation (Smith & Kendall, 1963). Behavioral scales, when developed properly, are content valid and job related (Goodale, 1977; Latham, Farr, & Saari, 1979).

- Research on the psychometric properties of BES suggests that they have demonstrated medium to high reliability (Burnaska & Hollman, 1974; Smith & Kendall, 1963). In at least one study, BES correlated highly with objective performance measures (Cascio & Valenzi, 1978). BES appear to possess adequate convergent validity but have questionable discriminate validity (Campbell, Dunnette, Arvey, & Hellervik, 1973; Zedeck & Baker, 1972). Field tests indicate that BES are superior to typical, graphic rating scales (in terms of reliability, validity, and freedom from halo and leniency error) (Borman & Vallon, 1974; Campbell, Dunnette, Arvey, & Hellervick, 1973).

Several apparent disadvantages also are worth mentioning. According to several sources, BES are not clearly superior to other, more traditionally, and more easily developed rating formats (Atkin & Conlon, 1978; Bernardin & Beatty, 1984).

- BES and BOS assess only behavior. Individual contributions to program or agency goals are better assessed by means of a goal-setting system, such as management by objectives (MBO). A comprehensive management plan could include an integrated BES and MBO system (Baird, Beatty, & Schneier, 1982.

- The development of BES is costly and time-consuming. The development of BES for college-instructor performance generally requires many hours of participant time (to create and scale incident descriptions) and as many as eighty hours of professional and clerical time (for editing, questionnaire development, data tabulation, statistical analysis, and final construction). Two shortcut methods for BES development are discussed by Green, Sauser, Fagg, and

Champion (1981) and, according to those researchers, the alternative methods do not significantly jeopardize the quality of behavioral-item development.

- The developmental procedures for BES create item wastefulness. According to DeCotiis (1977), current BARS scaling procedures "inevitably result in the rejection of a large percentage of the behavioral item pool" (p. 684). The development of behavioral observation scales (BOS) eliminates this problem by using more of the item pool (Latham & Wexley, 1977). A significant disadvantage with BES and BOS is that the rater must attempt to recall employee behavior over a six- to twelve-month rating period. If the rater does not make systematic observations at consistent intervals over time, he or she is inviting "virtually every type of rating error possible" (Bernardin & Smith, 1981, p. 463).

Some of the problems associated with behavioral expectations sales (BES) can be overcome with the development of behavioral observation scales (BOS). As has been discussed earlier, a BES is a vertical, graphic, rating scale (see Exhibit 1), with the behavioral scales being a seven-point continuum. The rater reviews the performance dimensions (for example, "planning and organizing," "interpersonal relations") and behavioral anchors for each dimension. The rater then checks the behavioral anchor that best describes what the employee could be expected to demonstrate. According to Latham and Wexley (1977), "A potential problem is that the behaviors that the manager has seen the employees demonstrate may not resemble the specific anchors on any of the scales. Thus the manager is required to extrapolate from observed behaviors those that could be 'expected' as defined by the scale anchors" (p. 267).

The BOS format utilizes a five-point scale for each behavioral anchor (see Table 2), and the rater indicates the frequency with which the behavior was observed. Thus, only observed behaviors are rated, and the rater is not required to infer or extrapolate actual behaviors. An additional advantage of BOS is that the final scale utilizes more behavioral items than does the BES format. In at least one study, BOS were rated by users as more practical than BES (Fay & Latham, 1982).

Taming the Beast of Rating Errors

Academicians and practitioners alike for years have been obsessed with taming the beast of rating errors (Ronan & Prien, 1971). Errors associated with idiosyncratic rating effects include leniency, strictness, halo, central tendency, regency of events, and range restriction. Leniency, as pointed out by Bass (1956), is especially problematic.

Understanding the source of idiosyncratic rating behaviors is reinforced by Smith (1976, p. 757) with the astute observation that "human judgment enters into every criterion from productivity to salary increases." The initial conclusion one could reasonably make based on the empirical and applied research is that it is less the type of rating scale used than it is that the rater receive training to reduce errors (Fay & Latham, 1982).

The traditional approach for reducing specific rating errors has been to provide training. Overcoming problems associated with certain types of errors and their effects and with accuracy of observations of performance is the goal of rater training programs. Cascio and Aquinis (2004) assert that the first step in the design of *any* training program is to specify objectives.

In the context of rater training there are three broad objectives: (1) to reduce or eliminate judgmental biases; (2) to improve the observational skills of raters by teaching them *what* to attend to; and (3) to improve the ability of raters to communicate appraisal information in an objective, constructive manner with ratees (Cascio & Aquinis, 2004).

Several creditable studies demonstrate that training reduces rating distribution errors (Borman, 1975; Ivancevich, 1979). Bernardin and Pence (1980) designed workshops to reduce the most common rating errors. Emphasis was on increasing skill to observe, record, and assess performance. Unfortunately, the decay rate for maintenance of skills after training has been shown to be quite short, as quickly as one rating period (Bernardin, 1979) and at six and twelve months (Ivancevich, 1979). Successes with rater training are offset with examples from the literature in which rater training was not successful (Sauser & Pound, 1979). Consistent with assertions by Bernardin and Buckley (1981) and Borman (1975), rater error training was likely to result in less accuracy and increased leniency.

The essence of these types of rater training programs is to change the response set of the raters (the tendency to commit idiosyncratic errors of observation) (Bernardin & Buckley, 1981). The unintended consequence of the message to raters could be "you need to avoid excessively high ratings" and the training results in a new response set of highly correlated job dimensions. Instead of being lenient, the raters are now stricter. We end up trading one effect error for another effect error.

According to Borman (1979), changing response sets is fairly straightforward; however, getting raters to be more accurate in their observations is more difficult. The issue here is that changing the response set through training impacts accuracy of the reported observations. Bernardin and Pence (1980) believe that emphasis "should be placed more on training raters to observe behavior more accurately and fairly than on providing illustrations of how to or not to rate" (p. 65). As an aid to increasing accuracy, Bernardin and Buckley (1981) suggest that raters increase observational skills through diary keeping of observations, providing a common frame of reference for raters in which they learn to be critical observers.

Frame of Reference Training

The most promising training intervention to date for improving rater accuracy is frame of reference training (FOR). The overall purpose of FOR training is to remove idiosyncratic standards used by raters who are instructed to use a "common frame of reference" for making ratings. The intent of this approach is to align individual perceptions and cognitions to be congruent with the norms, culture, expectations, and context of the organization. The design of instruction consists of the following components: (1) making important dimensions of the job visible and illustrating the dimensions with observable behaviors; (2) discussing levels of each dimension in terms of observable behaviors; (3) providing practice using the new frame of reference; and (4) providing feedback on the accuracy of the rating (Bernardin & Buckley, 1981; Pulakos, 1986; Schleicher, Day, Mayes, & Riggio, 2002; Sulsky & Day, 1992). Frame of reference training differs from previous attempts to improve rater effectiveness. This approach focuses on the multiple dimensions of the job and determining accuracy of ratings, whereas earlier attempts focused on reducing rating errors.

Significant support for frame of reference training is reported in the literature. Woehr and Huffcutt (1994) developed a meta-analysis model of rater training methods that includes four general categories: (1) rater error training; (2) performance dimension training; (3) frame of reference training; and (4) behavioral observation training. Dependent variables identified for the study were halo error, leniency error, rating error, rating accuracy, and observational accuracy. A meta-analysis of these variables resulted in a conclusion by Woehr and Huffcutt (1994) that "frame of reference training appears to be the most effective single training strategy with respect to increasing rating accuracy" (p. 198). This research determined an average effect size of .83 in favor of FOR training compared to control or no training groups. Studies supporting the effectiveness of FOR training include Cardy and Keefe (1994) and Woehr (1994).

Given that FOR training is generally supported by empirical and applied research, the questions are "How does it work, why does it work, and for what specific purpose?" (Campbell, 1989, p. 484). The underlying theory supporting FOR training is based in social learning theory (Bandura, 1977), in which ways are created to strengthen "expectations of personal efficacy [with] the conviction that one can successfully execute a behavior in order to produce a certain outcome" (Bernardin & Buckley, 1981, p. 209).

The underlying tenets supporting FOR training are based in cognitive psychology, more specifically schema, impression, and information processing theories (Cardy & Keefe, 1994; Woehr, 1994). A basic operating premise is that raters forget specific information over time (Feldman, 1986) and that absence of specific performance dimensions learned prior to observation of performance results in bias of recall. More specifically, if managers do not have a specific theory of performance *to call on* when recall of performance is required, then they will likely rely on a single "global" impression of the employee being evaluated (Woehr, 1992). In this context, a theory of performance is an articulated expectation developed and shared within an organization and is codified as dimensions of job performance (Sulsky & Day, 1994). Furthermore, according to Woehr (1992, 1994), research suggests that managers make judgments as the behavior occurs rather than at a time later when recall requires an evaluation of performance (that is, performance appraisal at a later date). These idiosyncratic judgments lie fallow until recalled as global impressions, thus introducing bias into the recall of observed behavior. Absent a theory of performance that includes an understanding of levels of performance within each dimension, it is likely that judgments formed at the time of observation will result in recall of global impressions.

Frame of reference training is designed to provide job dimensions as role schema or prototypical categories that enable the rater to more accurately match observed behaviors with levels within multiple job dimensions, more specifically the organization's theory of performance (Sulsky & Day, 1992). These cognitive knowledge structures are learned and stored in long-term memory. Frame of reference training requires that raters learn the job in question and understand the multiple dimensions of the job and levels within each dimension. This shared understanding by raters in FOR training has demonstrated improvements in accuracy of recall (Woehr & Huffcutt, 1994).

Summary

Several factors should be considered when using behaviorally based scales in a performance-appraisal system. Human resource management (from recruitment to termination) must rely on timely and accurate performance information.

Performance appraisal affects not only the person being appraised; it also should encourage each manager to provide feedback that is behaviorally specific, consistent, and thorough. The critical-incident method is useful for monitoring performance on a regular basis.

The appraisal process is one of many ways in which employees are socialized into the organization's culture. Rating error (for example, consistent leniency or harshness; prejudice regarding race, sex, or age; the tendency to rate everyone "average") indicates an unhealthy organizational culture.

No performance-appraisal system is perfect or without tradeoffs. BARS assess only behavior. Individual contributions to organizational results may be better assessed through some form of goal setting such as management objectives. A comprehensive organization development intervention could include an integrated BARS and MBO system.

The effects of poor rater training can be offset with frame of reference training. This approach appears to avoid the early issues associated with rater training and has strong empirical support.

The development of behaviorally based scales may be time-consuming; however, such scales provide a relevant and legally job-related, performance-assessment system that is consistent with the assumptions and objectives of human resource management and development.

References

Atkin, R.S., & Conlon, E.J. (1978). Behaviorally anchored rating scales: Some theoretical issues. *Academy of Management Review, 3,* 119–128.

Baird, L.S., Beatty, R.W., & Schneier, C.E. (1982). *The performance appraisal sourcebook.* Amherst, MA: Human Resource Development Press.

Bandura, A. (1977). *Social-learning theory.* Englewood Cliffs, NJ: Prentice-Hall.

Bass, B.M. (1956). Reducing leniency in merit ratings. *Personnel Psychology, 9,* 359–369.

Bernardin, H.J. (1979). The predictability of discrepancy measures of role constructs. *Personnel Psychology, 32,* 139–153.

Bernardin, H.J., & Beatty, R.W. (1984). *Performance appraisal: Assessing human behavior at work.* Boston, MA: Kent.

Bernardin, H.J., & Buckley, M.R. (1981). Strategies in rater training. *The Academy of Management Review, 6,* 205–212.

Bernardin, H.J., & Pence, E.C. (1980). The effects of rater training: Creating new response sets and decreasing accuracy. *Journal of Applied Psychology, 65,* 60–66.

Bernardin, H.J., & Smith, P.C. (1981). A clarification of some issues regarding the development and use of behaviorally anchored rating scales (BARS). *Journal of Applied Psychology, 66*(4), 458–463.

Blood, M.R. (1974). Spin-offs from behavioral expectation scale procedures. *Journal of Applied Psychology, 59,* 513–515.

Borman, W.C. (1975). Effects of instructions to avoid halo error on reliability and validity of performance evaluation ratings. *Journal of Applied Psychology, 60,* 556–560.

Borman, W.C. (1979). Format and training effects on rating accuracy and rating errors. *Journal of Applied Psychology, 64,* 410–421.

Borman, W.C., & Vallon, W.R. (1974). A view of what can happen when behavioral expectation scales are developed in one setting and used in another. *Journal of Applied Psychology, 59,* 197–201.

Burgar, P.S. (1978). Have behavioral expectation scales fulfilled our expectations? A theoretical and empirical review. *JSAS Catalog of Selected Documents in Psychology, 8,* 75–76 (Ms. NO 1745.).

Burnaska, R.G., & Hollman, T.D. (1974). An empirical comparison of the relative effects of rater response biases on three rating scale formats. *Journal of Applied Psychology, 59,* 307–312.

Campbell, J.P. (1989). The agenda for theory and research. In I.L. Goldstein & Associates (Eds.), *Training and development in organizations* (pp. 469–486). San Francisco, CA: Jossey-Bass.

Campbell, J.P., Dunnette, M.D., Arvey, R.D., & Hellervik, L.V. (1973). The development and evaluation of behaviorally based rating scales. *Journal of Applied Psychology, 57,* 15–22.

Cardy, R.L., & Keefe, T.J. (1994). Observational purpose and evaluative articulation in frame-of-reference training: The effects of alternative processing modes on rating accuracy. *Organizational Behavior and Human Decision Processes, 57,* 338–357.

Cascio, W.F., & Aquinis, H. (2004). *Applied psychology in human resource management* (6th ed.). Upper Saddle River, NJ: Prentice-Hall.

Cascio, W.F., & Bernardin, H.J. (1981). Implications of performance appraisal litigation for personnel decisions. *Personnel Psychology, 34,* 211–226.

Cascio, W.F., & Valenzi, E.R. (1978). Relations among criteria of police officers. *Journal of Applied Psychology, 63*(1), 22–28.

DeCotiis, T.A. (1977). An analysis of the external validity and applied relevance of three rating formats. *Organizational Behavior and Human Performance, 19,* 247–266.

Dunn, D.M. (1992). Assessing and training at work. *Health Manpower Management, 18*(3), 7–15.

Dunnette, M.D. (1976). Aptitudes, abilities and skills. In M.D. Dunnette (Ed.), *Handbook of industrial and organizational psychology.* Chicago, IL: Rand-McNally.

Engelbrecht, A.S., & Fischer, H. (1995). The managerial performance implications of a developmental assessment center approach. *Human Relations, 48*(4), 387–404.

Fay, C.H., & Latham, G.P. (1982). Effects of training and rating scales on training errors. *Personnel Psychology, 35,* 105–116.

Feldman, J.M. (1986). Instrumentation and training for performance appraisal: A perceptual-cognitive viewpoint. *Research in Personnel and Human Resources Management, 4,* 45–99.

Flannagan, J.C. (1954). The critical incident technique. *Psychological Bulletin, 51,* 327–358.

Fogli, L., Hulin, C.L., & Blood, M.R. (1971). Development of first level behavioral job criteria. *Journal of Applied Psychology, 55,* 3–8.

Friedman, B.A., & Cornelius, E. T. (1976). The effect of rater participation in scale construction of the psychometric characteristics of two rating scale formats. *Journal of Applied Psychology, 61,* 212–216.

Goodale, J.G. (1977). Behaviorally based rating scales: Toward an integrated approach to performance appraisal. In W.C. Hammer & F.L. Schmidt (Eds.), *Contemporary problems in personnel* (rev. ed.). New York: John Wiley & Sons.

Goodstone, M.S., & Lopez, F.N. (2001). The frame of reference approach as a solution to an assessment center dilemma. *Consulting Psychology Journal: Practice and Research, 53*(2), 96–107.

Green, S.B., Sauser, W.I., Fagg, J.N., & Champion, C.H. (1981). Shortcut methods or delivering behaviorally anchored rating scales. *Educational and Psychological Measurement, 41,* 761–765.

Harari, O., & Zedeck, S. (1973). Development of behaviorally anchored rating scales for the evaluation of faculty teaching. *Journal of Applied Psychology, 59,* 764–766.

Ivancevich, J.M. (1979). A longitudinal study of the effects of rater training on psychometric errors in ratings. *Journal of Applied Psychology, 64,* 502–508.

Katzell, R.A., & Austin, J.T. (1992). From then to now: The development of industrial-organizational psychology in the United States. *Journal of Applied Psychology, 77*(6), 803–835.

Kearney, R.C., & Whitaker, F. (1988). Behaviorally anchored disciplinary scales (BADS): A new approach to discipline. *Public Personnel Management, 17*(3), 341–351.

Kent, T.W., & Davis, T.J. (2002). Using retranslation to develop operationally anchored scales to assess the motivational context of jobs. *International Journal of Management, 19*(1), 10–17.

Latham, G.P., Farr, J.L., & Saari, L.M. (1979). The development of behavioral observation scales for appraising the performance of foreman. *Personnel Psychology, 32,* 299–311.

Latham, G.P., & Wexley, K.N. (1977). Behavioral observation scales for performance appraisal purposes. *Personnel Psychology, 30,* 255–268.

Leat, M.J., & Lovell, M.J. (1997). Training needs analysis: Weaknesses in the conventional approach. *Journal of European Industrial Training, 21*(4), 143–153.

Maiorca, J. (1997). How to construct behaviorally anchored rating scales (BARS) for employee evaluations. *SuperVision, 58*(8), 15–18.

Maurer, S. (2002). A practitioner-based analysis of interviewer job expertise and scale format as contextual factors in situational interviews. *Personnel Psychology, 55*(2), 307–327.

McGregor, D. (1957). An uneasy look at performance appraisal. *Harvard Business Review, 35,* 89–94.

McLagan, P.A. (1983). *Models for excellence.* Alexandria, VA: American Society for Training and Development.

Michell, P.C. (1987). Creativity training: Developing the agency-client creative interface. *European Journal of Marketing, 21*(7), 44–57.

Naffziger, D.W. (1985). BARS, RJPs and recruiting. *Personnel Administrator, 38*(8), 85–96.

Pulakos, E.D. (1986). The development of training programs to increase accuracy with different rating tasks. *Organizational Behavior and Human Decision Processes, 38,* 76–91.

Ronan, W.W., & Prien, E.P. (1971). *Perspectives on the measurement of human performance.* New York: Appleton-Century Crofts.

Sauser, W.I., & Pound, S.B. (1979). *Effects of rater training and participation on cognitive complexity: An exploration of Schneier's cognitive reinterpretation.* Paper presented at the annual meeting of the Southeastern Psychological Association, New Orleans.

Schleicher, D.J., Day, D.V., Mayes, B.T., & Riggio, R.E. (2002). A new frame for frame-of-reference training: Enhancing the construct validity of assessment centers. *Journal of Applied Psychology, 87*(4), 735–746.

Schwab, D.P., Hennemann, H.G., & Decotiis, T. (1975). Behaviorally anchored rating scales: A review of the literature. *Personnel Psychology, 28,* 559–562.

Smith, P.C. (1976). Behaviors, results, and organizational effectiveness: The problem of criteria. In M.D. Dunnette (Ed.), *Handbook of industrial and organizational psychology.* Chicago, IL: Rand-McNally.

Smith, P.C., & Kendall, L.M. (1963). Retranslation of expectations: An approach to the construction of unambiguous anchors for rating scales. *Journal of Applied Psychology, 47,* 149–155.

Sulsky, L.M., & Day, D.V. (1992). Frame of reference training and cognitive categorization: An empirical investigation of rater memory issues. *Journal of Applied Psychology, 77,* 501–510.

Sulsky, L.M., & Day, D.V. (1994). Effects of frame-of-reference training on rater accuracy under alternative time delays. *Journal of Applied Psychology, 79,* 535–543.

Toops, H.A. (1944). The criterion. *Educational and Psychological Measurement, 4,* 271–297.

Wade v. Mississippi Cooperative Extension Service, 528 F2nd 508 (5th Cir. 1976).

Warmke, D.L., & Billings, R.S. (1979). A recomparison of training methods for altering the psychometric properties of experiential and administrative performance ratings. *Journal of Applied Psychology, 64,* 124–131.

Woehr, D.J. (1992). Performance dimension accessibility: Implications for rating accuracy. *Journal of Organizational Behavior, 13*(4), 357–367.

Woehr, D.J. (1994). Understanding frame-of-reference training: The impact of training on the recall of performance information. *Journal of Applied Psychology, 79*(4), 525–534.

Woehr, D.J., & Huffcutt, A.I. (1994). Understanding frame of reference training: The impact of training on the recall performance of performance information. *Journal of Applied Psychology, 67*(3), 189–206.

Zedeck, S., & Baker, H.T. (1972). Nursing performance as measured by a behavioral expectation scale: A multitrait-multirater analysis. *Organizational Behavior and Human Performance, 7,* 457–466.

John Sample, *Ph.D., SPHR, has extensive consulting and training experience in the private and public sectors. His most recent challenge has been to convert a traditional face-to-face program in human resource development to a distance learning option for graduate students. Research interests include adult learning strategies and legal liability associated with training and program development.*

About the Editor

Robert C. Preziosi, D.P.A., is a professor of management and chair of the master of science in human resource management degree program in the H. Wayne Huizenga School of Business and Entrepreneurship at Nova Southeastern University. He teaches at the graduate level and has taught human resource management, HRD, leadership theory and practice, and the capstone MBA course. Before entering academia, he had been a line manager, director of human resources, and a vice president of management development and training for a Fortune 50 company. He owns Preziosi Partners, Inc., with his wife.

Dr. Preziosi is an award-winning professor, having received his school's first Excellence in Teaching award in 1997. He was Faculty Member of the Year in 2003 and Professor of the Decade in 2000. In addition, he is the only person to have been given ASTD's Torch Award twice for his leadership in ASTD.

Dr. Preziosi is a frequent presenter at academic and professional conferences. He has been quoted in *Fortune* magazine and has written for publications such as *National Productivity Review, Training and Development,* the Pfeiffer *Annuals,* and the McGraw-Hill *Sourcebooks.* He has been on the editorial boards of the *Journal of Leadership Studies* and *New Horizons in Adult Education.* He was the co-founder and co-editor of the *Journal of Applied Management and Entrepreneurship.* He was the editor of the first *HRM Annual.*

Contributors

Laurie Bassi
McBassi & Company
129 Eldridge Way
Golden, CO 80401
  (303) 278-8811
  Fax: (303) 279-5733
  email: lbassi@mcbassi.com

Douglas Buck
1720 Pine Log Road
Aiken, SC 29803
  (803) 648-7055
  email: buck@sbe.nova.edu

Thomas D. Cairns, D.B.A.
Senior Vice President
Human Resources
Digital, Television & Studio Operations
NBC Universal
100 Universal City Plaza
1280/10
Universal City, CA 91608
  (818) 777-3116
  Fax: (818) 866-3318
  email: Thomas.Cairns@nbcuni.com

Linsey Craig-Willis, D.P.A.
P.O. Box #1628
Boca Raton, FL 33429-1628
  (561) 750-8669
  Fax: (561) 391-5077
  email: lowillis@lijcraig.com

Elizabeth Doty
WorkLore
926 Madison Street
Albany, CA 94706
  (510) 558-7032
  email: elizabeth@worklore.com

Ronald C. Fetzer, Ph.D.
7985 Preble County Line Road
Germantown, OH 45327
  (937) 787–9190
  Fax: (937) 787–9180
  email: ron-fetzer@worldnet.att.net

Jack L. Howard, Ph.D.
Illinois State University
MQM Department, Campus Box 5580
Normal, IL 61790–5580
  (309) 438–8954
  email: jlhowar@ilstu.edu

Jack N. Kondrasuk, Ph.D.
Dr. Robert B. Pamplin, Jr. School
  of Business Administration
University of Portland
5000 N. Willamette Boulevard
Portland, OR 97219
  (503) 943-7278
  Fax: (503) 943-8041
  email: kondrasu@up.edu

Kat Koppett
StoryNet LLC
30 Grant Hill Court
Clifton Park, NY 12065
  (518) 383–8322
  email: kat@thestorynet.com

Richard P. Kropp, Ed.D.
Vice President, Human Resources
Cape Cod Health
46 Forest Lane
Scituate, MA 82066
  (508) 862-5716
  email: rkropp@capecodhealth.org

Bob Losyk, M.B.A., M.Ed., C.S.P.
Innovative Training Solutions, Inc.
2422 Retriever Lane
Greensboro, NC, 27410
  (800) 995–0344
  email: bob@boblosyk.com

Daniel McMurrer
Vice President, Research
McBassi & Company
129 Eldridge Way
Golden, CO 80401
  (303) 278-8811
  fax: (303)279-5733)
  email: dmcmurrer@mcbassi.com

Bahaudin G. Mujtaba, D.B.A.
Assistant Professor of Management
Nova Southeastern University
3301 College Avenue
Fort Lauderdale, FL 33314
  (954) 262-5045
  email: Mujtaba@nova.edu

Melissa A. Parris
School of Management,
  College of Law and Business
University of Western Sydney
9/253 Dunmore St.
Pendle Hill NSW 2145
Australia
  +61 2 97 67 1661
  email: melissaparris@bigpond.com

Stephen M. Paskoff, Esq.
ELI®
2675 Paces Ferry Road, Suite 470
Atlanta, GA 30339
  (770) 319–7999
  Fax: (770) 319–7905
  email: paskoff@eliinc.com

Linda M. Raudenbush
7201 Kindler Road
Columbia, MD 21046
  (410) 381-2747
  email:
  Linda_Raudenbus@nass.usda.gov

Jim Rhodes
Vice President of Compliance
  in Human Resources
Publix Super Markets Inc.
P.O. Box 407
Lakeland, FL 33802–0407
  (863) 688–7407, ext. 53011.
  email: jim.rhodes@mail.publix.com

Rick Rocchetti
Organization Development and
  Training Manager
City of Raleigh
222 West Hargett Street
Raleigh, NC 27602
  (919) 890–3625
  email: Rick.Rocchetti@ci.raleigh.nc.us

John Sample, Ph.D., SPHR
College of Education
Florida State University
114A Stone Building
Tallahassee, FL 32306
  (850) 644–8176
  email: sample@coe.fsu.edu

Roslyn Vargas
14203 S.W. 16th Court
Davie, FL 33325
  Phone/fax: (954) 423–9143
  email: jrvargas@bellsouth.net

Margaret H. Vickers, Ph.D.
Associate Professor
School of Management,
  College of Law and Business
Parramatta Campus, Building EK,
  Room G22
University of Western Sydney
Locked Bag 1797
Penrith South DC, NSW 1797
Australia
  +61 2 9685 9008
  Fax: +61 2 9685 9625
  email: m.vickers@uws.edu.au

How to Use the CD-ROM

System Requirements

PC with Microsoft Windows 98SE or later
Mac with Apple OS version 8.6 or later

Using the CD with Windows

To view the items located on the CD, follow these steps:

1. Insert the CD into your computer's CD-ROM drive.

2. A window appears with the following options:

   Contents: Allows you to view the files included on the CD-ROM.

   Software: Allows you to install useful software from the CD-ROM.

   Links: Displays a hyperlinked page of websites.

   Author: Displays a page with information about the Author(s).

   Contact Us: Displays a page with information on contacting the publisher or author.

   Help: Displays a page with information on using the CD.

   Exit: Closes the interface window.

If you do not have autorun enabled, or if the autorun window does not appear, follow these steps to access the CD:

1. Click Start -> Run.

2. In the dialog box that appears, type d:<\\>start.exe, where d is the letter of your CD-ROM drive. This brings up the autorun window described in the preceding set of steps.

3. Choose the desired option from the menu. (See Step 2 in the preceding list for a description of these options.)

In Case of Trouble

If you experience difficulty using the CD-ROM, please follow these steps:

1. Make sure your hardware and systems configurations conform to the systems requirements noted under "System Requirements" above.

2. Review the installation procedure for your type of hardware and operating system.

It is possible to reinstall the software if necessary.

To speak with someone in Product Technical Support, call 800-762-2974 or 317-572-3994, M–F 8:30 a.m.–5:00 p.m. EST. You can also get support and contact Product Technical Support through our website at www.wiley.com/techsupport.

Before calling or writing, please have the following information available:

- Type of computer and operating system

- Any error messages displayed

- Complete description of the problem.

It is best if you are sitting at your computer when making the call.

Pfeiffer Publications Guide

This guide is designed to familiarize you with the various types of Pfeiffer publications. The formats section describes the various types of products that we publish; the methodologies section describes the many different ways that content might be provided within a product. We also provide a list of the topic areas in which we publish.

FORMATS

In addition to its extensive book-publishing program, Pfeiffer offers content in an array of formats, from fieldbooks for the practitioner to complete, ready-to-use training packages that support group learning.

FIELDBOOK Designed to provide information and guidance to practitioners in the midst of action. Most fieldbooks are companions to another, sometimes earlier, work, from which its ideas are derived; the fieldbook makes practical what was theoretical in the original text. Fieldbooks can certainly be read from cover to cover. More likely, though, you'll find yourself bouncing around following a particular theme, or dipping in as the mood, and the situation, dictate.

HANDBOOK A contributed volume of work on a single topic, comprising an eclectic mix of ideas, case studies, and best practices sourced by practitioners and experts in the field.

An editor or team of editors usually is appointed to seek out contributors and to evaluate content for relevance to the topic. Think of a handbook not as a ready-to-eat meal, but as a cookbook of ingredients that enables you to create the most fitting experience for the occasion.

RESOURCE Materials designed to support group learning. They come in many forms: a complete, ready-to-use exercise (such as a game); a comprehensive resource on one topic (such as conflict management) containing a variety of methods and approaches; or a collection of like-minded activities (such as icebreakers) on multiple subjects and situations.

TRAINING PACKAGE An entire, ready-to-use learning program that focuses on a particular topic or skill. All packages comprise a guide for the facilitator/trainer and a workbook for the participants. Some packages are supported with additional media—such as video—or learning aids, instruments, or other devices to help participants understand concepts or practice and develop skills.

- *Facilitator/trainer's guide* Contains an introduction to the program, advice on how to organize and facilitate the learning event, and step-by-step instructor notes. The guide also contains copies of presentation materials—handouts, presentations, and overhead designs, for example—used in the program.

- *Participant's workbook* Contains exercises and reading materials that support the learning goal and serves as a valuable reference and support guide for participants in the weeks and months that follow the learning event. Typically, each participant will require his or her own workbook.

ELECTRONIC CD-ROMs and web-based products transform static Pfeiffer content into dynamic, interactive experiences. Designed to take advantage of the searchability, automation, and ease-of-use that technology provides, our e-products bring convenience and immediate accessibility to your workspace.

METHODOLOGIES

CASE STUDY A presentation, in narrative form, of an actual event that has occurred inside an organization. Case studies are not prescriptive, nor are they used to prove a point; they are designed to develop critical analysis and decision-making skills. A case study has a specific time frame, specifies a sequence of events, is narrative in structure, and contains a plot structure—an issue (what should be/have been done?). Use case studies when the goal is to enable participants to apply previously learned theories to the circumstances in the case, decide what is pertinent, identify the real issues, decide what should have been done, and develop a plan of action.

ENERGIZER A short activity that develops readiness for the next session or learning event. Energizers are most commonly used after a break or lunch to stimulate or refocus the group. Many involve some form of physical activity, so they are a useful way to counter post-lunch lethargy. Other uses include transitioning from one topic to another, where "mental" distancing is important.

EXPERIENTIAL LEARNING ACTIVITY (ELA) A facilitator-led intervention that moves participants through the learning cycle from experience to application (also known as a Structured Experience). ELAs are carefully thought-out designs in which there is a definite learning purpose and intended outcome. Each step—everything that participants do during the activity—facilitates the accomplishment of the stated goal. Each ELA includes complete instructions for facilitating the intervention and a clear statement of goals, suggested group size and timing, materials required, an explanation of the process, and, where appropriate, possible variations to the activity. (For more detail on Experiential Learning Activities, see the Introduction to the *Reference Guide to Handbooks and Annuals*, 1999 edition, Pfeiffer, San Francisco.)

GAME A group activity that has the purpose of fostering team spirit and togetherness in addition to the achievement of a pre-stated goal. Usually contrived—undertaking a desert expedition, for example—this type of learning method offers an engaging means for participants to demonstrate and practice business and interpersonal skills. Games are effective for team building and personal development mainly because the goal is subordinate to the process—the means through which participants reach decisions, collaborate, communicate, and generate trust and understanding. Games often engage teams in "friendly" competition.

ICEBREAKER A (usually) short activity designed to help participants overcome initial anxiety in a training session and/or to acquaint the participants with one another. An icebreaker can be a fun activity or can be tied to specific topics or training goals. While a useful tool in itself, the icebreaker comes into its own in situations where tension or resistance exists within a group.

INSTRUMENT A device used to assess, appraise, evaluate, describe, classify, and summarize various aspects of human behavior. The term used to describe an instrument depends primarily on its format and purpose. These terms include survey, questionnaire, inventory, diagnostic survey, and poll. Some uses of instruments include providing instrumental feedback to group members, studying here-and-now processes or functioning within a group, manipulating group composition, and evaluating outcomes of training and other interventions.

Instruments are popular in the training and HR field because, in general, more growth can occur if an individual is provided with a method for focusing specifically on his or her own behavior. Instruments also are used to obtain information that will serve as a basis for change and to assist in workforce planning efforts.

Paper-and-pencil tests still dominate the instrument landscape with a typical package comprising a facilitator's guide, which offers advice on administering the instrument and interpreting the collected data, and an initial set of instruments. Additional instruments are available separately. Pfeiffer, though, is investing heavily in e-instruments. Electronic instrumentation provides effortless distribution and, for larger groups particularly, offers advantages over paper-and-pencil tests in the time it takes to analyze data and provide feedback.

LECTURETTE A short talk that provides an explanation of a principle, model, or process that is pertinent to the participants' current learning needs. A lecturette is intended to establish a common language bond between the trainer and the participants by providing a mutual frame of reference. Use a lecturette as an introduction to a group activity or event, as an interjection during an event, or as a handout.

MODEL A graphic depiction of a system or process and the relationship among its elements. Models provide a frame of reference and something more tangible, and more easily remembered, than a verbal explanation. They also give participants something to "go on," enabling them to track their own progress as they experience the dynamics, processes, and relationships being depicted in the model.

ROLE PLAY A technique in which people assume a role in a situation/scenario: a customer service rep in an angry-customer exchange, for example. The way in which the role is approached is then discussed and feedback is offered. The role play is often repeated using a different approach and/or incorporating changes made based on feedback received. In other words, role playing is a spontaneous interaction involving realistic behavior under artificial (and safe) conditions.

SIMULATION A methodology for understanding the interrelationships among components of a system or process. Simulations differ from games in that they test or use a model that depicts or mirrors some aspect of reality in form, if not necessarily in content. Learning occurs by studying the effects of change on one or more factors of the model. Simulations are commonly used to test hypotheses about what happens in a system—often referred to as "what if?" analysis—or to examine best-case/worst-case scenarios.

THEORY A presentation of an idea from a conjectural perspective. Theories are useful because they encourage us to examine behavior and phenomena through a different lens.

TOPICS

The twin goals of providing effective and practical solutions for workforce training and organization development and meeting the educational needs of training and human resource professionals shape Pfeiffer's publishing program. Core topics include the following:

Leadership & Management

Communication & Presentation

Coaching & Mentoring

Training & Development

e-Learning

Teams & Collaboration

OD & Strategic Planning

Human Resources

Consulting